TWA

LEONARD

5

TWA

9

GATES 8-15

CHICAGO
LOS ANGELES

ARRIVALS
OKLAHOMA CITY
BOSTON
HELICOPTER SERVICE

DEPARTURES
3:15 11
2:45 9
now boarding
14 LOS ANGELES
now boarding
10
now boarding
6 BOSTON
15
10 DAYTON
8 non stop INDIANAPOLIS
4
10 CLEVELAND
CINCINNATI

OXX-969

Designing TWA

Designing TWA

Eero Saarinen's Airport Terminal in New York

Kornel Ringli

PARK BOOKS

Contents

Designing TWA

1 Cover of a restaurant menu, TWA, ca. 1962

Around the mid-1950s, a new era begins in the aviation industry. In the hotly contended US market, the airlines increasingly try to use their corporate image to set themselves apart from each other in the competition for customers. Architecture and interior design of the airlines begin to play an important role.[1] This is reflected by the fact that air carriers like Trans World Airlines (TWA) hire industrial designers to comprehensively modernize and unify their corporate design. A peak in the aviation industry development toward differentiation through outward appearance is reached at New York's Idlewild Airport (today John F. Kennedy International Airport), where America's largest airlines, including TWA, are able to build their own terminals.[2] As TWA opens their Trans World Flight Center to great media attention on May 28, 1962, the terminal, designed by Eero Saarinen and Associates (ES&A), manifests new demands on architecture.[3] **Fig. 1** The striking building silhouette stands out among all the different designs and architecturally sets the airline apart from the competition in the overall complex. Thanks to its extraordinary form, which when seen from the outside evokes a giant bird, the building comes across as an easily understood and recognizable symbol of flying—like an advertisement for TWA. Inside the building, the air travelers find themselves amidst a spatial composition of curved lines that merge into one another, and they are accompanied everywhere by the authenticating red corporate color of TWA. Given increasing visual equalization in civil aviation and the airline's desire for visual distinguishing features, Saarinen designs a distinctive building as part of the corporate design.

The TWA Flight Center meanwhile fits seamlessly into a development that, in 1960, two years before completion of the Saarinen terminal,

2 Lever House, New York, Skidmore, Owings and Merrill, 1952

Architectural Forum identifies as a "corporate 'showpiece' movement," whose vanguard, according to the professional journal, is Lever House (1952) by Skidmore, Owings and Merrill (SOM).[4] **Fig. 2** Company buildings advance in the 1950s to become essential components of corporate marketing, because the desired corporate image can be vividly represented through the building's appearance: not only in the

3 IBM Manufacturing and Training Facility, Rochester, MN, ES&A, 1958

glassy facade of Lever House, the corporate headquarters of a detergent manufacturer, but also in the first facade manufactured entirely of aluminum for the administrative offices of Alcoa (Aluminum Company of America, Harrison and Abramovitz, 1953), in the stainless-steel facade of the headquarters of Inland Steel (SOM, 1957), facades of COR-TEN steel for the agricultural machinery manufacturer John Deere (ES&A, 1964), or an almost endless series of modules in two shades of blue as a formal analogy to the patterns of digital data processing at the IBM Building in Rochester (ES&A, 1958).[5] **Fig. 3** Eero Saarinen (1910–1961) significantly shapes this trend by designing buildings for each of his clients that are tailored specifically to them in terms of their outward appearance. **Fig. 4** Consequently, in 1962 he is dubbed "the first patron saint of the 'style-for-the-job' faction" by the English architecture critic Reyner Banham.[6] The architect deserves

4 Eero Saarinen, year unknown

this epithet based on his use of a recurrent method: a unique outward appearance for each specific client, marketable technical and design innovations, and sometimes project-specific art objects.[7] After generating extremely effective publicity upon testing this "style-for-the-job" recipe for success with his work on the General Motors Technical Center (1956), Saarinen prompts other designs to follow a very similar pattern. The corporate campus for General Motors is followed by Kresge Auditorium (1955) and a chapel for the Massachusetts Institute of Technology (MIT) (1955) **Fig. 5**, and later, in addition to the TWA Terminal, various other buildings for clients from the business and education sectors, most notably IBM, which commissions him twice, first for their office in Rochester and then for the one in Yorktown Heights (1961).

But the TWA Flight Center shares more with these buildings than just a unique outward appearance (corporate design) tailored specifically to the client. This is because representatives of American corporate culture from the realms of management, design, and marketing impose new conceptual demands on architecture in the interests of corporate identity at different levels. Commensurate with the complex and fast-paced organization, flexible but standardized spatial modules that can be optimally adapted to the working processes are desired.[8] **Fig. 6** In view of this, the

5 Kresge Chapel, MIT, Boston, MA, ES&A, 1955

buildings also need to follow an internal logic of organization (corporate architecture). For the terminal, this principle is already emblematically reflected in TWA's catalog of requirements, but also manifests itself later in the spatial concept as well as in the technical facilities. Given the incipient mass market in civil aviation, the building is supposed to ensure efficient passenger handling and thus efficient operational management. Corporate boards like that of TWA ultimately seek to employ a business organization optimized in such a way and the intended technical progress to strengthen their corporate identity through strategic corporate communications. With essential support from Eero Saarinen, and above all from his wife Aline B. Saarinen (1914–1972), the airline intensively uses its new terminal

6 Deere and Company Administrative Center, Moline, IL, ES&A, 1963

to improve their damaged public reputation. Thus corporate design and corporate architecture target not just the creation of aesthetically and functionally satisfying objects, but importantly also the production of a corporate image in the public eye.

Even though Eero Saarinen's airport terminal is so typical of postwar corporate architecture—in that it engages the realms of corporate architecture, corporate design, and corporate communication—in one essential point it differs from all the other contemporary company buildings. Although the TWA Terminal advances to become an attraction that is accessible to the masses thanks to its unique form and extensive marketing, it captivates mainly due to its unmistakable visual appearance, while its underlying operating technology does not stand out from that of the competition. Hence the building is similar to the successful consumer goods with attractive packaging that the then-growing American consumer society prefers over products with the same core utility. **Fig. 7** Unlike other

7 Sunbeam Mixmaster mixer, 1953

iconic buildings of the postwar period, which continue to serve their original purpose to this day (e. g. Seagram Building, 1958), the terminal building, which was advertised as suitable for jet aircraft, loses its functional capacity within just a few years. **Fig. 8** By 1970 at the latest, as the first jumbo jets need to be served, the terminal proves to be inefficient and unsuitable to accommodate the ever-increasing numbers of passengers. Whereas the terminal building increasingly suffers from its operational shortcomings and is decommissioned in 2001, its unique exterior fascinates the public to this very day. Eero Saarinen's TWA Flight Center ranks as an icon of the jet age, even though it never did justice to this in terms of operational logistics. Its declaration as a landmark in 1994 firmly established the intrinsic architectural and historical significance of the

8 Seagram Building, New York, Mies van der Rohe, 1958, photo from 2015

airport terminal. As a prime example for the central purpose of today's corporate headquarters—bestowing the owner with public attention through an eye-catching, easily recognizable building—Saarinen's airport terminal is paradigmatic for a breed of sensational buildings that are meanwhile the order of the day. Beyond the impact of the TWA Terminal at the time, this book also pursues its influence on subsequent and current architectural phenomena, especially because Saarinen himself repeatedly emphasized the importance of his buildings maintaining enduring validity.[9] Consequently, this treatise looks at the Trans World Flight Center as a building of the postwar era that is both typical of its time and has far-reaching architectural-historical significance. By comprehensively analyzing Saarinen's airport building for the first time in terms of the nexus of corporate architecture, corporate design, and corporate communication, the myth of the terminal as an icon of the jet age is scrutinized and corrected.

An overview of the existing literature on Eero Saarinen's work shows that the current state of research does not do justice to this ambition. What is striking at first is how Saarinen's presence in the trade and general press already rapidly diminishes shortly after his unexpected death in 1961. The reasons for this lie primarily in the highly controversial reception of his works. On the one hand, during his lifetime he becomes known far beyond professional circles thanks to wide media coverage in major popular magazines such as *Time, Holiday, Playboy,* and others, and on the other hand, he sees himself as subjected throughout his lifetime to sometimes fierce criticism by his professional colleagues, who accuse him of formal arbitrariness as well as an overly pronounced client focus and promotional spirit.[10] **Fig. 9** Bearing in mind the relatively clear stylistic principles of the International Style, Saarinen's notion of a style that varies from task to task is suspect at the least to many critics. Their mistrust grows all the more so because his "style for the job" is allegedly commercially motivated, focused solely on marketable buildings for his clients. At the time of the best-selling book *The Hidden Persuaders* (1957) by Vance Packard, which denounces the seduction of consumers through advertising, Saarinen is thus relegated to the sidelines of architectural criticism.[11] The result is that Eero Saarinen fades into obscurity, and his work long remains unnoticed and unexplored.[12] Architecture critics have only displayed a renewed interest in him beginning at around the turn of the millennium. With *Eero Saarinen: Shaping the Future*, the most detailed and profound study of his oeuvre to date appears in 2006.[13] Thus Saarinen had indeed secured the place in architectural history which, by his own admission, he had desired. Today he is again familiar to a wider audience in the US. Taking Saarinen's repeated appearance in crossword puzzles in the *New York Times* as an indicator, he may even be the best-known architect.[14]

Reflected in the longtime discrepancy between Saarinen's public and professional reception are two predominant patterns that also apply to assessments of the TWA Flight Center made thus far. The

9 Eero Saarinen (third from left) with George Nelson, Edward Wormley, Harry Bertoia, Charles Eames, and Jens Risom, feature article in *Playboy*, 1961

design of the terminal is either highly praised as a masterpiece by an artistic form-giver—most commonly by the popular press but also by trade journals—or, equally rash, dismissed by architecture critics as superficial, excessively client-oriented, and promotional.[15] Over time, however, the public perception of the building changes and coalesces. Although at the outset the terminal is sometimes inundated with malice, the reviews increasingly devolve into uncritical and glorifying representations of the airport building. This development leads to today's perception of the TWA Terminal as "a jet age icon."[16] The glorification of the building is supported by the publications issued to date, which either predominantly feature large-format illustrations—a photo of the terminal often decorates the cover—and whose explanatory texts, by contrast, play a minor role, or the publications contain detailed text contributions, but these disregard the basic historical context. Thus, the fundamental operational and economic conditions, which can be traced back to consequential aeronautical developments during the Second World War, have largely gone without consideration until now. Equally little attention has focused thus far on the building's significance for corporate communications and the media's influence on public perception. The TWA Flight Center, which Reyner Banham deemed "the essential Saarinen design," accordingly lacks a well-founded academic publication.[17] In contrast to previous publications, the present study takes the first comprehensive look at the TWA Terminal from the viewpoints of business organization (corporate architecture), design (corporate design), and media (corporate communications).

This treatise is arranged into three main chapters corresponding to these three perspectives. The first chapter focuses on the operational, technical, and logistical changes in civil aviation after the Second World War and their effects on the design of the terminal. TWA, which often flies in the red despite rising passenger numbers, makes new demands for increased efficiency and profitability, initially aimed at the passenger cabins, then the ground infrastructure. The new guiding principles are automated and mechanized processes modeled on the cargo industry. The goal is an airport terminal that functions efficiently and reliably, like a machine. The design of the TWA Flight Center by ES&A is clear evidence of this. The internal spatial arrangement is based on an extensive study of the professional literature and takes into account the most important operational criteria for a successful terminal that were known at the time. And more: developed on the basis of elaborate process studies at airports, the TWA Terminal is equivalent to a direct spatial translation of the delineated flow diagrams. The various handling stations correspond to specific zones, analogous to the flow charts, that are strung together. The goal of fast and trouble-free ground handling results in a spatial sequence that is nearly free of thresholds and doors, but equipped with diverse technical facilities. In this way, the terminal building is conceived to withstand the demands of the mass market in civil aviation.

The second chapter is devoted to the corporate design of TWA. In view of leveling tendencies among the air carriers, TWA discovers corporate image as a differentiating factor of economic importance. The line of argumentation begins with TWA's development of the Constellation, a propeller aircraft that is, after the Second World War, initially unique from a technical and visual standpoint. **Fig. 10** By 1958 at the latest, however, with the introduction of jet aircraft—which, in contrast to the Constellation, no longer have an eye-catching appearance—TWA loses the visual unique selling point it previously had. Consequently, the comprehensive design program conceived by Raymond Loewy (1893–1986) is meant to provide a distinction from its competitors. Moreover,

10 Lockheed Constellation L-1649, TWA, ca. 1960

TWA engages Eero Saarinen as the architect of its new terminal at Idlewild Airport. Since Saarinen designs a building that evokes the image of a bird taking flight, it reads like an appeal from an advertisement to fly with TWA. The terminal's ability to have a positive effect on the company's image is the economic capital of the popular and mediagenic building. In this regard, it is committed to a new form of economy. It is not based on constructive efficiency or sparing use of building materials, as the four supposedly thin roof vaults may suggest. Rather, the TWA Terminal has economic value for the airline thanks to its striking and recognizable shape. With the public attention it brings, the building's appearance offers a commodity that is particularly in demand at Idlewild Airport in the face of other airlines competing with their own terminals.

The main focus of the third chapter is the public relations work of Aline Saarinen and TWA. **Fig. 11** It shows that Eero Saarinen, who aspires to a permanent place in the history of architecture, finds an ideal PR professional in his wife. Not only does the former *New York Times* journalist have excellent contacts in the media world. Thanks to her own publications and those of others—she is able to skillfully influence the latter for her own purposes to serve the intended goal—she also succeeds in increasing the renown of her husband considerably within less than a decade. **Fig. 12** Now the general public knows him as

11 Aline B. Saarinen, Lincoln Center, New York, 1962

an architect and not, as before, first and foremost as a furniture designer. Because TWA likewise benefits from the publicity garnered by Eero Saarinen's growing fame, the terminal project proves to be an excellent marketing tool for both closely cooperating sides. The PR specialist uses the building project throughout all its stages of development in order to

12 Eero Saarinen, year unknown

reach her goal of establishing an Eero Saarinen legend, which finally finds an apt expression in a commemorative plaque in the terminal for the deceased architect. The TWA Flight Center becomes a monument to the architect. For its image campaigns, TWA takes advantage of the markedly increased renown of the architect, but also of the building itself. First, the terminal building is intended to make people forget the failed procurement of jet aircraft, although the building—still conceived in the Constellation era—is by no means tailored to the new generation of aircraft. Second, the publicity measures, which culminate in a veritable array of events for the opening, aim to position the company as an exclusive airline with global operations.

The closing words discuss the origins of the building's legend, which began with the joint marketing of the terminal by Aline Saarinen and TWA and which continues today. Reproductions of the building are found in surveys of twentieth-century architecture and travel guides to New York, as well as in the popular press. In the monographs on Saarinen's work, too, the terminal occupies a prominent place. Hence the building, which has been widely published in various media channels, advances to become a place of interest and the epitome of airport architecture par excellence. **Fig. 13** Since the building's operational efficiency decreases inversely to the rapid growth in passengers served, its media exposure—and less the building's actual purpose of providing for the rapid handling of passengers and cargo—increasingly constitutes the intrinsic value of the TWA Flight Center. This manifests itself today more than ever. Although the airport building stands

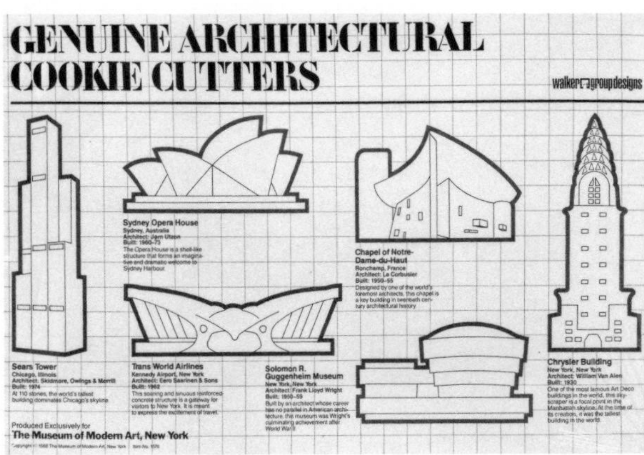

13 Box of cookie cutters in the form of iconic buildings, 1988

empty since 2001, it is still a source of great fascination for both professionals and laypeople alike. Eero Saarinen's TWA Terminal is considered an icon of the jet era, even though it was never really up to the task in an operational sense.

Endnotes

1 For an overview of the development of corporate design in civil aviation, see **Eisenbrand**, Jochen: "Airlines and Corporate Design," in: **Vegesack**, Alexander von (ed.): *Airworld: Design and Architecture for Air Travel*, Weil am Rhein: Vitra Design Museum, 2004, pp. 144–174.
2 The airport is indeed officially opened as New York International Airport, but Idlewild, the former name of the once marshy tract of land, remains in common use.
3 The terminal is also called TWA Flight Center or Trans World Flight Center by its owner. But in the vernacular it is known as the TWA Terminal.
4 **Anonymous**: "Good Architecture is Good Promotion," in: *Architectural Forum*, vol. 113, no. 1 (July 1960), pp. 88–89, 186–187, p. 88.
5 See **Martin**, Reinhold: *The Organizational Complex: Architecture, Media, and Corporate Space*, Cambridge, MA: MIT Press, 2003, pp. 95–105, 159–167.
6 **Banham**, Reyner: "The Fear of Eero's Mana," in: *Arts Magazine*, vol. 36, no. 5 (February 1962), pp. 70–73, p. 73.
7 See **Albrecht**, Donald: "The Clients and Their Architect," in: **Pelkonen**, Eeva-Liisa; **Albrecht**, Donald (eds): *Eero Saarinen: Shaping the Future*, New Haven, CT: Yale University Press, 2006, pp. 44–55, p. 47.
8 See **Martin**, Reinhold: *The Organizational Complex: Architecture, Media, and Corporate Space*, Cambridge, MA: MIT Press, 2003, pp. 81–90.
9 See e.g. **Saarinen**, Eero: "Architecture of the Future," in: *Cleveland Engineering*, vol. 46, no. 19 (May 7, 1953), pp. 6–8, 10–11, p. 7.
10 See e.g. **Lessing**, Lawrence: "The Diversity of Eero Saarinen," in: *Architectural Forum*, vol. 113, no. 1 (July 1960), pp. 94–103, p. 95. His designs are, almost without exception, greeted with skepticism, above all by the European trade journals. See e.g. **Zevi**, Bruno; **Richards**, J. M.; **Giedion**, Sigfried: "Three Critics Discuss M.I.T.'s New Buildings," in: *Architectural Forum*, vol. 104, no. 3 (March 1956), pp. 156–157, 174, 178, 182, p. 157.
11 **Packard**, Vance: *The Hidden Persuaders*, New York: Pocket Books, 1958 (5th ed.).
12 Jayne Merkel attributes Saarinen's fall into oblivion less to the architecture critics than the public at large: "The disillusionment with the Vietnam War created a loss of faith and doubt, so Saarinen's work didn't mean so much to people—they just didn't get it." **Makovsky**, Paul [interview with Jayne Merkel]: "Reconsidering Eero," in: *Metropolis*, vol. 25, no. 2 (October 2005), pp. 134–139, 173, p. 135.
13 See **Pelkonen**, Eeva-Liisa; **Albrecht**, Donald (eds): *Eero Saarinen: Shaping the Future*, New Haven, CT: Yale University Press, 2006.
14 See **Knight**, Richard: "Once Upon a Time ...," in: **idem**: *Saarinen's Quest: A Memoir*, San Francisco, CA: William Stout Publishers, 2008, pp. 17–64, p. 166 (remark to footnote 85, p. 63).
15 See e.g. **Colquhoun**, Alan: "TWA Terminal Building, Idlewild, New York," in: *Architectural Design*, vol. 32, no. 10 (October 1962), pp. 465–469, p. 465.
16 "A jet age icon is threatened," calls a flock of illustrious architects surrounding Philip Johnson as demolition excavators threaten the terminal in 2001. **Anonymous**: "A Jet Age Icon is Threatened," 2001, http://www.jetset-modern.com/twa.htm (accessed February 3, 2015).
17 **Banham**, Reyner: "The Trouble with Eero," in: *New Statesman*, vol. 64, no. 1654 (November 23, 1962), pp. 745–746, p. 746.

1 Diagrams of Passenger and Baggage Movements

Until well into the 1930s, flying is reserved for the happy few—a spectacular and singular adventure. Flying is expensive, dangerous, and uncomfortable. The small, low-flying propeller-driven planes are vulnerable to turbulence and cause a multitude of aviation accidents. The pioneer airlines make their money first and foremost with postal deliveries. Until the outbreak of the Second World War, prestigious national aviation companies are established in both Europe and the United States, but due to the technologically rudimentary planes, aviation safety remains inadequate.[18] As with the First World War, the Second World War would also give important stimuli to civil aviation in this respect. Whereas the planes had previously reached their limits on a flight across the Atlantic, they manage the trip easily after the war. The various American airlines now take turns outperforming each other with new nonstop routes and higher-performance versions of their aircraft types.[19]

As transatlantic flights become routine, a new market opens; nevertheless, the competition remains as tough as before, especially among US air carriers. They struggle to survive. In 1947, the American airlines generate a total deficit of more than $20 million. Trans World Airlines (TWA), which has often operated at a loss since its inception in 1930, is no exception in this regard.[20] After a period of temporary financial relief in the early 1950s, the airline records high losses once more until 1961. Given the strained financial conditions, the airlines seek new sources of revenue—and modify their business model. Business at a large scale is expected to create new sales opportunities. While Europe is busy rebuilding, the United States becomes the largest growth market in the aviation industry. The two postwar decades become the proverbial "golden age of passenger aviation."[21] But this was to demand a lot from TWA and its infrastructure in the air and on the ground.

14 The first propeller airplanes fly low, offer a bumpy ride, and are also unsafe. Besides the high ticket prices, people's fear keeps them from flying.

15 Well-heeled travelers debarking a Douglas DC-3 in 1937. Until the Second World War, the airplanes only offered space for about two dozen passengers.

16 After 1945 transatlantic flights become routine. But with their exclusive offerings, the airlines generate substantial losses—business on a large scale aims to remedy this situation.

17 Mass tourism demands optimization of the work process. Uniforms are designed not only according to fashion but also for practicality, by facilitating necessary movements—as this page from the employee magazine *Skyliner* in 1960 reveals.

18 To optimize economic factors, the behavior of the personnel is to be standardized and monitored. The hostesses must have certain body measurements.

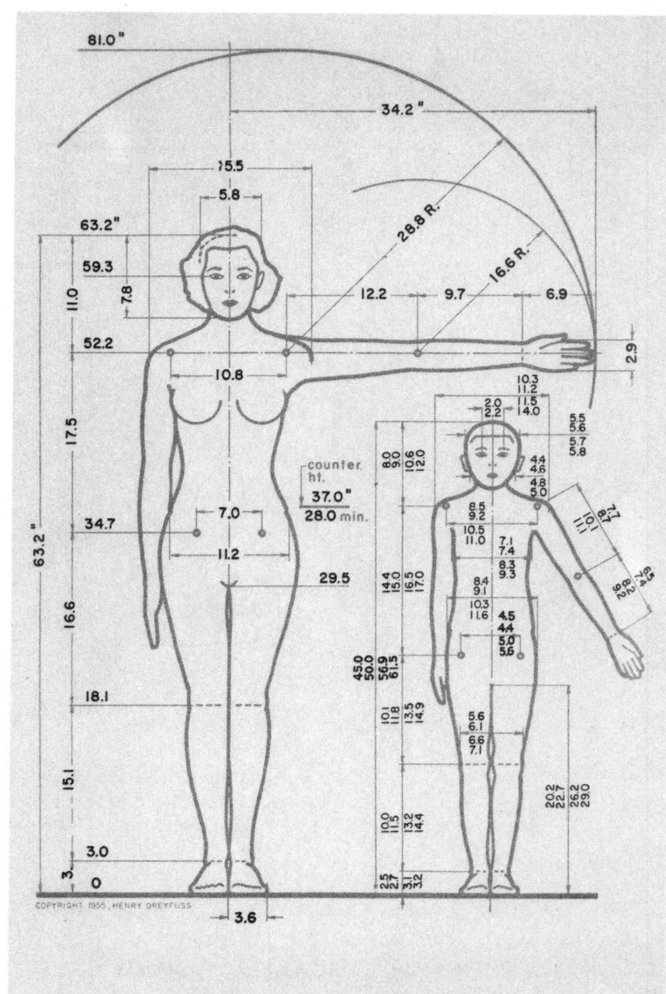

19 In order to accommodate passenger growth, the passenger cabins must be spatially optimized. Measurements of the human body help designers like Henry Dreyfuss to design airline seats.

20 TWA standardizes the actors as well as the activities to be carried out. On the basis of these parameters, the desired operational efficiency is to be established.

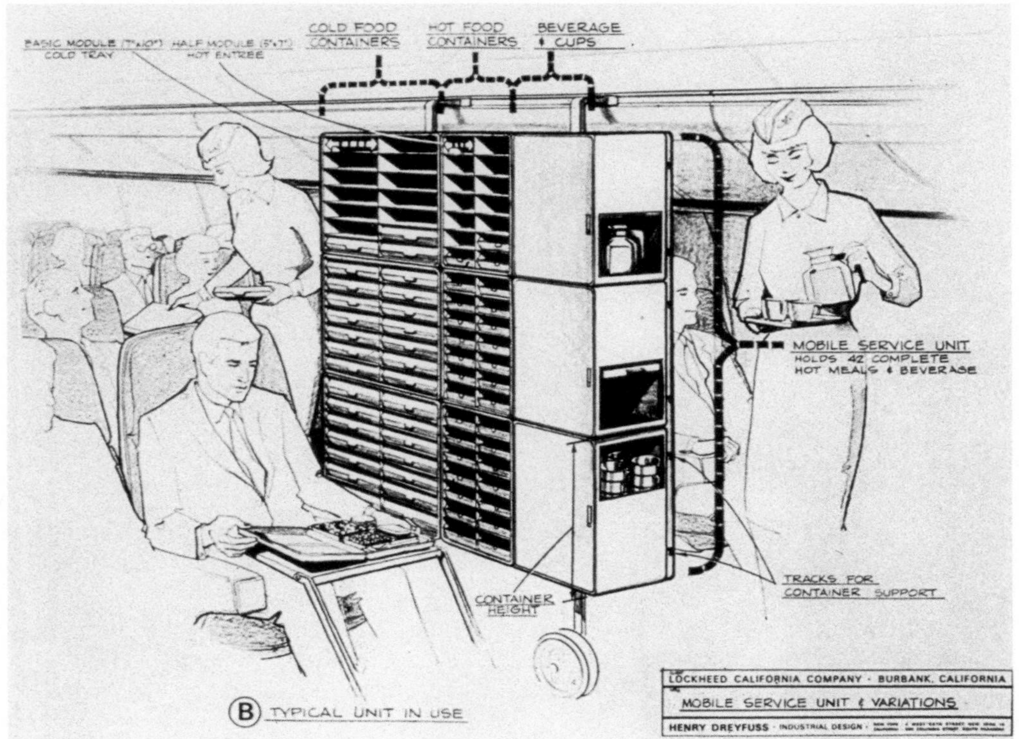

21 In 1965, to optimize the process of serving food, Henry Dreyfuss designs a new type of serving cart for the cabin of the Lockheed L-2000. The airplane, however, remains on the drawing board.

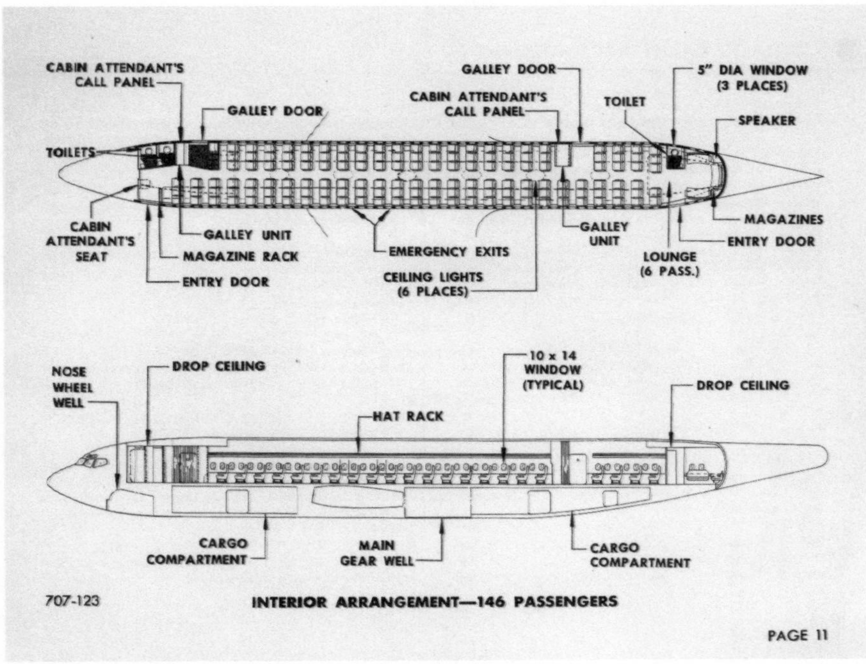

22 In order to be able to transport more passengers, the airlines introduce space-saving rows of seats, all oriented in the direction of flight, and reduce the width of the seats and the distance between rows.

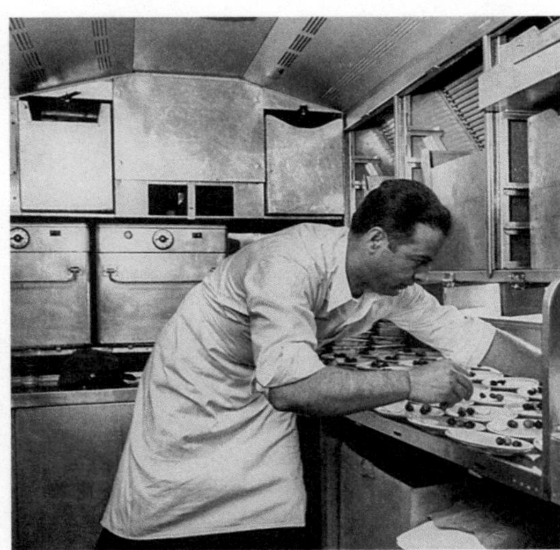

23 As in this galley of a Lockheed Constellation from 1952, the other parts of the cabin interior are also optimized to achieve the best arrangement.

24 This mock-up of the Boeing 707 by Teague Associates from 1956 demonstrates that as a result of the optimizations, the aircraft interior, once subdivided several times, is now transformed into a longitudinal tube-like space.

25 The passenger cabin—here a mock-up of the Lockheed L-1011 from 1968—sheds its visual borrowings from railroads and living rooms in favor of a sleek appearance.

26 This caricature from 1965 illustrates that in addition to seats that continually become more sophisticated, other technical innovations are also introduced in the seating area. Call buttons to summon the hostess, loudspeakers, fresh-air outlets, backlit symbols, and more are intended to make on-board service more efficient and more pleasant.

27 Airplanes like this TWA Constellation, seen in a photo from 1952, park at a distance from the departure building, meaning that passengers must walk a long way while being exposed to the weather.

28 **Waiting in line—after rationalization of the passenger cabin, the bottlenecks shift to passenger handling on the ground.**

29 **Check-in at a New York airport in 1952: Because the terminals are unable to cope with mass-market throngs, the response is to accelerate the handling process.**

13

IDLEWILD
Architectural Engineering

PASSENGERS AND BAGGAGE

To get six million passengers a year and all their baggage on and off planes and through customs without loss or damage or exposure to weather requires some large spaces and ingenious devices: telescopic corridors from lounge to plane, conveyor belts that think, acres of customs counters

PASSENGER LOADING

(Left) Truck-motorized stairways for fair-weather passengers on BOAC
(Right) Self-propelled, telescoping corridors to and from lounge nuzzle up to UAL jets

(Left) PAA's canopy-protected ramps swing on radius to plane position
(Right) AAL has short, enclosed, telescoping ramp with weather seal at plane door

BAGGAGE HANDLING

(Left) Check-in counter at PAA where baggage is weighed, then belt-conveyed to lower level for loading
(Right) Supermarket counters and carts for customs inspection area

(Left) Hand delivery from trucks to sloped metal pick-up counter
(Right) Belt delivery to pick-up area with automatic kicker that spaces bags on sloped counter. Visible at far end, kicker mechanism proceeds along belted track as bags are delivered

ARCHITECTURAL RECORD *September 1961* 189

30 **This page from *Architectural Record* (1961) illustrates how passenger boarding and baggage handling is to be simplified at Idlewild with the aid of technological means.**

31 At Idlewild, the largest American airlines, including TWA, can build their own terminals and optimize their ground handling processes.

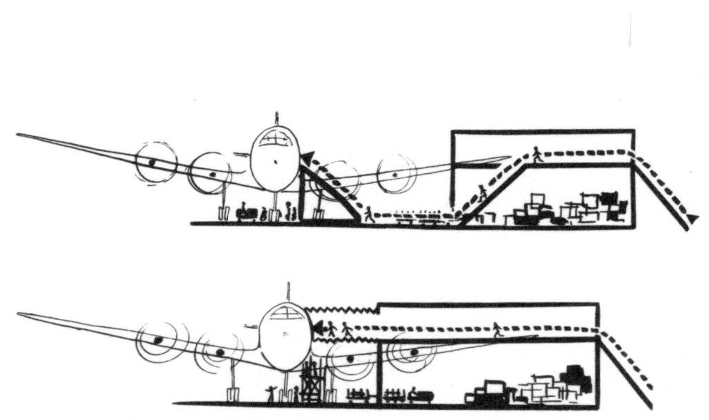

32 The jetway establishes itself as an efficient and effective resource that enables passengers to board and exit the plane without climbing steps or getting their feet wet.

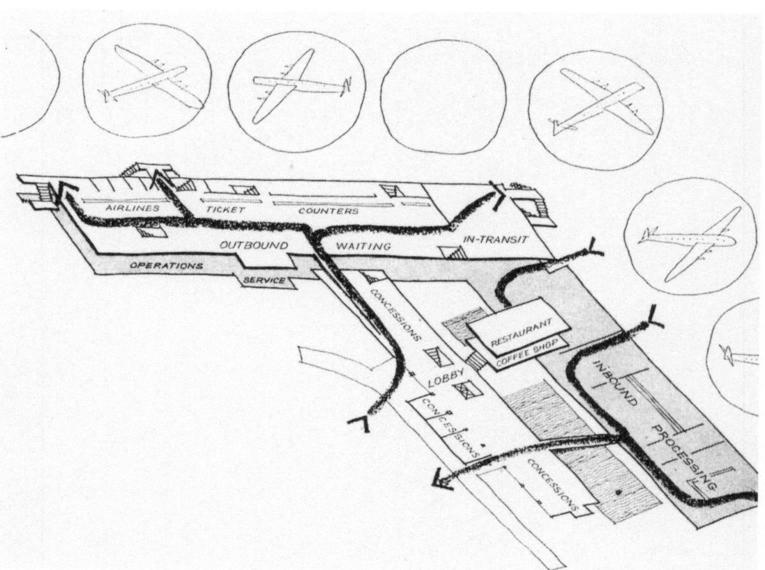

33 This axonometric diagram from 1956 shows an ideal airport without walls. Arrows symbolize one-way traffic with clear destinations. The modern airport terminal corresponds to a barrier-free spatial continuum.

SUMMARY

	Number of Values Used for Average	Average
Terminal		
Date		
Equipment Type		
Flight Number		
Pass Off		24
Pass On		27
Touch Down		
	8	0:30
Begin Taxi		
	8	2:20
Plane in Position		
	19	0:56
Door Opened		
	19	2:24 *
Last Pass Out		
Pass Load'g Begun		
	11	10:22
Pass.Load'g Complete		
Button Up		
	13	2:44
Leave Ramp		
	6	2:31
Wait for T.O.		
	6	1:22
Begin T.O.		
	3	0:24
Wheels Off		
Aero Bridge		
Start		
	3	1:55
Stop		
Start		
	2	1:34
Stop		

* MAJORITY OF FLIGHTS OBSERVED INDICATE THAT
A) LAST 10 PASS. REQ'D 1:30 MIN.
B) ALL OTHERS REQ'D 3 SEC. EA.
∴ 60 PASS REQ = 1:30
+ (60 − 10)(0:03) = 2:30
TOTAL TO DEPLANE = 4:00 MIN

34 In order to derive the ideal spatial relationships for the TWA Terminal, ES&A survey the process times at various airports.

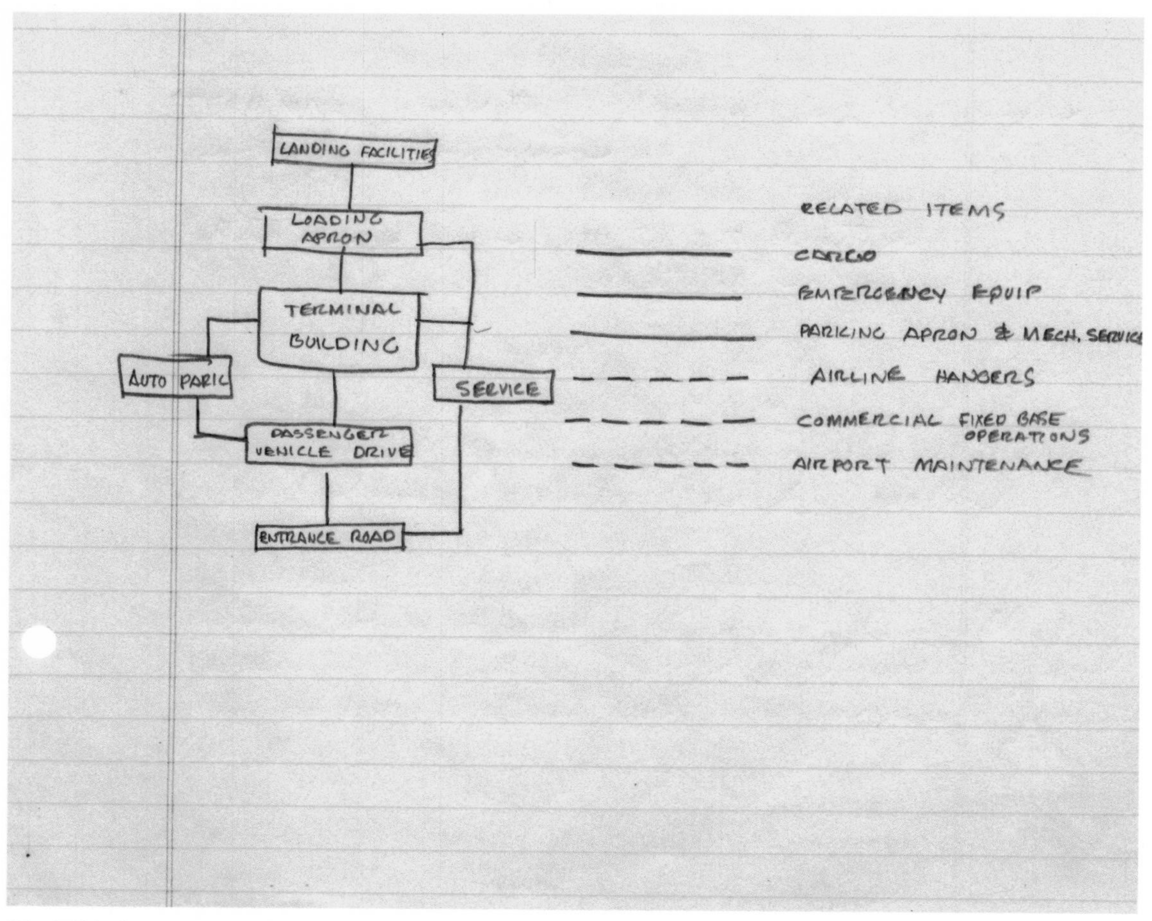

35 **ES&A abstract the different handling stations of an ideal terminal, depicting them as schematic sketches and flow diagrams.**

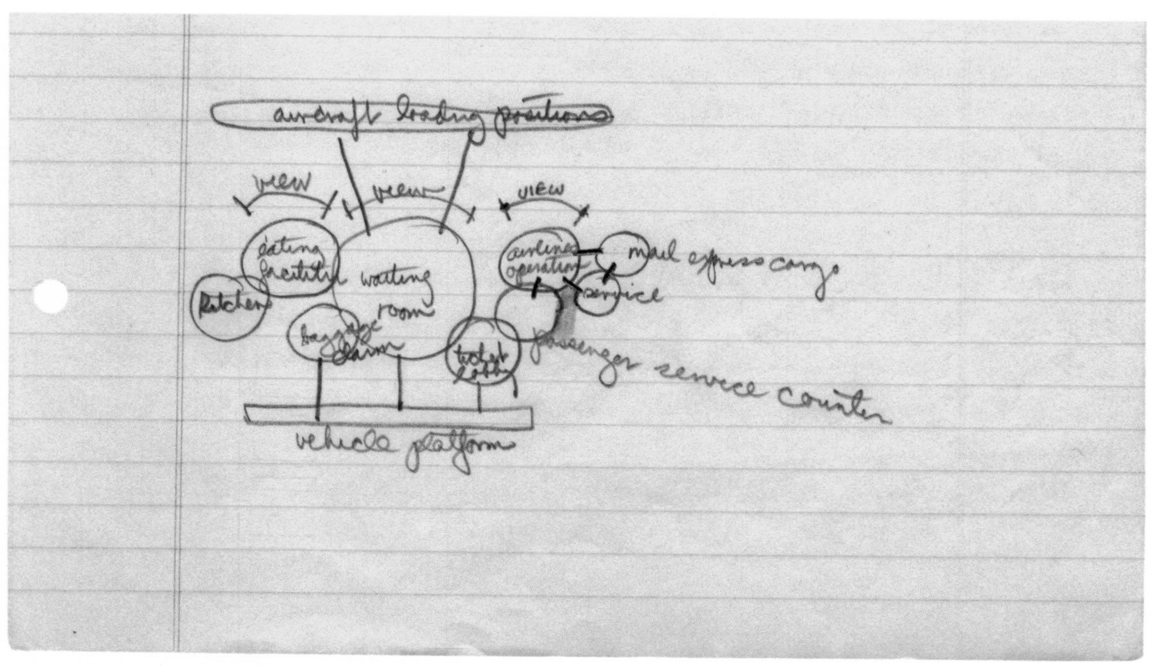

36 **The process studies lead to this scheme of various handling stations (check-in, waiting, baggage claim, food service, etc.).**

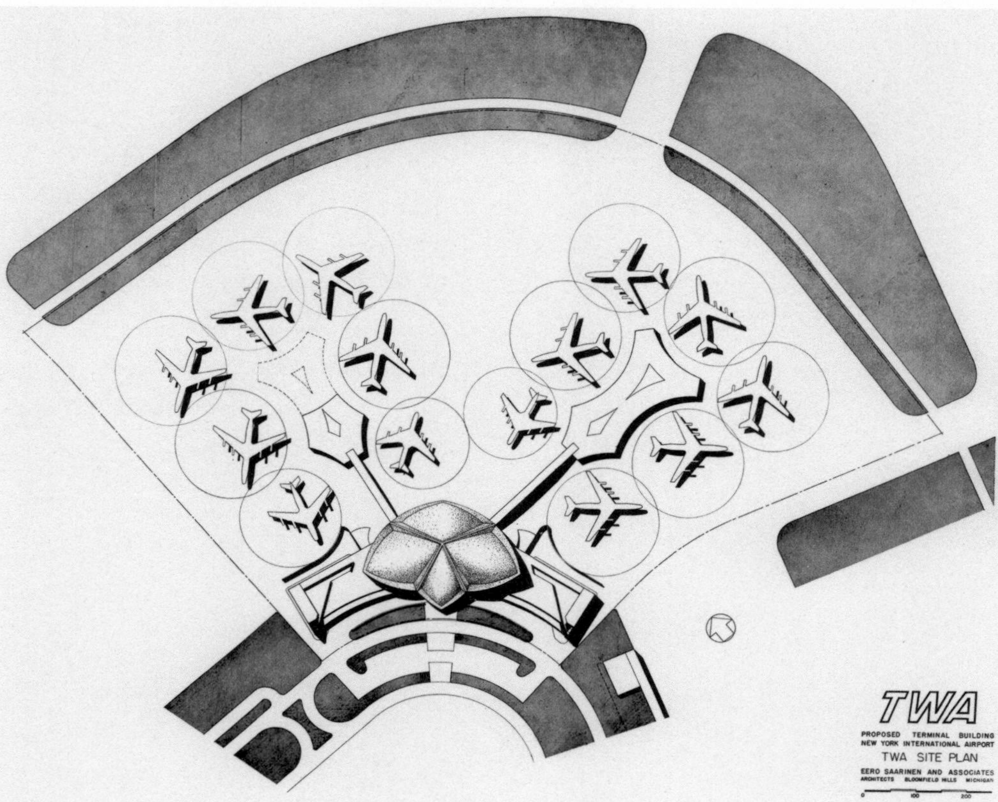

37 This preliminary design is the first to be presented to TWA by ES&A. It largely anticipates the arrangement of uses in the terminal building as it was ultimately built.

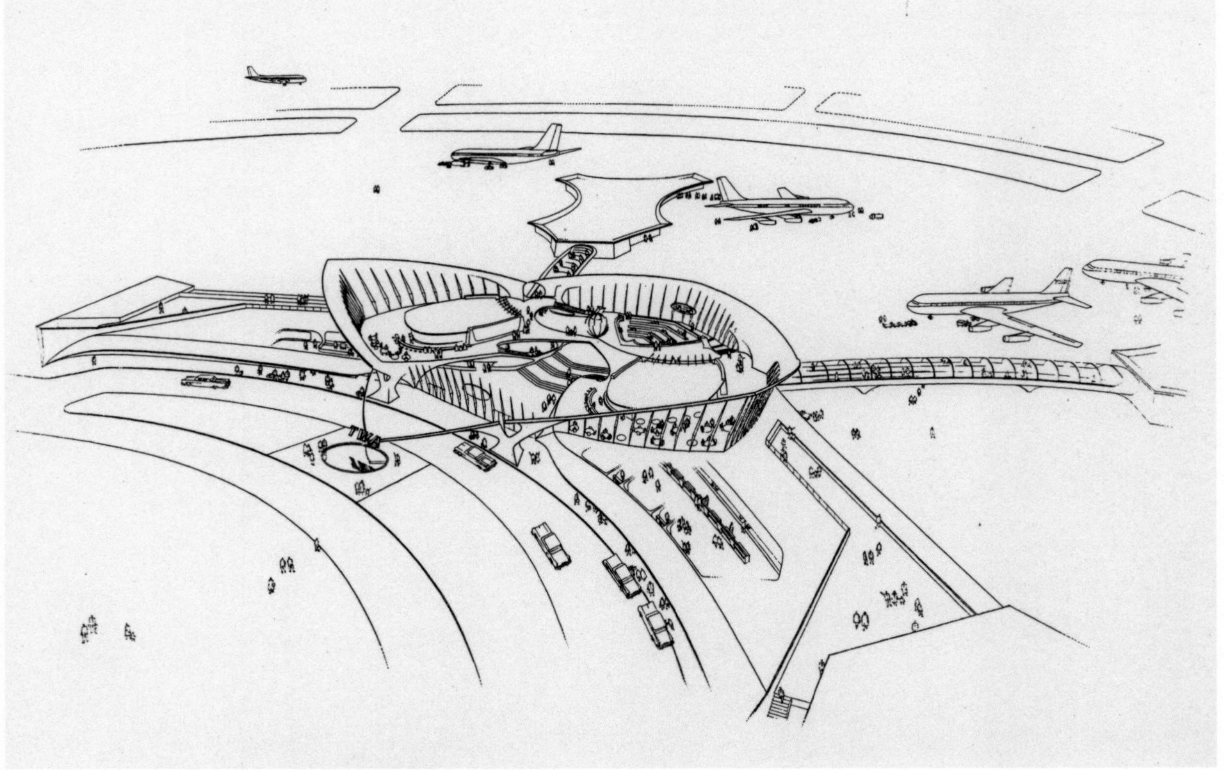

38 The goal of expeditious ground handling leads to a spatial sequence that is nearly free of thresholds and doors. The various handling stations are connected in a series that is almost seamless and without restriction.

39 The employees of TWA are eliminated from the handling process to the greatest extent possible. At check-in, a computer calculates whether any bags are overweight and processes flight reservations in just seconds.

40 What previously required manpower is now accomplished by a machine. A baggage conveyor system transports the travelers' luggage into one of three self-service baggage carousels.

41 Airline passengers encounter only one single glass door on their way from their car to the airplane. They receive flight information from a centrally controlled arrivals and departures board. Passenger flow is handled by a spatially and technically optimized, highly specialized built structure.

1.1 Passenger Cabins Optimized for the Masses

In the development of flight offerings suitable for the masses, TWA plays a pioneering role. In 1949 it first introduces a tourist class on domestic routes, followed by the international routes in 1952.[22] With their "Go now, pay later" program, the airline allows its air passengers to pay for their plane tickets in installments. Fig. 42 Moreover, package deals that are more

42 TWA advertisement for air travel paid in installments, *This Week Magazine*, 1954

cost-effective make it easier for travel-hungry customers to make air journeys abroad. Due to price reductions, air travel is in some cases ultimately almost equally affordable as traveling by train. Owing to adjustments in the supply and because airplanes have not only become faster, but also increasingly more reliable, efficient, and comfortable due to simplified operation, increased travel speed, smoother turbine operation, and better flight safety, the confidence of the traveling public in the means of transportation—and thus the share of the flying population—increases significantly.[23] Furthermore, the economic recovery causes business travel to intensify and brings higher incomes to Americans, with the result that flying moves within reach of the middle class.[24]

Even in 1945, global passenger traffic had more than doubled compared to prewar levels. In 1946, the first full year of peace, 538,000 Americans fly abroad, whereas it is more than a million in 1950 and again almost twice as many by mid-1954. By the mid-

43 Ralph S. Damon, president of TWA 1949–1956, 1954

1950s, a veritable boom develops. *Life* magazine dubs the summer of 1955 "the greatest vacation exodus ever."[25] And in the following year, for the first time more Americans cross the Atlantic on an airplane than on a ship. TWA, too, records impressive growth figures in the decade following the war, which lead among other things to a doubling of the passengers carried within an annual period.[26] In 1952, according to President Ralph S. Damon (1897–1956), TWA has already come a stately step closer to its goal of transforming the airline business into a mass market.[27] Fig. 43 In 1954 the employee magazine *Skyliner* runs the headline "Passenger traffic jumps 10% as business booms in 1954." [28] In the 1960s the trend continues, so that from 1945 to 1972, the number of air passengers in the US climbs from 7 to 32 million, and the percentage of Americans with flight experience clambers to 50 percent. Between 1951 and 1966, the passenger airline industry is the fastest-growing sector of the economy in the United States.[29]

A central prerequisite for the marked increase in passenger capacity is the spatial, procedural, and technical optimization of the aircraft cabin. For this purpose, the aircraft manufacturers and airlines hire all the big names in industrial design: TWA commissions Raymond Loewy (Constellation), Henry Dreyfuss (Super Constellation), and Harley Earl (Convair CV 880); Boeing puts its faith in Walter

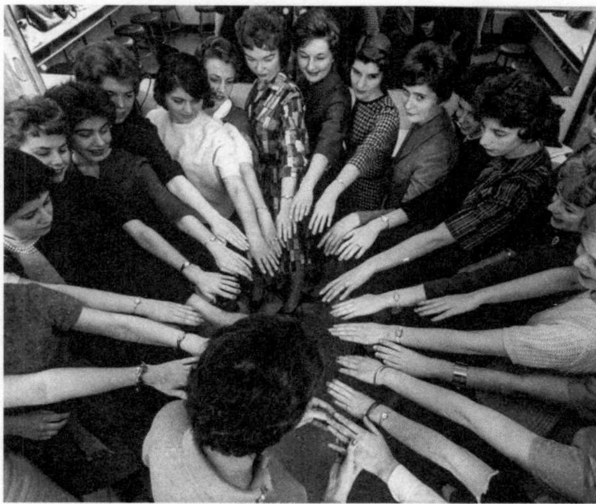

44 Future TWA hostesses at the training center in Kansas City, MO, 1961

Dorwin Teague (Boeing 707); United also chooses Raymond Loewy (Douglas DC-6); and Continental relies on Charles Butler (Vickers Viscount).[30] Their task consists of creating smooth workflows in the passenger cabin and to reduce symptoms of fatigue for the crew and passengers.[31] Maximum space utilization and economic operational processes inside the aircraft become the highest imperative. Thus, via reorientation to the mass market, the loss-making course of business leads to the operational requirement to achieve cost reductions through more efficient processes and automation, where time savings of mere seconds are of value.

An initial starting point for economic optimization is the desire of the airlines to guide and supervise the behavior of their (cabin) staff along standardized paths. Fig. 44 This is clearly reflected in TWA's human resource management during the postwar years. TWA hones and standardizes its service regulations into mandatory staff manuals for the flight crew as well as instruction manuals and operating manuals for navigation, refueling, communication, and loading the airplanes.[32] For a TWA manager in the Transportation Division, for example, job description "Job No. 5-636, Chart Ref. 75B" stipulates in detail the operating hierarchies, mandatory reporting duties, primary and secondary scope of duties and responsibilities, down to internal and external cultivation of relationships.[33] The effort to monitor and control the activities of the employees also leads to the definition of certain body dimensions for certain occupational groups. This is shown, for instance, by the fact that TWA uses newspaper advertisements to seek flight attendants with precisely defined personal qualities and body characteristics such as age (21 to 26), body size (5'-2" to 5'-6"), and weight (100 to 130 pounds).[34] Along the same vein, TWA categorizes and standardizes its employees based on elaborate evaluation schemes or mathematically calculated average values, which is demonstrated by a computer-based profile from 1965 of their standard flight attendant:

> "Miss Average TWA Hostess is 21 years old, five feet five and a third inches tall, weighs 118.1 lbs. She has brown hair and blue eyes. She's had two years of college and has been with TWA for 23 months and two days. Her home state is California." [35]

Inasmuch as the company standardizes the actors as well as the activities to be carried out, not only are the processes precisely defined, executable, and controllable, but above all, the desired operational efficiency can be established based on these parameters.[36] Deviations from the standard, like individual behaviors, are disruptive to the performance of the organization and should therefore be avoided through supervision and the threat of sanctions. Industrial designers proceed from this principle of scientific management in order to ensure the required efficiency in the face of pronounced passenger growth. An example of this is the work of Henry Dreyfuss, who conducted measurement studies to define average human bodies (he calls them Joe and Josephine). Their body dimensions are then used by the designer for the design of seats or the arrangement of shift levers in the cockpit.[37] With the aid of motion studies of work in kitchens and aircraft cabins, as well as other processes in an airplane, the necessary functional elements are optimized for the most favorable configuration.

On the basis of such activity studies, TWA has the work clothes of its hostesses trimmed for operational efficiency. For the uniform designed in collaboration with Don Loper in 1960, Raymond Loewy analyzes the movements of the hostesses to find out what kind of clothes are best suited for their work. Press releases emphasize not only the new uniform's appearance but also the importance of its durability, comfort,

45 Passenger cabin, Douglas DC-6, probably United Airlines, ca. 1954

ease of care, quality, and versatility. The result is a uniform with sleeves that consist of a single piece of fabric in order to avoid seams that restrict motion. The skirt is buttoned to the camisole so it cannot slip out of the skirt. As TWA sees it, these elements of clothing, like the snap mechanism of the uniform's cuff links, promote a rational and efficient workflow for those wearing them.[38] Even more far-reaching are the effects that time and motion studies have on the cabin layout. By the end of the 1950s, the special day and night interiors that were the former standard disappear in favor of flexible furnishings. With the introduction of jet planes, the spacious lounges in first class vanish almost entirely. The airlines compensate for the price reductions in tourist class by installing space-saving rows of seats all pointing in the direction of flight, like those that travelers know from buses. **Fig. 45** The goal: a reduction of spacing, width, and legroom for the rows of seats. After the Second World War, the seat pitch recommended by IATA, the airline industry trade association, measures 120 centimeters in tourist class, while at the beginning of the 1960s it is 99 and a decade later just 86 centimeters.[39] The reason for the new seating concept is—in addition to saving space—the flexibility to divide the passenger cabin according to customer demand. In 1955, TWA namely becomes the first provider to switch over to accommodating two different booking classes in the passenger cabin instead of operating separate first-class and tourist flights.[40] Later, at least on short-haul flights, the merging of tourist and first class proceeds by using the same seats throughout the entire cabin. In the course of such optimizations, a spatial transformation takes place: The aircraft interior, once subdivided several times but now no longer in need of being adapted to changing requirements, transforms itself more and more into a single, preferably uninterrupted, longitudinal tube-like space.

46 Plastic molded seat by designer E. Gilbert Mason for TWA, 1961

Under the banner of economic efficiency, adaptability, as well as interchangeability, lightness, and ease of maintenance mutate into decisive criteria for the cabin environment. Upon discontinuing the comfortable lounge seats, the airlines regularly introduce ever more technically sophisticated seats, yet they do not lose sight of properties such as their weight and the space they occupy. **Fig. 46** The mass-produced wall and ceiling cladding is now made of plastic, which not only facilitates cleaning and replacement, but also shortens the needed maintenance time. The fabric curtains also fall victim to maintenance friendliness and are replaced by easier-to-care-for synthetic blends. And the in-flight meal service also comes into the focus of operational optimization. **Fig. 47** Emphasis is given to the lightness and space-saving dimensions of serving utensils. The introduction of folding tray tables in the late 1950s and serving carts in the 1960s provides another significant operational simplification. Additional technical innovations in the passenger's seating area are designed to make on-board service even more efficient: the hostess can be summoned simply by pressing a button, passenger information comes from loudspeakers, oxygen masks automatically fall down from their holders in an emergency, and electric light symbols indicate when smoking must be discontinued and the seatbelts must be fastened. But these represent only a temporary climax. Soon, the airline industry is thinking about new types of serving carts, which are intended to speed up the meal service, and microwave ovens are introduced to shorten the preparation time needed for in-flight meals.[41] In 1972 TWA aptly describes their Lockheed L-1011 as "virtually an automatic airplane."[42]

47 In-flight catering prior to the introduction of folding tables and serving carts, 1952

As a result, the standards for the interiors of commercial aircraft are fundamentally transformed. Henry Dreyfuss formulates a revealing new model in 1955: "An airplane interior that looks and performs like a machine racing through the stratosphere rather than the front parlor it imitates today."[43] In the course of development, the passenger cabin not only sheds its optical borrowings from railroads and living rooms in favor of a sleek appearance, but its operational layout is also increasingly guided by the ideal of a reliable and smoothly functioning machine. Being able to handle large numbers of people creates new conditions for the ground infrastructure.

1.2 New Requirements for Ground Infrastructure

Idlewild New York International Airport is the City of New York's second airport (alongside La Guardia), and soon after it opens in 1948, plans are already underway for a fundamental renewal of the just-opened but undersized facility. In February of 1955, the Port of New York Authority (PONYA), which operates the city's two airports, provides information about its reorganization plans.[44] A concept of smaller terminal buildings that are capable of being individualized, dubbed "Terminal City," shall be built according to the plans of Wallace K. Harrison, a partner of Harrison and Abramovitz. Larger domestic airlines are given an opportunity to build terminals according to their own concepts and requirements. Smaller airlines and foreign carriers are accommodated in the International Arrivals Building or share a terminal building, so their freedom to act is more limited. With the Terminal City airport concept, the planning authority explores new ground. Individual pioneer airlines had already set up their own terminals at remote outposts, yet in most cases, airlines share the ground infrastructure placed at their disposal by the operator of the airport. It is a novelty that in Idlewild, air carriers can operate their own terminal buildings, so-called unit terminals.[45]

As the fourth-largest airline in the US, TWA is also given the opportunity to build its own unit terminal that meets its operational needs.[46] Toward the end of 1955, TWA commissions Eero Saarinen and Associates (ES&A) with the design work.[47] As with the master plan for the entire airport, the operational requirements for the terminal defined by the carrier are also high, which is not surprising given the airline's economic situation. During the entire time when the terminal was being developed, TWA would be burdened not only with financial problems. An internal letter from 1961 documents that

48 Criticism of the complexity of modern airports of the day, *Architectural Record,* 1951

after optimizing its airplanes, TWA also identifies a need for improving ground handling:

> "Since TWA currently is able to offer almost everything that any other airline can in the way of in-flight service and on-time performance, it is reasonable to assume that no small part of our inability to match competitors' loads in major markets is the result of sub-standard terminal facilities at principal cities, notably Idlewild, O'Hare and Los Angeles."[48]

The airline does not blame the capacity of its airplanes for their inadequate seat load factor—the passenger occupancy rate of airplanes—but its obsolete airport infrastructure. The airline is not alone with this problem, however. Given strong passenger growth during the 1950s, many airports are no longer able to cope with the steadily increasing aircraft capacity and are bursting at the seams. In contrast to the service on board, the ground handling at US airports is miserable according to popular opinion. "As the bottleneck is relieved in the air," remarks *Business Week* in 1954, "it's merely moved to the ground."[49] The airport planners and architects have not been able to keep pace with the increase in passengers and the technological changes in the air. The various terminals are obsolete soon after their completion.[50] One critic sums it up accordingly in 1956: "In the air the consumer may be treated like a king. But on the ground he still has to fight his way through a chamber of horrors."[51] **Fig. 48**

This assessment not only encapsulates the discrepancy between ground and air infrastructure, but in a significant way it also refers indirectly to the model of modern airport architecture prevalent at the time. The airport of the future, the article continues, waits with untangled flows of passengers, baggage, and cargo; short, direct, broad, and well-marked footpaths; and technical support such as moving walkways, automatic doors, conveyor belts, etc.[52] Instead of labyrinthine spatial cells, the author postulates the ideal of a contiguous sequence of spacious halls following operational logic, combined with clear and short connecting paths separated by direction. An axonometric drawing fittingly illustrates the ideal airport terminal as having no walls, and lines with arrows represent distinct directions of movement with clear destinations.[53] In place of the earlier airport, with its confusing juxtaposition of small rooms, we now have a new understanding: the vision of a modern airport terminal corresponds to a barrier-free spatial continuum of zones flowing into one another, which follow each other as directly as possible in an operationally logical sequence corresponding to the different steps in the handling process. The underlying guiding principle is formulated by an airport expert this way: "Air transport's primary product is speed—speed in transporting the businessman, the traveller, mail and more and more cargo anywhere in the world."[54] The handling process should be accelerated in view of rising numbers of passengers, so that the passengers and their baggage move without obstacle and rapidly from ground transport to air transport (and vice versa).

Fundamental to this ideal, as with the aircraft cabin, is the idea of a machine. "An air terminal is a machine and its principal job is to simplify the transfer of passengers and cargo from ground to air transportation."[55] Albert Heino, one of the best-known airport planners of his time, is not alone with his appeal. Colleagues postulate in 1953: "Whatever the operational system adopted, it is clear that the air station must function precisely—it is basically a machine to facilitate transfer of passengers from the ground to the air and vice-versa."[56] Until now, and antithetical to these demands, the ground handling of airplanes and passengers takes place substantially without the use of auxiliary mechanical means. For example, passengers who have landed are personally given their luggage by an airport employee after it has been heaved, also by hand, from the plane onto a cart, then transported from there to the luggage room, and finally unloaded. **Fig. 49** The stipulations of the specialist engineers do not bring concrete results until the early 1950s. "To get over the technical hurdles of quadrupled airspeeds and zooming volume of air transport," *Business Week* declares in 1954, "airports are looking more and more to the engineers."[57] Trials are undertaken at American airports to accelerate the ground handling of airplanes by using technical equipment.

49 Manual loading of cargo, Atlanta Municipal Airport, GA, 1956

A major problem of ground handling since the dawn of civil aviation, namely bringing passengers from the terminal to the waiting aircraft (and back) without getting wet—constitutes a developmental focus for the airport engineers. It is a problem because the airplanes park at a distance from the departure building, thus exposing the passengers to the elements on the sometimes long route in between.[58] **Fig. 50**

Given this problem, the engineers are faced with a fundamental question: "Whether it is better to bring the people to the planes or the planes to the people."[59] Initially, trials pursue the latter option as the Whiting Corporation introduces its "Loadair" airplane parking system in 1950. Fig. 51 A pilot maneuvers the airplane onto trolleys standing at the ready, which are then drawn along rails to the terminal with the aid of winches. Finally, the airplane comes to a halt alongside the terminal, enabling access to the front and rear aircraft doors. *Aviation Week* describes the parking system as an "automatic plane parking device" and promises time savings of 50 percent. Despite this promising prediction, deployment does not move beyond experimental use, first in the Colombian city of Barranquilla, then at Idlewild (in the United Terminal). [60]

50 Criticism of the lack of weather protection at airports at the time, *Architectural Record,* 1951

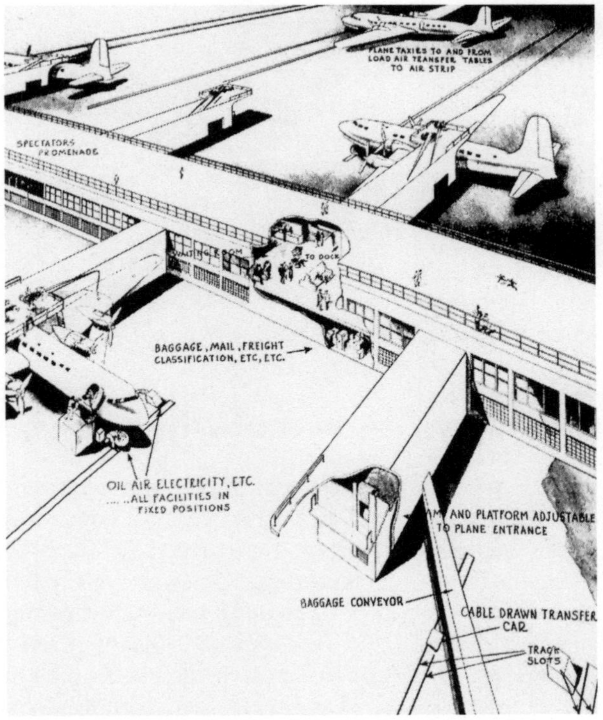

51 "Loadair" docking system, Whiting Corporation, 1950

Instead, it is the opposite approach, of taking the passengers to the airplane, that leads to a breakthrough. American Airlines experiments in 1959 with a telescopic connection between the terminal building and the front cabin door of the parked aircraft. In the same year, the passenger boarding bridge (also called jetway) goes into service in San Francisco and New York, establishing itself as an efficient and effective resource that enables passengers to board and exit the plane without climbing steps or getting wet.[61] Fig. 52 It is revealing that the passenger boarding bridge prevails over the "Loadair" system. As a mechanical appendix to the terminal building, the jetway testifies to the technical adaptation of airport architecture to meet the needs of the aircraft. Meanwhile, the "Loadair" parking system, a mechanical intermediary detached from the terminal, cannot close the gap between the terminal and airplane in a way that optimally meets the operational criteria. In other words: the terminal itself must, in accordance with the requirements of the airport planners, be integrated with contrivances like the jetway to form a machine. Because the economic success of an airport facility can be measured by its ability to enable a quick and efficient transition between ground and air transportation, the conclusion is that a passenger handling machine conceived on the basis of precise spatial and passenger parameters should mechanize and automate as fully as possible the sought-after process ideal of direct and seamless passenger flows separated by direction.

52 Douglas DC-8 docked to the terminal via jetways, San Francisco, CA, ca. 1965

This criterion for success of the terminal, based on operational logic that airport engineers have posited since the 1940s, was to decisively influence the requirements TWA presented to ES&A. The airline essentially has free rein in defining its specifications. One indication of this is that the planning guidelines issued by the airport authority are incorporated into a document comprising only six pages. The basis of TWA's catalog of requirements for ES&A are various traffic forecasts and the spacial needs these entail, as revealed by an internal report from October 3, 1956. TWA's additional needs include maximizing the num-

53 Dockworkers on a stack of freight pallets, New York, 1947

ber of departure gates, locating the gates as close as possible to the terminal building, and ensuring that the "largest aircraft under consideration by TWA" can take its waiting position and leave again under its own power. Furthermore, the report contains the client's considerations about optimal arrangements for parking its aircraft on the site. Finally, the future adaptability of the terminal to the projected capacity is an important criterion for designing the departure gates and the passenger handling facilities. In summary, the report states: "Space requirements were the basis of the Architect's plan and determined the general scope of the project."[62]

The importance given to quantitative targets in the spatial program reflects the fierce competition TWA confronts, inasmuch as it aims to reduce costs through efficient operational procedures and gain an advantage in the battle for customer patronage with satisfactory space conditions. Its requirements are indebted to the mindset of airport architect and engineer Walther Prokosch, the co-author of one of the first planning manuals for airports (*Airport Planning*, 1946). In 1951, Prokosch writes an article in *Architectural Record* with planning recommendations, which also appear, almost to the letter, in TWA's building specifications. "Every study must begin with preparation of traffic forecasts for passenger, airmail and cargo volumes," advises Prokosch, for example, who also enjoins a shift from "planes flying" to "people flying."[63] What the planner has in mind, and what sounds hopeful for the airline passenger, is demonstrated by a change in the ground handling process introduced at the beginning of the 1950s. In order to shorten the planes' ground time, the airlines conduct ticket checks at the gate instead of inside the airplane. The airline industry calls the areas established for this purpose "hold areas," like the cargo compartments in airplanes. Like cargo, the flight passenger is accordingly dispatched and then transported via the "batch method" onto the airplane.[64]

From this perspective, the passenger seems like cargo to be transported according to a logistical model. On the other hand, Francis Meisch, a colleague of Prokosch, derives from this a call that the passenger—just like the freight pallets that found common use in the United States beginning in the late 1920s and especially during the Second World War **Fig. 53**—be regarded as a standardized unit whose transport through the terminal must be controlled to increase process efficiency: "The passenger, a mobile unit, must be controlled and guided for safety and operating efficiency, in his own interest."[65] Through control and guidance of passengers standardized to the average, deviations from the standard should be avoided during handling so as to come to terms with rapid passenger growth and to manage operations economically. According to this principle, ES&A should address operational optimization of the terminal as well.

1.3 Analysis and Research

54 Grand Central Terminal, New York, 1941

Even though Eero Saarinen emphasizes that every project has its own priorities for analysis and development, the design work at ES&A follows a recurring pattern.[66] Apart from thorough research, the analysis and documentation of operational processes with the aid of flow diagrams emerges as an important part of the planning. For TWA, a client facing operational challenges, Saarinen is a particularly suitable architect in this respect, which would manifest itself concisely in the TWA Flight Center.[67] As the design work for the Trans World Flight Center begins in the first quarter of 1956, employees of Saarinen's firm visit several newly opened airports, equipped with notebooks and stopwatches.[68] Their objective is to record the functional routines and, from them, derive the optimal spatial connections and the shortest and smoothest circulation paths for the terminal they will be planning. Saarinen's employees not only collect data at airports—including Chicago O'Hare, Pittsburgh, and Philadelphia—however, but also in New York's Grand Central Terminal train station, which also lends itself to movement and time studies due to an even larger number of passengers.[69] **Fig. 54** Saarinen is likely compelled to pursue these extraordinary efforts not only to

55 Eero Saarinen leaving an airplane, ca. 1960

meet the demands of his client, but also due to his personal assessment of the existing airport terminal, which he repeatedly describes as awkward and impractical. The ways of the frequent flyer demand more efficient terminal buildings: "Eero believes it's immoral to waste time arriving before the airplane motors are being tuned up. Even on transatlantic flights," knows his wife, Aline Saarinen.[70] **Fig. 55** The Principal Design Associate, Kevin Roche (born 1922), recalls in an interview that Saarinen carried a stopwatch with him on his air travels, so he could measure for himself the various sequences during ground handling.[71] Optimizing the ground handling process at the TWA Terminal is of top priority.

The studies lead to an exhaustive inventory of passenger handling on what were then the most modern airports in the United States. Saarinen's estate includes an analysis report on the subprocess between landing

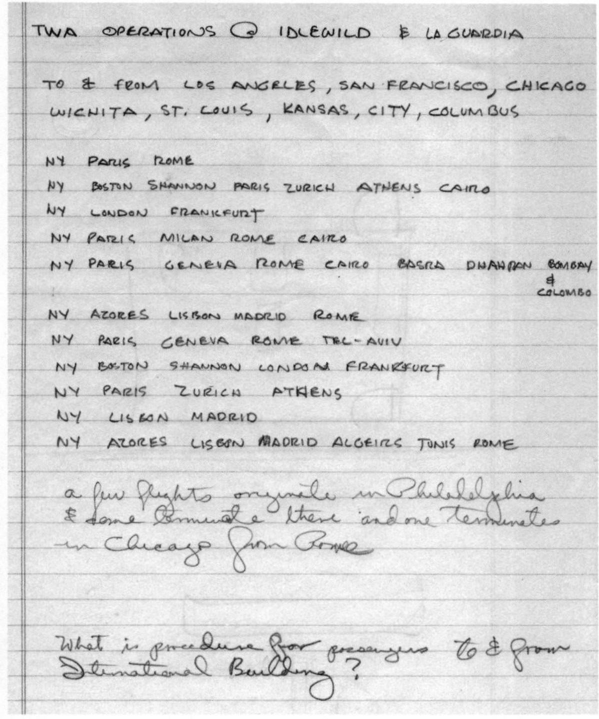

TWA OPERATIONS @ IDLEWILD & LA GUARDIA

TO & FROM LOS ANGELES, SAN FRANCISCO, CHICAGO
WICHITA, ST. LOUIS, KANSAS, CITY, COLUMBUS

NY PARIS ROME
NY BOSTON SHANNON PARIS ZURICH ATHENS CAIRO
NY LONDON FRANKFURT
NY PARIS MILAN ROME CAIRO
NY PARIS GENEVA ROME CAIRO BASRA DHAHRAN BOMBAY & COLOMBO
NY AZORES LISBON MADRID ROME
NY PARIS GENEVA ROME TEL-AVIV
NY BOSTON SHANNON LONDON FRANKFURT
NY PARIS ZURICH ATHENS
NY LISBON MADRID
NY AZORES LISBON MADRID ALGEIRS TUNIS ROME

a few flights originate in Philadelphia & some terminate there and one terminates in Chicago from Rome

What is procedure for passengers to & from International Building?

56 Analysis of air routes to/from Idlewild and La Guardia, ES&A, ca. 1956

and deplaning (the other subprocesses appear to have been lost) that provides detailed information about the findings of the investigation. The average times for the various segments of the process between "touch down," "begin taxi," "plane in position," "door opened," "last pass out," and so on are based on two to nineteen field surveys. ES&A conclude in summary that four minutes elapse on average between touchdown and debarking, whereby the last ten occupants of the aircraft each require disproportionately more time.[72] Furthermore, according to the collected data, at the ten airports that were inspected, distance traveled by foot totals an average of 940 feet (287 m).[73] In order to understand the operational requirements of TWA even more precisely, Saarinen has their air routes from La Guardia and Idlewild analyzed. **Fig. 56** That he is once again interested in the underlying operational processes is indicated by the question jotted next to a list, wondering how the transiting airline passengers get from the future TWA Terminal to the International Arrivals Building.

Besides this empirical survey, ES&A make an extensive review of the professional literature in order to understand the procedural, technical, and typological standards of airport terminals. They study numerous architecture magazines and reference books as well as the planning recommendations of

57 Aline and Eero Saarinen (back) with Kevin Roche at work, probably at the office in Bloomfield Hills, MI, ca. 1957

professional trade associations and government agencies. If one believes a statement from Roger Johnson, an architect at ES&A from 1953 to 1956 and involved in the research, the results were unsatisfactory.[74] With a total of around sixty magazine articles and books, however, the research covers a considerably broad spectrum, and from today's perspective it proves to be extremely thorough. Saarinen's manuscripts confirm this impression: the ensuing handwritten notes summarize, on about forty pages, the state of knowledge on the ideal arrangement of aircraft at the time. They also reflect the demand for speed and efficiency, the principle of separating passenger, visitor, and cargo flows, considerations of weather protection, and the imperative of mechanization. Beginning with elementary statements such as "The time element is a most important reason for an efficient airport layout" or "Speed is the offering of air transportation," and continuing with the procedural principle that "Incoming & outgoing passengers must be separated (two levels or divided concourses)" as well as a call for mechanization—"Better to use conveyors than chutes in baggage handling"—these notes illustrate that ES&A derive the essential operational criteria for success from the technical literature.[75] Last but not least, they also study the article by Walther Prokosch, whose key demands find their way, virtually unchanged, into TWA's performance-driven collection of requirements, and additionally make a note of another key sentence: "Airports have become facilities for handling people rather than airplanes." Prokosch is not, however, the only well-known airport engineer that ES&A carefully examine. Their research also leads the architects to the previously cited publications by Francis Meisch and Albert Heino, as well as to other standard works of contemporary airport planning, such as *Airport Planning* by Charles Froesch and Walther Prokosch and *Airports: Design, Construction and Management* by Horace K. Glidden. The basic principles for the procedural and technical organization of airport facilities that ES&A recorded thus comprehensively reflect the state of knowledge at the time.

Except in text notes, ES&A record what has been read in various graphic diagrams. For one thing, the architects examine around thirty-five aircraft-parking schemes.[76] Schematic linear, curved, and pier-like terminal layouts are analyzed in terms of necessary walking distances and the number of possible parking positions. For another, ES&A abstract the horizontal and vertical relationships of the varied handling stations of an ideal terminal to a series of schematic sketches or flow diagrams. Saarinen's sequence plans symbolize the flows of people and materials with solid, dashed, or dotted lines and arrows, while geometric shapes such as rectangles and circles denote different activities or actions. When those at ES&A do not consistently adhere to the presentation rules which had become standard within the company's organization by this point in time, their flow diagrams illustrate the clear intention to graphically visualize complex operational processes, relationships, and dependencies in a clear and standardized way.[77] Among the flow diagrams, one stands out in particular; it depicts the ideal pedestrian flows of not only departing, arriving, and connecting passengers, but also airport visitors. Different options for separating the passenger and freight flows from each other vertically, as several of the studied sources do, are also examined. Ultimately, the studies lead to a scheme of various handling stations (check-in, waiting, baggage claim, food service, etc.). Aline Saarinen, who is often present in the studio **Fig. 57**, writes the following in summary of this stage of design to an unknown recipient: "When you were here TWA had progressed to studies and diagrams of passenger and baggage movements, timing, plane clearance and parking, etc.—all the results of a long period of investigation."[78] Design of the terminal can begin.

1.4 Passenger Handling Machine

Under the guidance of Eero Saarinen and Kevin Roche, Leon Yulkowski designs the site plan first of all, on the basis of the identified airport standards and in dialogue with TWA. The architects develop a system that is substantially different from the passenger terminals that are common at the time, which usually extend along the main access road or protrude into the airfield like a pier.[79] Instead, ES&A create a fragmented complex: a main building (reception, main waiting hall), one wing each for arriving and departing passengers (check-in, baggage drop-off/claim), and two detached "satellite" buildings (departure gates) on the apron to the runway. The latter are linked to the main building by two bridge-like connecting corridors.[80] Fig. 58

This layout, like the initial process analysis, testifies to the operational requirements of the client: For an apron area of a given size, the building arrangement maximizes the aircraft parking positions and minimizes the required building area. Since the paths

58 Connecting corridor between the main building and the satellite, TWA Flight Center, 1962

between the main building and the satellites have clear start and end points, they are ideal for the use of moving walkways. A split-level solution unbundles passenger and goods flows at least in part on two stories, which, thanks to one-way traffic, affords improved utilization of land, higher frequencies, and safety for the passengers.[81] Whereas the split-level arrangement divides operational processes vertically, the two wings of the building are intended to separate the departing and arriving air travelers horizontally. In combination with the jetways employed here, the bridge-like connections between the main building and the satellites enable the processes to be distributed on two stories, which optimizes the handling of cargo and passengers on the air side.[82] Furthermore, the separate cargo level on the ground floor has a positive effect on the handling efficiency of the proposed airport terminal. Even the restaurants, bars, and entertainment facilities located on the gallery level, which, for the sake of promoting sales ought to obstruct the most direct route of flight customers as they move through the terminal (as already recognized by contemporary airport planners), do not interrupt the flow of movement.[83] Along with the sequence of spaces, the room sizes are ultimately also conceived for optimal material flow according to plan. Based on the various peak capacities and maximum passenger volumes specified by TWA, the spaces are laid out by accordingly adjusting the parameters of area, length, and number of seats for the anticipated passenger and freight flows. And, last but not least, ES&A also give consideration to passenger growth, proceeding under the premise that the terminal could one day be expanded by adding another level to the single-story wings or extending a satellite (although neither were to happen).[84]

The first preliminary design presented in the late summer of 1956 already largely anticipates the arrangement of uses in the terminal building as it was ultimately built. As a rendition of production (check-in), storage (waiting), and transport (arriving and departing), the sequential chain of passenger activities in the course of embarking (and analogously while disembarking) is consistent with the desired process ideal borrowed from the cargo industry. Saarinen arrays the various stations that the airline passenger must pass during the ground handling process into a sequence based on operational logic: The departing air passenger arrives in a vehicle—either directly in front of the departure hall or at the Terminal City parking lot—proceeds to the check-in area, then goes to a sunken waiting area, one of the restaurants or the first-class lounge, continues out to one of the two satellites, and finally boards a waiting airplane. The design represents a direct spatial translation of the flow diagrams delineated in the course of the research. The activities at the different handling stations correspond to separate areas of the building, arranged sequentially analogous to the flow diagrams. The goal of expeditious and trouble-free ground handling leads to a spatial sequence that is nearly free of thresholds and doors. The only spatial barriers that an airline passenger in the terminal encounters are a glass door and shallow cascading stairs.[85] Otherwise, the various handling stations spatially merge into one another seamlessly and without restriction.[86]

The intent to make the routes within the terminal as short and free of obstacles as possible is most plainly expressed in the two passageways running in midair, connecting the satellites to the main building. Here, the process ideal of a straight and unobstructed point-to-point connection, as it is idealized in the flow diagram, is given its most immediate architectural expression. The connecting corridors comply with the process theory model of a direct, uninterrupted, linear, and mechanizable subprocess with a clear beginning and end (main building and satellite) as well as precisely defined inputs and outputs (number of aircraft passengers). Even though the spatial organization accepts certain compromises in relation to the theoretically ideal ground handling—as will be shown in the chapter "Jet Propaganda"—the plan of the TWA Terminal nevertheless marks a fundamental departure from the cell-like spatial concepts of previous airports. Architecture critic Edgar Kaufmann, Jr. consequently describes the route of the airline passengers in the Trans World Flight Center as "channels of life" within a "complex yet clearly organized . . . entity."[87] From this perspective, the airport terminal appears to be an architectural translation of the sequence plans that Saarinen and his colleagues had previously drawn on paper.

But the terminal is meant to accelerate not only the transition between ground and air transportation, but also that from one airplane to another. In this regard, the TWA Flight Center exploits its traits as a process-optimized transfer point even more explicitly. For a passenger changing from one TWA flight to another within the satellite (transit passengers to other airlines must change terminals), the distance between the two airplanes is eliminated almost entirely. With the transfer process from car to plane, Saarinen seeks to minimize the transit distance, and with the satellite concept he nearly eliminates it. Seen in this light, the satellites conform to the ground handling ideal of a localized transfer point and represent the direct expression of Saarinen's endeavor to enable an effortless transition from one means of transportation to another for the traveler in the terminal. According to the same ideal concept of transferring at one and the same place, TWA also makes plans for a heliport, which, however, would only temporarily go into operation in 1964 for the New York World's Fair.[88]

Aside from its spatial disposition, the TWA Terminal is organized by its technical equipment based on the model of an efficient machine.[89] The building has a control tower of its own, located above the northern satellite, that guides the airline passengers on their way through the terminal.[90] A TWA press release aptly titled "Control Tower at TWA Flight Center Directs Operations" characterizes the central control

59 Arrivals and departures board with information desk, TWA Flight Center, ca. 1962

room as "a factor which assures the traveling public of the utmost in efficient operations, coordinated terminal service, and on-time flight arrivals and departures."[91] The flight control in the tower directs travelers to the correct departure gate by means of two display boards, whose flight information can be synchronously adjusted via keyboard input. Fig. 59 An internal network of monitors, which is likewise operated from the control tower, also broadcasts the arrival and departure information in all the other areas of the terminal. A public address system, consisting of a central loudspeaker in the middle of the hall and additional ones in the washrooms, restaurants, and satellites, accomplishes the same. Fig. 60

The employees of TWA, who receive their work instructions from the same control room via radio equipment, microphones, telephones, and a branched pneumatic tube transport (PTT) system, are eliminated from the handling process to the greatest extent possible. Not only are they lacking entirely in TWA's public statements about the terminal, but in view of the goal of a process that is automated to the greatest possible degree and which requires no

60 Speakers hanging from the vaults of the departure hall, TWA Flight Center, ca. 1962

human intervention, they see themselves as actually being expelled from various handling stations. Although the electronically controlled doors that were planned for the building entrance were ultimately not installed, at check-in, a computer calculates whether any bags are overweight and prints out a corresponding receipt; and an automatic reservation system processes flight reservations, which used to take up to two hours, in just seconds.[92] On one hand, travelers are informed by recorded announcements, and on the other hand, a modern video system relays current information about flight schedules.[93] Furthermore, TWA has a baggage conveyor system installed that transports the travel goods to one of three self-service

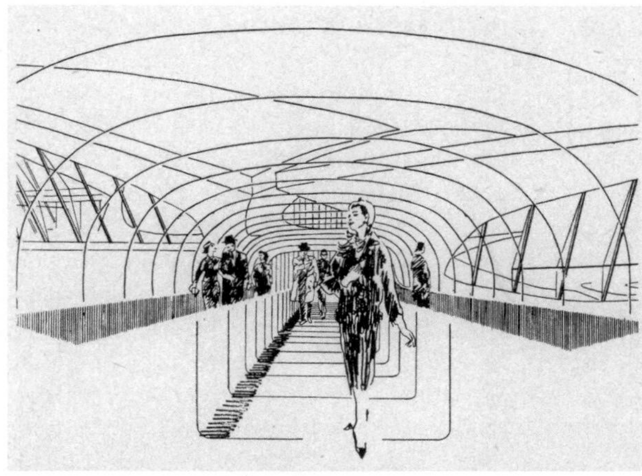

61 **Sketch visualizing the moving sidewalk, TWA Flight Center, 1957**

baggage carousels, where landed passengers can reclaim them. A second conveyor belt running in the opposite direction transports departing travelers' baggage from the check-in counter to a luggage collection point in the rear part of the departure hall. Conveyor belts of a different sort are envisaged between the main building and the satellites. The idea is to enable air travelers to traverse the 310-feet (95 m) distance of the connecting corridors along moving sidewalks.[94] **Fig. 61** And on the apron of the runway, an underground fueling system would be employed, as well as in-pavement heating designed to melt obstructive snow in the maneuvering area of the airplanes quickly ("25 tons of snow an hour") and cost-effectively ("a saving of about $50 over trucking methods").[95]

Thus by first using process studies and flow diagrams and then utilizing a layout that follows operational logic, the technical facilities aim for the greatest possible automation of all the sequentially linked activities involved in passenger handling: checking-in, obtaining information, consuming food and drink, moving through the terminal, and dropping-off (or claiming) baggage. The passengers should be handled by a facility precisely optimized to the building's purpose, thus making it a highly specialized built structure created on the operational model of a smoothly functioning machine.

Endnotes

18 See **Rhoades**, Dawna L.: *Evolution of International Aviation: Phoenix Rising*, Aldershot: Ashgate, 2003, p.17.

19 See **Davies**, R. E. G.: *Airlines of the United States Since 1914*, London: Putnam, 1972, p.383.

20 Upon establishing the company, TWA is still called Transcontinental and Western Air (fusion of Transcontinental Air Transport and Western Air Express). In 1950 the company is renamed Trans World Airlines.

21 See e.g. **Spode**, Hasso: "'Let Us Fly You Where the Sun Is': Air Travel and Tourism in Historical Perspective," in: **Vegesack**, Alexander von (ed.): *Airworld: Design and Architecture for Air Travel*, Weil am Rhein: Vitra Design Museum, 2004, pp.12–34, p.24.

22 See **Transworld Airlines Flight Operations Department**: *Legacy of Leadership: A Pictorial History of Trans World Airlines*, Marceline, MO: TWA/Walsworth Publishing Company, 1971, pp.160, 165. Domestically the service is called "Sky Coach"; abroad it is called "Sky Tourist." The word "coach" presumably refers to the seating arrangement, which is similar to that of a train or a bus. The term persists until around the end of the 1960s (although it is still used sporadically in the US), then today's commonly used terms "economy" and "tourist class" take root.

23 In addition to the costs, a condition for the selection of the aircraft is safety. The claim made by Pan American World Airways (Pan Am) of being "the world's most experienced airline" or TWA's attempt to sell their transatlantic flights as "routine stuff" must be understood against this backdrop. Promoting the safety of flying poses a tricky task at that time for marketing specialists: They must underscore the reliability of the airplanes without giving so much attention to the subject that people become suspicious.

24 On the economic grounds for the growth in passenger air traffic, see **Pompl**, Wilhelm: *Luftverkehr: eine ökonomische und politische Einführung*, Berlin: Springer, 2002, p.1.

25 **Anonymous**: "Europe, Here They Come," in: *Life*, vol.38, no.26 (June 27, 1955), pp.34–39, p.34.

26 See e.g. **TWA**: "All-Time Atlantic Travel Mark Set," in: *Skyliner*, vol.11, no.41 (October 12, 1950), p.1; **TWA**: "New Record High Set in September for Miles Flown," in: *Skyliner*, vol.15, no.41 (October 9, 1952), p.1; **TWA**: "Tourist Mileage Hiked on Jan. 9 Schedule Pattern," in: *Skyliner*, vol.17, no.1 (January 7, 1954), p.1. The issues of the employee magazine *Skyliner* (between 1946 and 1947 it was called *Starliner*, between September 1970 and April 1974 *TWA Today*) cited in this work come from the Trans World Airlines (TWA) Records (KC0453) at the University of Missouri-Kansas City.

27 See **Damon**, Ralph S.: "Trans World Airlines," in: *Flight International*, vol.61, no.2260 (May 16, 1952), p.591.

28 **TWA**: "Passenger Traffic Jumps 10% as Business Booms in 1954," in: *Skyliner*, vol.18, no.1 (January 6, 1955), p.1.

29 See **Mecklin**, John: "U.S. Airlines: Into the Wild Blue What?" in: *Fortune*, vol.73, no.5 (May 1966), pp.146–151, 187–188, 192, 194, p.147.

30 Aircraft manufacturers also awarded commissions to external industrial designers at the end of the 1930s. Douglas Aircraft Company, for instance, hires Howard Ketcham for development of the DC-4. See **Bilstein**, Roger E.: *Flight in America: From the Wrights to the Astronauts*, Baltimore, MD: Johns Hopkins University Press, 1994 (second ed.), pp.94–96.

31 For an overview of the different designers and their

work in the service of various airlines, see **Christian**, George: "Comfort in Airline Cabin Design Makes Dollar Sense," in: *Aviation Week*, vol. 64, no. 20 (May 14, 1956), pp. 92–101, p. 92. Of course, the task of industrial designers is also to visually enhance the passenger cabin. This is pursued in the chapter "A Focal Point of Attention."

32 See **Williams**, J. E. D.: *The Operation of Airliners*, London: Hutchinson and Co., 1964, pp. 220–221.

33 **TWA**: "Manual of Organization: Position Description; Manager Transportation Training Audio-Visual Aids," June 1, 1960, Trans World Airlines (TWA) Records (KC0453), WHMC-KC, University of Missouri-Kansas City, box 131.

34 **TWA**: "TWA Air Hostess Qualifications," September 20, 1945, http://library.duke.edu/digitalcollections/adaccess_T1960 (accessed February 5, 2015).

35 **TWA**: "TWA's Average Hostess" [press release], May 10, 1965, Trans World Airlines Collection (M-234), The Saint Louis Mercantile Library, University of Missouri-St. Louis, box 1-55.

36 Starting from the recognition that large bureaucratic companies (such as TWA) shape employment roles with their functional logic, William Whyte also notes in his 1956 book *The Organization Man* a shift in the personal identity and private existence of employees. Whyte criticizes that professional success now no longer accrues primarily to those individuals who—in the American tradition of the Protestant work ethic—seek personal independence in gainful employment and rely mainly on their internalized self-discipline, but to those employees who seek to fit in by conforming to the dense normative field of the organization and who are willing to remain steadfastly loyal to their employer in exchange for lifelong material security. See **Whyte**, William H.: *The Organization Man*, New York: Simon and Schuster, 1956.

37 See **Dreyfuss**, Henry: *Designing for People*, New York: Simon and Schuster, 1955, pp. 28, 131.

38 See **Blanck**, Katherine: "Hostess Couture, Classrooms Go Modern: New in Look and Book," in: *Skyliner*, vol. 23, no. 17 (August 18, 1960), p. 4; and **Entwistle**, Joanna: "Fashion Takes Flight: The Air Stewardess and Her Uniform," in: **Vegesack**, Alexander von (ed.): *Airworld: Design and Architecture for Air Travel*, Weil am Rhein: Vitra Design Museum, 2004, pp. 176–210, p. 182.

39 Today the standard is 79 centimeters or even less. See **Hewitt**, Ed: "The Shrinking Airline Seat," n. d., www.independenttraveler.com/travel-tips/travelers-ed/the-shrinking-airline-seat (accessed February 3, 2015). But even then, criticism becomes loud in the face of increasingly cramped conditions on board. See **Johnson**, George: *The Abominable Airlines*, New York: Macmillan, 1964, p. 180.

40 See **Conley**, Gordon: "TWA Hopes to Double Tourist Volume," in: *Aviation Week*, vol. 63, no. 10 (September 5, 1955), pp. 97–98.

41 On the flexibility and ease of maintenance of airplane interiors, see **Fitton Hauss**, Barbara: "A Trip Through Time in the Aircraft Cabin," in: **Vegesack**, Alexander von (ed.): *Airworld: Design and Architecture for Air Travel*, Weil am Rhein: Vitra Design Museum, 2004, pp. 82–122, p. 107; **Anonymous**: "Boeing Shows Luxurious 707 Interior," in: *Aviation Week*, vol. 64, no. 23 (June 4, 1956), pp. 80–83.

42 **TWA**: "TWA Inaugurates L-1011 Service Between St. Louis and Los Angeles" [press release], June 23, 1972, p. 2, Trans World Airlines Collection (M-234), The Saint Louis Mercantile Library, University of Missouri-St. Louis, box 1-28.

43 **Dreyfuss**, Henry: *Designing for People*, New York: Simon and Schuster, 1955, pp. 131, 132.

44 PONYA was established in 1921 and is the joint port authority for the US states of New York and New Jersey. In addition to air and sea ports, it also operates many important components of the regional transport infrastructure, such as bridges, ferries, ferry stations, and tunnels. Since 1972 it has been operating as the Port Authority of New York and New Jersey (PANYNJ).

45 See **Blacklock**, Mark: *Recapturing the Dream: A Design History of New York's JFK Airport*, London: M. Blacklock, 2005, pp. 4–7.

46 TWA is the contracting body for the terminal, which is financed by the Port Authority. See **TWA**: "Summary of Planning Data: proposed TWA Unit Terminal," October 3, 1956, p. 5, Trans World Airlines Collection (M-234), The Saint Louis Mercantile Library, University of Missouri-St. Louis, box 1-65.

47 Details of the initial contact between TWA and Saarinen are obscure. Research done to date identifies 1956 as the year when the TWA project began. This is true only in regard to the early design work begun by ES&A in February 1956. In all likelihood, programming discussions must have already begun in 1955, especially since it is certain that Ralph S. Damon, who died suddenly on January 4, 1956, played a key role in the contract awarding process and also because the Port Authority announces its plans for Terminal City as early as February 1955.

48 **TWA**: "Public Relations Planning for 1961–62" [internal concept paper], July 25, 1961, p. 2, Gordon L. Gilmore Papers, 1946–1973, Wisconsin Historical Society, Administrative Records, box 2, folder 3.

49 **Anonymous**: "Airports Turn to the Engineers," in: *Business Week*, no. 1287 (May 1, 1954), pp. 92–98, p. 94.

50 For a concise portrayal of how airports are constantly lagging behind the development of airplanes, see **Banham**, Reyner: "The Obsolescent Airport," in: *Architectural Review*, vol. 132, no. 788 (October 1962), pp. 252–253.

51 **Anonymous**: "The Airport Scramble," in: *Architectural Forum*, vol. 104, no. 6 (June 1956), pp. 116–131, p. 117.

52 See ibid., p. 119.

53 See ibid., pp. 119, 129 (axonometric).

54 **Borger**, J. G.: "Jet Transport Economics: Influence on Airport and Airway," in: *ASCE Proceedings*, vol. 79, no. 241 (1953), pp. 1–12, p. 1.

55 **Heino**, Albert F.: "Designing the Large Terminal," in: *Architectural Record*, vol. 97, no. 4 (April 1945), pp. 80–83, pp. 80, 82.

56 **Arroyo**, Nicholas R.; **Grisdale**, John; **Heino**, Albert F.; **Meisch**, Francis R.; **Prokosch**, Walther: "Airport Terminal Buildings," in: *Progressive Architecture*, vol. 34, no. 5 (May 1953), pp. 69–121, p. 88.

57 **Anonymous**: "Airports Turn to the Engineers," in: *Business Week*, no. 1287 (May 1, 1954), pp. 92–98, pp. 92, 93.

58 Attempts to protect passengers from the effects of the weather are as old as civil aviation itself. A prime example of this is Berlin's Tempelhof Airport from the 1930s, with its deeply overhanging roof for the protection of the airplanes as well as the embarking and disembarking passengers. Another idea envisages the planes rolling in on one side of the terminal and out on the other side, like trains using a through station.

59 See **Raney**, Don: "People and Planes! Can Airports Bridge the Gap?" in: *Progressive Architecture*, vol. 50, no. 9 (September 1969), pp. 92–115, p. 95.

60 See **Anonymous**: "Details of Automatic Plane Parking Device," in: *Aviation Week*, vol. 56, no. 4 (January 28, 1952), pp. 59–60; **Christian**, George: "Loadair Dock Goes into Operation," in: *Aviation Week*, vol. 62, no. 3 (January 17, 1955), pp. 63–64.

61 Engineers are already in the late 1920s experimenting with forerunners, initially in the form of covered walkways on the ground. Shortly thereafter the first connecting bridges follow in Burbank and Gatwick, but these still lack a weatherproof mechanism for connecting to the aircraft door and thus leave a small gap open. It is not until after the Second World War that the passenger boarding bridge is perfected. Leading the development is United, which uses the device for the first time at O'Hare Airport. The device, known as the "Aero-Gangplank," is based on an arrangement in which the airplanes park laterally along the terminal, thus giving access to all the aircraft doors. Then, in 1959, American tests a version in San Francisco with which the airplanes park pointing forward. The passenger boarding bridge admittedly only gives access to the front aircraft door, but parking is easier and takes up less space. The two parking directions initially divide the airlines into two camps, but "nose-in parking" ultimately prevails. See **Blacklock**, Mark: "Bridging the Gap," in: *Airways*, vol. 13, no. 10 (December 2006), pp. 44–49.

62 **TWA**: "Summary of Planning Data: Proposed TWA Unit Terminal," October 3, 1956, pp. 1–2, Trans World Airlines Collection (M-234), The Saint Louis Mercantile Library, University of Missouri-St. Louis, box 1-65.

63 **Prokosch**, Walther: "Airport Design: Its Architectural Aspects," in: *Architectural Record*, vol. 109, no. 1 (January 1951), pp. 112–117, p. 112. Prokosch, formerly an architect in the engineering department of Eastern Airlines, is the responsible engineer for Pan Am's Idlewild terminal, which was designed and built simultaneously with the TWA Terminal.
64 **Thompson**, Arnold W.: "Evolution and Future of Airport Passenger Terminals: *Journal of the Aero-Space Transport Division* (series: "Proceedings of the American Society of Civil Engineers"), no. 4064, AT 2 (October 1964), pp. 127–134, p. 130. See also **Dixon**, John Morris: "Air Terminal for Jet Travel: New Problems and Trends," in: *Progressive Architecture*, vol. 42, no. 11 (Nov. 1961), pp. 128–131, p. 131.
65 **Meisch**, Francis R.: "Architecture and Air Transportation," in: *Pencil Points*, vol. 24, no. 11 (November 1943), pp. 36–69, p. 43. On the history of the pallet, see **Dommann**, Monika: "'Be Wise—Palletize': die Transformationen eines Transportbretts zwischen den USA und Europa im Zeitalter der Logistik," in: *Traverse: Zeitschrift für Geschichte*, vol. 16, no. 3, "Gesteuerte Gesellschaft" (2009), pp. 21–35, esp. pp. 22, 24.
66 **Saarinen**, Eero: "General Statement About Architecture (Eero, dictated weekend of January 3 [1954])," [p. 1], Eero Saarinen Collection (MS 593), Manuscripts and Archives, Yale University Library, series II, box 28, folder 118. The external differences of his designs, says Saarinen, arise from the different requirements and varied possibilities of each particular building task, while his fundamental attitude remains the same.
67 See interview by Marc Guberman with Robert and Pat Burley, ES&A employees 1956–1963, December 13, 2004, Waitsfield, VT, unpublished (conducted as part of the research project "Eero Saarinen: Shaping the Future" for the book publication and traveling exhibition of the same name).
68 In March 1956, TWA project number 5603 appears for the first time in ES&A's check ledger. Furthermore, a trip to New York that could be associated with the project is booked for February 2–8, 1956. See Eero Saarinen Collection (MS 38), Manuscripts and Archives, Yale University Library, series III, box 38A, folders 51–57. The architectural contract between TWA and ES&A is apparently subsequently revised or not signed until December 5, 1956, as a letter by former TWA employee Rose Scotti suggests. See **Clark**, Robert Judson (ed.): *Design in America: the Cranbrook Vision 1925–1950*, New York: Abrams, 1983, p. 301. All in all, ten to twelve architects work on the design, whereas Kevin Roche, Cesar Pelli, Norman Pettula, and Edward Saad share the lead responsibility. The work is carried out under the supervision of John Dinkeloo, Ralph Price, and Chuck Parise. Key roles within ES&A are also taken up by Bill Gardner (project manager) as well as Ralph Yeakel and Leonard Bell. The latter takes over from Yeakel in 1960 as the on-site supervising architect in New York. See interview by Wesley Janz with Charles (Chuck) Parise, ES&A employee, 1956–1964, January 13, 1993, n. p., Wesley R. Janz Collection, Bentley Historical Library, University of Michigan.
69 See **Román**, Antonio: *Eero Saarinen: An Architecture of Multiplicity*, New York: Princeton Architectural Press, 2003, p. 43.
70 **Saarinen**, Aline B.: "Homey Stuff," unpublished, n. d. [1956], Aline and Eero Saarinen Papers, 1906–1977, Archives of American Art, Smithsonian Institution, series 1, box 2, folder 7, sheets 7–13.
71 Author interview with Kevin Roche, August 2, 2007, Hamden, CT.
72 See **ES&A**: "Summary," [typewritten document], n. d., Eero Saarinen Collection (MS 593), Manuscripts and Archives, Yale University Library, series IV, box 460, folder 1288.
73 See **Dorr**, Maude: "Portraits in Architecture: A Review of the Most Recent Buildings of the Late Eero Saarinen," in: *Industrial Design*, vol. 10, no. 5 (May 1963), pp. 62–71, p. 68.
74 See Roger Johnson, ES&A employee, 1953–1956, cited in: **Price**, Cathy (ed.): *Saarinen Swanson Reunion Proceedings*, Bloomfield Hills, MI: Cranbrook, 2001, p. 32.
75 See **ES&A**: [handwritten notes], n. d. [1956], Eero Saarinen Collection (MS 593), Manuscripts and Archives, Yale University Library, series IV, box 460, folder 1288. Emphasis in original.
76 See **TWA**: "Summary of Planning Data: Proposed TWA Unit Terminal," October 3, 1956, p. 2, Trans World Airlines Collection (M-234), The Saint Louis Mercantile Library, University of Missouri-St. Louis, box 1-65.
77 In the military service regulations of the US Army, vertical lines are intended for the flow of material, and auxiliary operations are separated into secondary flows. In addition, the geometric symbols circle (transport), triangle (storage), and square (inspection) are used. See **Dommann**, Monika: "'Be Wise—Palletize': die Transformationen eines Transportbretts zwischen den USA und Europa im Zeitalter der Logistik," in: *Traverse: Zeitschrift für Geschichte*, vol. 16, no. 3, "Gesteuerte Gesellschaft" (2009), pp. 21–35, esp. p. 24.
78 **Saarinen**, Aline B.: Letter to unknown recipient, n. d., Aline and Eero Saarinen Papers, 1906–1977, Archives of American Art, Smithsonian Institution, series 1, box 2, folder 45, p. 34.
79 Neither of the two commonly used alternatives offers enough space on the trapezoidal building site along a sharp curve to provide the required fourteen aircraft parking spaces. Author interview with Kevin Roche, May 5, 2008, Hamden, CT.
80 According to Kevin Roche, the pier concept underlying the idea is influenced by the airport in San Francisco, which was the first to be inspected by ES&A. Author interview with Kevin Roche, August 2, 2007, Hamden, CT.
81 Because the stairway to the second floor is located within the departure hall, meaning that not the entire building has two stories, the TWA Terminal is described as a one-and-a-half-level operation. On the typology of airport terminals, see **Ashford**, Norman; **Wright**, Paul H.: *Airport Engineering*, New York: Wiley, 1979, p. 244.
82 Initially, TWA wants to forgo passenger boarding bridges because they view the costs as too high. But in July of 1958 the board of directors reverts to the earlier decision. See **TWA**: "Summary of Planning Data: Proposed TWA Unit Terminal," October 3, 1956, p. 3, Trans World Airlines Collection (M-234), The Saint Louis Mercantile Library, University of Missouri-St. Louis, box 1-65; **Saarinen**, Eero: Letter to Rex Raab, Anthroposophischer Architektenkreis, Stuttgart, July 22, 1958, p. 1, Eero Saarinen Collection (MS 593), Manuscripts and Archives, Yale University Library, series I, box 14, folder 227. Saarinen admires the jetways long before his client ultimately decides to adopt the new system, although he, too, expresses some skepticism: "American has a very good loading system if it works. But, boy, if something goes wrong with it, then the passengers and the company will be very unhappy." **Saarinen**, Eero: Letter to G. Richard Davis, Eero Saarinen Collection (MS 593), Manuscripts and Archives, Yale University Library, series II, box 18, folder 39.
83 Prokosch describes the interplay between the business situation and sales revenue at airports as follows: "Concessions will be more heavily patronized if the passenger must wend his way through a labyrinth of coffee shops and branch banks to get from door to ticket counter." **Prokosch**, Walther: "Airport Design: Its Architectural Aspects," in: *Architectural Record*, vol. 109, no. 1 (January 1951), pp. 112–117, p. 117.
84 In an internal planning document, the client lists virtually all the building characteristics of the ES&A design that are favorable to operating logic. See **TWA**: "Summary of Planning Data: Proposed TWA Unit Terminal," October 3, 1956, Trans World Airlines Collection (M-234), The Saint Louis Mercantile Library, University of Missouri-St. Louis, box 1-65.
85 In the neighboring Pan Am Terminal, the transition between inside and outside is even more immediate thanks to an air curtain. See **Hunt**, Dudley, Jr.: "Idlewild: New York International Airport," in: *Architectural Record*, vol. 130, no. 3 (September 1961), pp. 151–190, p. 187.
86 With the first airplane hijackings in the late 1960s and the stringent security checks that result, the idea of an unrestricted passenger flow increasingly becomes an illusion. See **Anonymous**: "Anti-Hijacking System Being Used by TWA," in: *Aviation Week & Space Technology*, vol. 91, no. 25 (December 22, 1969), p. 32.

87 **Kaufmann**, Edgar, Jr.: "Inside Eero Saarinen's TWA Building," in: *Interiors*, vol. 121, no. 7 (July 1962), pp. 86–93, p. 86. See also **Vidler**, Anthony: *Warped Space: Art, Architecture, and Anxiety in Modern Culture*, Cambridge, MA: MIT Press, 2000, pp. 178–180.

88 See **TWA**: "TWA and New York Airways Fly World's Fair Helicopters," in: *Skyliner*, vol. 27, no. 13 (June 22, 1964, 1957), p. 1.

89 This does not proceed without resistance, however, as a document in the Saarinen archive illustrates: "After long study of mechanical devices for baggage transportation and for second level entrance to the plane by mechanically operated bridges, it was determined by the architect and client jointly that the dangers of over-mechanization in passenger routing and baggage handling would result in inflexibility and that in the long run the simplest devices would save the most time." **ES&A**: "Building for public use: Trans World Airlines, Idlewild International Airport, New York, N.Y.," unpublished, n. d., Eero Saarinen Collection (MS 593), Manuscripts and Archives, Yale University Library, series IV, box 330, folder 933.

90 The control tower is not part of the original requirements, but is added during the course of carrying out the work. See interview by Wesley Janz with Charles (Chuck) Parise, ES&A employee, 1956–1964, January 13, 1993, n. p., Wesley R. Janz Collection, Bentley Historical Library, University of Michigan.

91 **TWA**: "Control Tower at TWA Flight Center Directs Operations" [press release], May 1, 1962, Trans World Airlines Collection (M-234), The Saint Louis Mercantile Library, University of Missouri-St. Louis, box 1-30.

92 See **TWA**: "New Innovations Improve Services at Idlewild's Trans World Flight Center" [press release], May 1, 1962, p. 1, Trans World Airlines Collection (M-234), The Saint Louis Mercantile Library, University of Missouri-St. Louis, box 1-30. On the increasing automation of business processes at the time, see **Shapiro**, Irving D.: "From the 20's to Automation," in: *Progressive Architecture*, vol. 38, no. 6 (June 1957), pp. 201–203. On the development of mechanical door systems, see **Stalder**, Laurent: "Turning Architecture inside Out: Revolving Doors and Other Threshold Devices," in: *Journal of Design History*, vol. 22, no. 1 (2009), pp. 69–77.

93 See **TWA**: "TWA Transfers to Larger Terminal Area at Idlewild" [press release], August 15, 1960, p. 1, Trans World Airlines Collection (M-234), The Saint Louis Mercantile Library, University of Missouri-St. Louis, box 1-65.

94 In addition to the moving sidewalk, other mechanical methods of transportation for conveying the passengers onto the plane are apparently studied, including a mobile lounge. The stimulus for this comes from Roger Johnson during his research for the TWA Terminal, after he comes across a corresponding transport system from a Swiss company. See **Price**, Cathy (ed.): *Saarinen Swanson Reunion Proceedings*, Bloomfield Hills, MI: Cranbrook, 2001, p. 32.

95 **TWA**: "TWA Idlewild Terminal Will Be Kept Free of Interference by Snow" [press release], July 8, 1961, Trans World Airlines Collection (M-234), The Saint Louis Mercantile Library, University of Missouri-St. Louis, box 1-65.

2 A Focal Point of Attention

On January 9, 1943, the big day has arrived. After three years of secret developmental work, the Lockheed Constellation takes off on its maiden flight. Impressed by the size and efficiency of the airliner, the *Washington Post* reports on its front page about the "new sky giant" and describes it as a "shark-bodied, triple-tailed ship."[96] This fascination for the new model of aircraft subsequently spreads rapidly, and Trans World Airlines (TWA) is given particular benefit, because it developed the Constellation together with aircraft manufacturer Lockheed, was able to be the first airline to place an order, and has the largest fleet of the planes. By the late 1950s, the aircraft makes up nearly three quarters of its fleet and decisively shapes the public image of the company. Accompanied by corresponding marketing actions, the Constellation thereby continues a tradition. Since the beginnings of civil aviation, the visual appearance of the airplanes and their livery graphics have shaped the public's image of the airlines.[97] Meanwhile, the ground infrastructure still plays a secondary role in the corporate image.

This is about to change in the 1950s. Beginning in the middle of the decade, the airline industry discovers the airport terminal as a means of corporate representation. The example par excellence for this is New York's Idlewild Airport. In 1962, *Architectural Forum* called it "one of a great ring of competing structures, each inhabited by rival airlines seeking to woo travelers to their ticket counters with design."[98] Every architect working in Idlewild has tried to outdo his predecessor, explains an executive of the airport authority in describing the logic at work.[99] And *Aviation Week & Space Technology* characterizes Idlewild as a "classic example of the airline industry's intense devotion to the preservation and perpetuation of the corporate image."[100] In this development that sees airport architecture moving from an operational organization principle to an architectural representation of the company, the terminal that Eero Saarinen erected for TWA between 1955 and 1962 plays a decisive role.

62 A Constellation above La Guardia in 1959. This aircraft type, with its unique tripartite tail fin, substantially shapes the public image of TWA in the decade following the Second World War.

63 The Constellation embellishes countless TWA advertisements. Meanwhile, the ground infrastructure still plays a secondary role in the airline's corporate image.

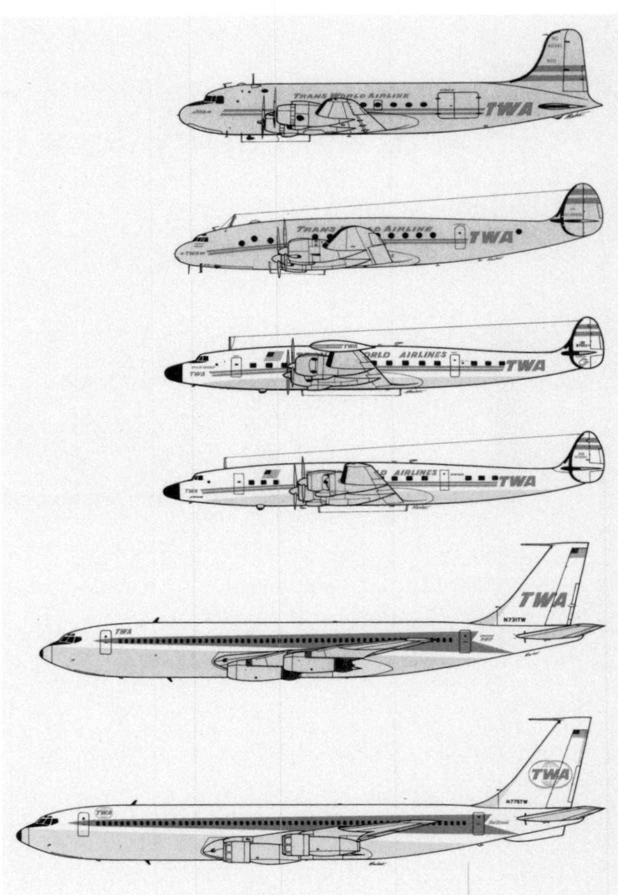

64 Earlier, TWA flew exclusive routes with exclusive airplanes. By the end of the 1950s, they have to share both with the competition.

65 Initially, jets like this Convair CV 880 still easily succeed in gaining the desired attention. But soon a new differentiating factor is needed.

A Look at the Loewy Look...

TICKET OFFICES . . . modern, colorful, spacious. Decorated in TWA red, white and gold, each ticket office will feature ticket counters of rosewood formica with indirect lighting under the front edges to give the illusion of floating. Behind the counters, a mural treatment supplanting the world maps will incorporate the theme of winds aloft. Borne on the winds will be names of TWA cities in geographic sequence. First to receive the Loewy Look will be the Chicago ticket office, shown above in full-scale model form. Below is an artist's rendering of the Fifth Avenue, New York, office of the future.

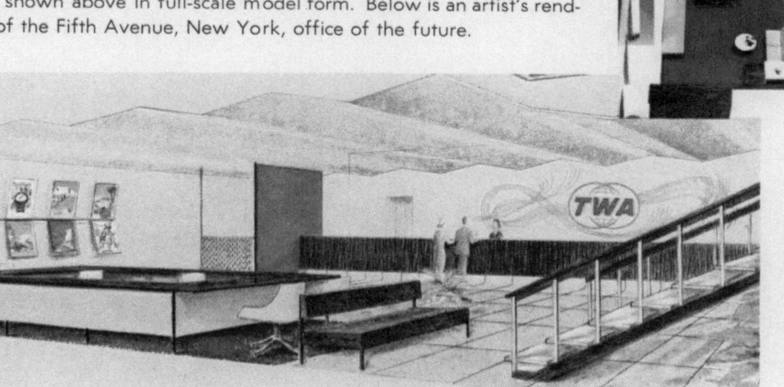

DECOR . . . bright, beautiful, breathtaking. Adrienne Artus, NYC receptionist, points out such decor innovations as the red all-wool carpeting designed especially for TWA, the rosewood-formica in all its rich elegance and the other fabrics and materials which add beauty to the design concept.

GROUND EQUIPMENT . . . neat, clean and eye-appealing. Every TWA vehicle and ramp will be completely redesigned and repainted in sun beige and ice white to convey the appearance of sparkling cleanliness. Admiring the proposed new look are (left to right) NYC secretary Ann De Carlo, steno-clerk Sandy Stousland, and receptionist Adrienne Artus.

66 **In 1960, Raymond Loewy receives the commission from TWA to design a new and consistent corporate look. His design is presented in a colorful special issue of the employee magazine *Skyliner* on October 20, 1960.**

67 The key feature of Loewy's design is a new company logo, which this advertisement from 1963 illustrates.

68 A model presents the hostess uniform, which Raymond Loewy has developed together with Don Loper, at Idlewild Airport.

69 Until the 1960s, TWA had not established any mandatory design guidelines for the ticket offices. This changed with Loewy's design program, which was implemented in this sales office at an unknown location.

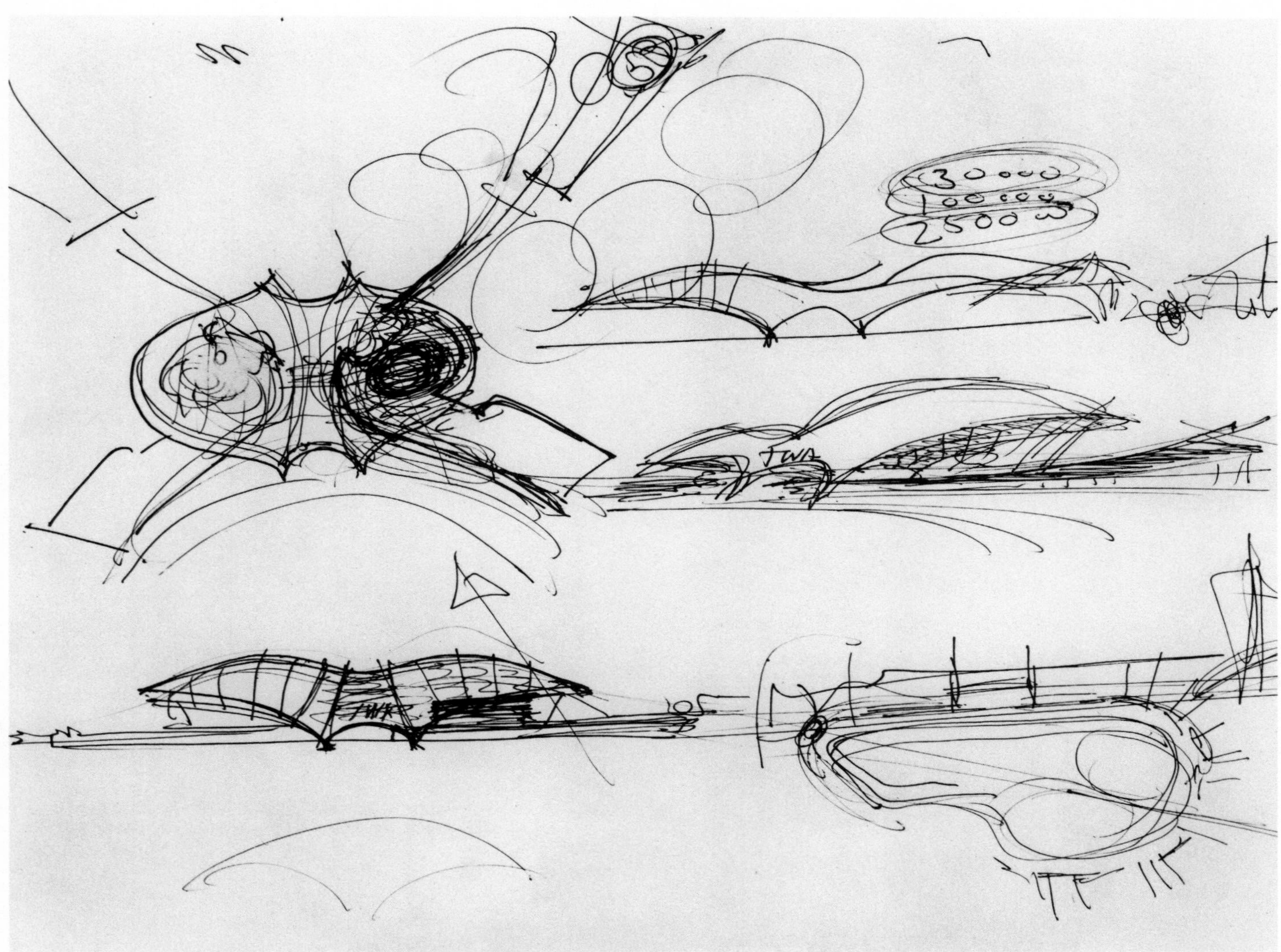

70 **The TWA Terminal is also to become part of the corporate identity. Eero Saarinen sketches his design ideas on the back of a restaurant menu in 1956. The TWA site, which lies directly opposite the airport entrance, for him has a decisive advantage that he illustrates at the bottom right.**

"No, that's the terminal. The 747 is around in back."

71 Eero Saarinen sees the opportunity to dramatize the terminal as a monumental eyecatcher for the arriving airline passengers, as conveyed by this cartoon from 1970.

72 Eero Saarinen seeks to tailor the appearance of his buildings to the respective clients. That is the goal which he and his staff pursue, also in the design for the terminal.

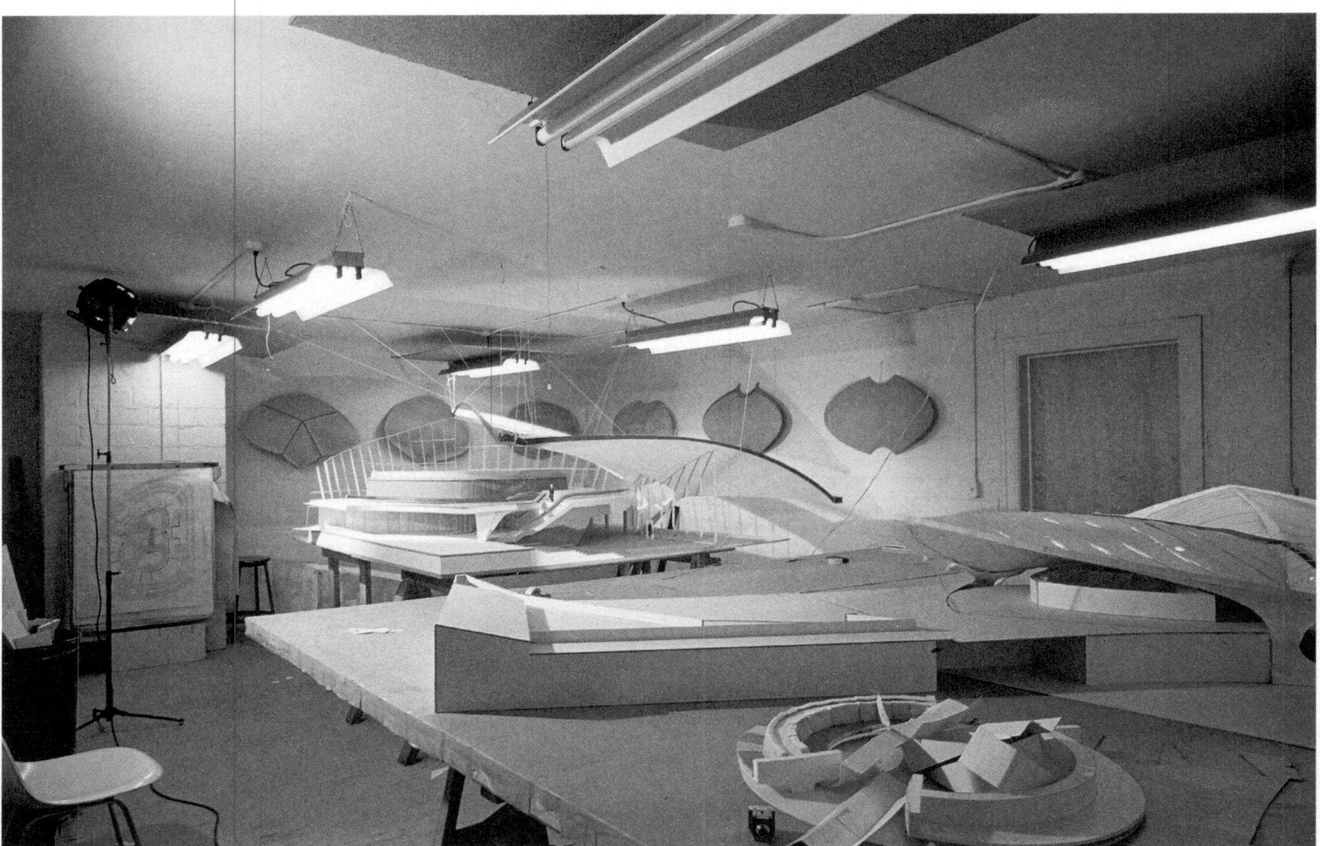

73 The TWA Flight Center is meant to stand out among the various airline terminals at Idlewild. For this purpose, Eero Saarinen chooses a shell structure and leases a sufficiently large studio space expressly for working on the design.

74 In order to achieve the desired coherent impression for the building, ES&A build several hundred models—from hand-sized plasticine models to this one.

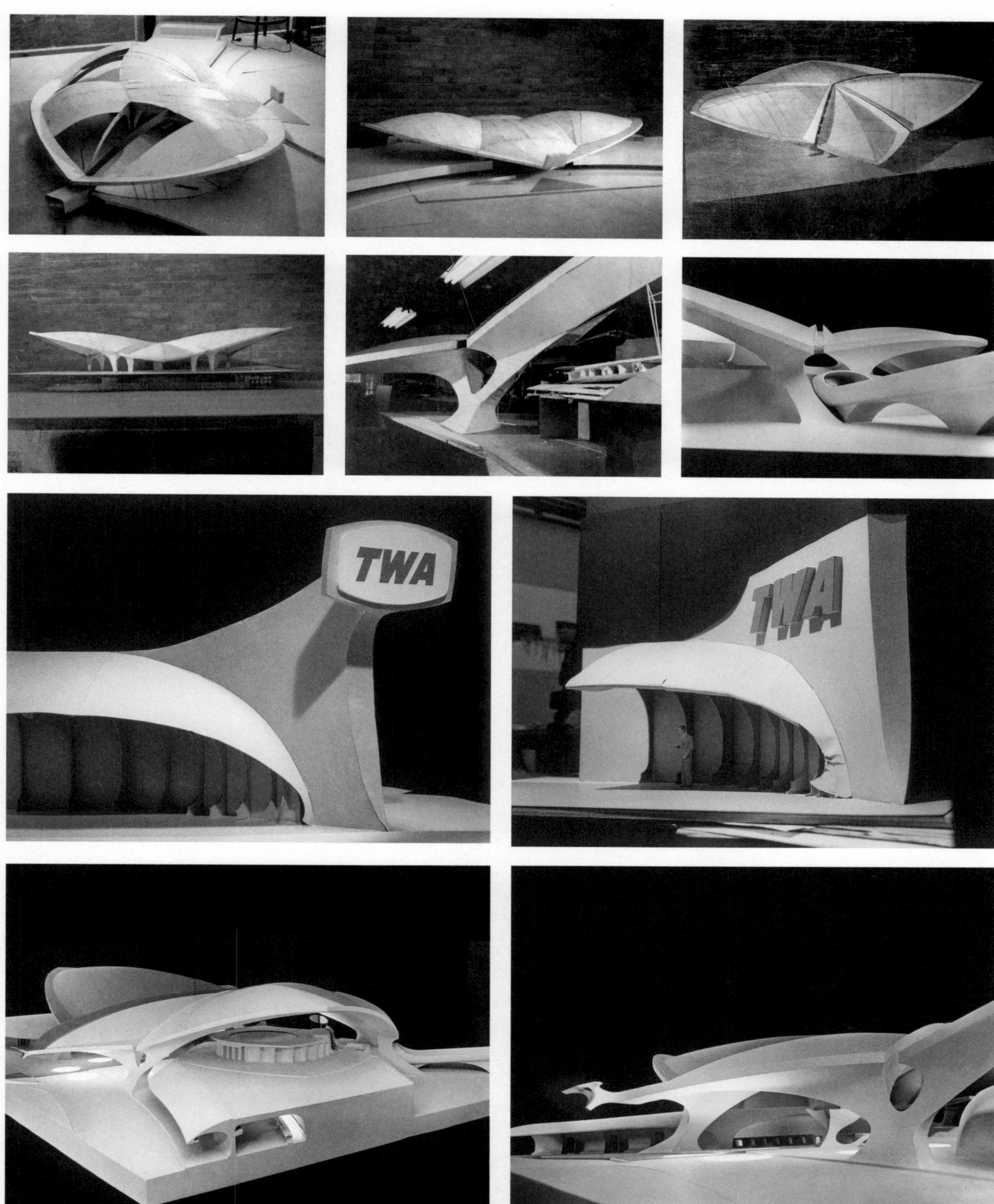

75 **Eero Saarinen designs the vaults of the terminal without regard to the ideal structural behavior, but instead with regard to the desired visual effect.**

76 With the same goal of fascinating the flying public with the building design, ES&A develop not only the building silhouette but also the interior space.

77 Red carpets and upholstery in an otherwise light gray or white interior space: The color scheme harmonizes with TWA's company colors.

78 Only the publicly accessible areas like the Ambassador Lounge are elaborately designed and conform to the TWA corporate look. The spaces which are accessible solely to staff members are, by contrast, conventional and orthogonal.

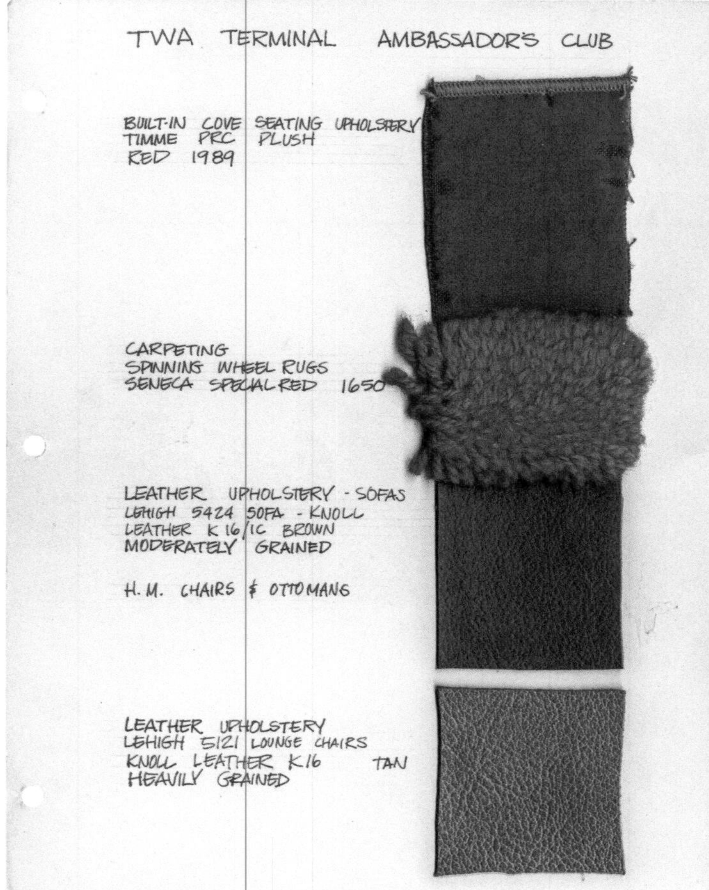

79 Color and material samples for the Ambassador Lounge, which contrary to earlier intentions (see fig. 78) is not furnished with "Womb" chairs.

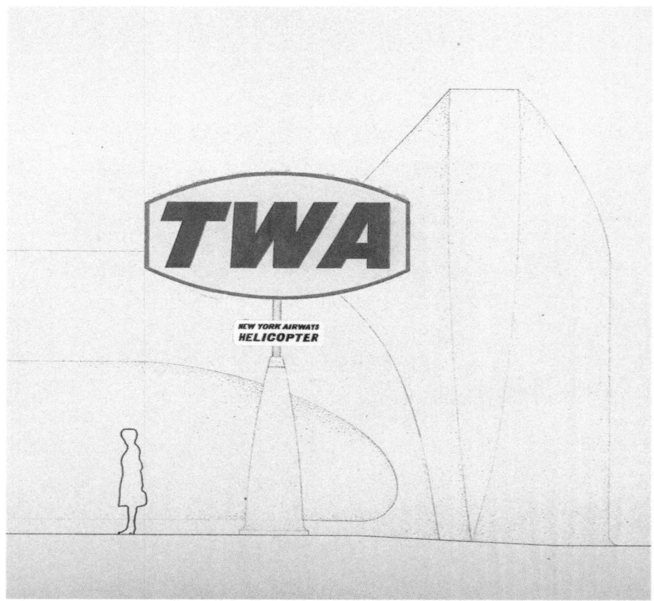

80 The positioning of the TWA signage is given much attention by ES&A. This underscores the significance of the corporate look and brand development for the design.

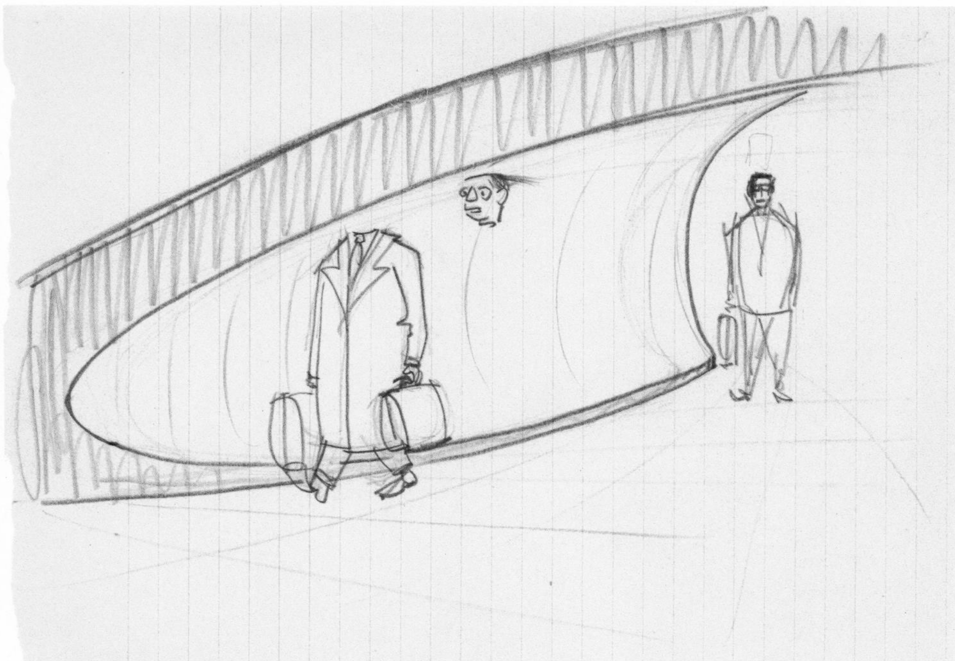

81 The sleek lines of the terminal remind Saarinen employee Claude DeForest of automotive design, and he gives expression to the design relationship with this sketch (1957).

82 Saarinen's terminal, just like the car bodies, is greatly determined by the sought-after visual impact on consumers. With its uncommon design, it resembles a consumer good.

83 With the one-legged "Pedestal" chair, Eero Saarinen wants to present the client with a previously unknown chair form.

84 The design illustrates Eero Saarinen's sense for the market value of novel shapes. The "Pedestal" chair is successfully promoted by furniture manufacturer Knoll.

85 As a successful furniture designer, Eero Saarinen—here seen in a discussion with Florence Knoll—internalized the principles of industrial design like hardly any other architect of his time.

"A nice try, but notice how it never got off the ground?"

86 The unique form of the terminal is reminiscent of a bird. This ensures public attention for the building—and economic value for TWA. Its value consists of the terminal's capability to have a positive impact on the company's image.

2.1 From the Constellation to a Comprehensive Corporate Look

When, in the course of 1955, TWA seeks an architect for its new terminal at Idlewild, the artistic director of the public relations department, Rex Werner (1909–2004), brings Eero Saarinen into play.[101] Fig. 87 This is indicative of an architectural paradigm shift. The mere fact that the PR department has a say in selecting the architect makes clear that the new Idlewild terminal is expected to have public impact.[102] The building program also follows entirely in this spirit. In addition to optimizing the ground

87 Rex Werner, TWA's Senior Director of System Design, 1964

infrastructure for optimal operations, it namely demands of Saarinen "that the building should be of a nature which would provide TWA with advertising, publicity and attention."[103] Saarinen's task, to create a building eminently good for publicity, can be seen, on the one hand, against the backdrop of the Idlewild development plan, which gives TWA the opportunity to display its architecture, and, on the other hand, it also reflects the growing rivalry among the airlines. Accompanied by far-reaching changes in civil aviation, the commissioning of Saarinen marks the beginning of a significant transformation in the way the company presents itself.

To begin with, the cause lies in an intensification of the market conditions in the already strongly competitive situation among the American airlines. Unlike most other countries at that time, which each only have a single national airline, a competitive aviation market with numerous participants has established itself in the USA since the beginnings of civil air transport. The rivalry comes to a head in 1955 with the liberalization of domestic landing rights, leading to a convergence of services.[104] Moreover, the airlines use their cartel-like trade association, the IATA, to obligatorily define aspects pertaining to virtually their entire range of services: from the physical dimensions of the passenger seat to the in-flight and ground services, aircraft capacity, and marketing and advertising efforts, as well as the airfares.[105] But that is not enough. After the Second World War, a profound technological transformation also begins, which leads in 1958 to the commissioning of the first American jet aircraft and to further increases in competitive pressure. This is because the cruising speed, range, and passenger capacity of the jets considerably exceed that of propeller-driven aircraft like the Constellation, causing the latter to rapidly lose its marketability. At the outset this is not so bad, because the ultra-modern jet aircraft easily succeed in

88 TWA advertisement with a Boeing 707, 1962

creating a sensation. Fig. 88 Thousands marvel at TWA's first two Boeing 707s before they take off on March 20, 1959, for their first scheduled flights.

Yet, what the visitors get to see differs little from the airplanes that the other airlines have put into service. First, the airlines are now equipped almost exclusively with jets of the types Boeing 707 or Douglas DC-8 and second, the appearance of both jet airliners is nearly identical. Fig. 89 The jet aircraft lack the eye-catching appearance of the Constellation, leading a trade journalist to note: "The American big jets are virtually indistinguishable from one another, at least in so far as external appearance is concerned."[106] Moreover, the new passenger handling procedures using the tunnel-like jetways mean that the air traveler hardly gets to see how the outside of the plane looks. By the end of the 1950s the airplane has had its day as a differentiating factor. After an era in which the pioneer airlines had different aircraft and flew to different destinations, and after a time when market regulations had once ensured exclusive air routes, now the airlines cannot distinguish themselves from their rivals—neither with the flights they offer nor with their airplanes.

89 TWA Boeing 707 and United DC-8, San Francisco International Airport, CA, 1959/1968

Against this backdrop, a high-ranking TWA executive's call for a new marketing approach is significant. Floyd D. Hall (1916–2012), responsible for flight operations on the ground and in the air for the airline, asserts that—unlike in the past—airline travel must be marketed like a consumer product, "just as if it were a cake of soap."[107] With this example, Hall aims at brand development in the aviation industry, of the sort that has already been successfully implemented by the consumer products industry with everyday products such as soap, which also has a highly undifferentiated base value. This new model ripens in TWA's leadership ranks in the second half of the 1950s; until then, brand development has received scant attention in civil aviation. Now, despite standardized mass check-in and processing, which the passenger airline industry prescribes for cost optimization after the Second World War, TWA's customers shall each be given a uniquely tailored travel experience. The goal: a subjectively perceived added value for the passenger when compared to competing offers, just like with brand products compared to unbranded goods. Airline travel should become a comprehensively conceived service with brand character. To implement this plan, TWA first gathers ideas in-house, through its communication agency, about the intended repositioning in order to then launch a program to promote its corporate image. As Gordon L. Gilmore (1908–1987), the PR chief of the airline who is directly subordinate to Hall, formulates the goal, "a good corporate image can have the effect of preselling a company, its product or services to customers, employees, community, government, or stockholders."[108] To promote the new image of the company, however, advertising slogans and taglines are not sufficient, as Gilmore adds. To this end, other measures are needed.[109]

To begin with, updated graphics for the aircraft livery and new trademark fleet designations like "SuperJet Airline" and "StarStream" are intended to give TWA's jet fleet the exclusive character that it otherwise lacks. But the airline is targeting far more ambitious and comprehensive design measures. "We want to project in a uniform, attractive manner our image around the world of a reliable, friendly airline offering good service everywhere," announces President Charles S. Thomas in 1960.[110] To this end, the air carrier promotes Rex Werner, the artistic director of the PR department, to Director of System Design in December 1959, and in 1964 to Senior Director. This gives Werner, who had joined TWA as a staff member of the photo department in 1943, an increasingly influential position in the company.[111] His mission is nothing less than the introduction of a unified corporate design. As with Pan American World Airways (Pan Am), which entrusts Edward Larrabee Barnes with this task in 1955, and later Lufthansa and KLM, TWA is now also seeking a progressive and comprehensive corporate appearance. In his new role, Werner occasionally develops his own designs—such as the

90 TWA Moonliner, Disneyland, Anaheim, CA, ca. 1955–1962

TWA Moonliner in Disneyland and special cutlery and dishes for the Boeing 707 Fig. 90—but the design commission for the new corporate image, which is of overriding importance, is given in 1960 to the industrial designer Raymond Loewy. Fig. 91

For TWA, Loewy designs the decorative color scheme for the ground vehicles as well as the hostess uniforms, the latter in collaboration with fashion designer Don Loper. The key features of Loewy's design, however—the client and designer agree—are a new company logo, consisting of the initials "TWA" and two interlocking golden hemispheres, and a design principle for all the ticket offices, where, until this point, a hodgepodge of different logos, typography, colors, and materials are employed. The airline's updated appearance is meant to elicit in the passenger that new travel experience envisioned by the client. Loewy writes: "One moves through miles by becoming somehow a slightly different person. Instead of being just plain old Joe, here he is an interesting

91 **Raymond Loewy, 1948**

stranger bent on some unknown mission."[112] The design of the equipment should consequently evoke the feeling of belonging to a flying elite. The "Loewy look," as the program is known, is thus consistent with the differentiating factor sought by TWA, namely that of a brand product which is capable of providing the owner with emotional added value beyond the identical base value of an undifferentiated object. Seen this way, the new corporate design becomes an essential hallmark of quality for air travel and a criterion of economic success for TWA.

Against this backdrop, the commissioning of Saarinen—which takes place roughly four years before that of Loewy but is advanced by the same key people, especially Rex Werner and Floyd D. Hall—can be seen in a broader context. Given the increasing similarities among the airlines, both visual and service-related, Saarinen's commissioning at the end of 1955 marks the start of a far-reaching transformation of TWA's public image. The aspirations that TWA placed on the terminal for serving as a corporate flagship reflect the change of view that would culminate in 1960 in granting Loewy his commission. At the same time, it signals that a significant change had been consummated. Whereas until then ground infrastructures had unfolded economic benefits for TWA at most through efficient operational logic, for its

92 **Charles C. Tillinghast, President of TWA 1961–1969, in front of the TWA Flight Center under construction, 1961**

93 **General Motors Technical Center, Warren, MI, ES&A, 1956**

Idlewild terminal the airline formulates another economic ambition: it should become part of the corporate identity and should support brand development. "There was a very definite reason behind TWA's asking Eero Saarinen to design its Idlewild terminal," announces President Charles C. Tillinghast, Jr. (1911–1998) **Fig. 92**, and continues:

> "Mr. Saarinen was recognized internationally as a creator of structures that achieved more than simple functional excellence. They were aesthetic monuments as well that conveyed feeling and emotion, and stirred something within those who looked upon them."[113]

The client strives to have a high-profile and attractive building similar to what General Motors (GM) and the Massachusetts Institute of Technology (MIT) received a short time earlier.[114] **Fig. 93** The expectations of the airline attest to Saarinen's ability to design buildings that can generate emotional added value for the viewer—similar to that of Loewy's corporate design or a brand-name item.

2.2 Spectacular Shells

"Eero cared for the opinion of his clients," recalls his then employee Cesar Pelli (born 1926). "If the client felt that certain aspects of the building design were not right, Eero would listen attentively and make changes."[115] The addressee clarifies: "I feel strongly that architecture has to be a personal service."[116] Saarinen fosters the intent to give each building an appearance that matches the respective building task. "Each building must have its own look," Saarinen is quoted as saying by *Time* magazine in 1956.[117] This attitude is an expression of a paradigm shift after the Second World War. While the International Style aspired to standardized designs along the lines of mass production, the clients' desires for a distinctive outward appearance for their buildings receives more and more importance.[118] Saarinen, a protagonist of this transformation, knows that companies in particular attribute growing importance to architecture as it relates to how they appear to the public. In contrast to painting and sculpture, he states in a 1960 lecture, architecture enjoys a high level of acceptance among the public, because it arouses "aspirations" and can satisfy "needs." Clients would have discerned new opportunities in architecture:

94 IBM Manufacturing and Training Facility, Rochester, MN, ES&A, 1958

> "The idea that a well-designed building is desirable and that it enhances the corporation or the university has become an accepted idea. The phrases 'prestige building' and 'showcase building' have entered the client's language. Good modern architecture is something that these clients are proud of."[119]

With this new perspective, Saarinen designs outwardly unique buildings for his clients. He searches for "an appropriate architectural expression" for General Motors, "a really good scheme for CBS," and the "character of the [John Deere] company," and he responds to IBM's desire for a building "which would not be architecturally obnoxious to its neighbors."[120] **Fig. 94** Also in the case of the Trans World Flight Center, Saarinen was to formulate his design goals with a view to the client—and he comprehends the building task as a challenge "to create, within the complex of terminals that makes up Idlewild, a building for TWA which would be distinctive and memorable."[121]

Fundamental to the design of the TWA Flight Center is the domed Kresge Auditorium at MIT (1955). **Fig. 95** When Eero Saarinen begins to design the latter in 1950, shell structures are admittedly no longer a new form of construction—they have been used for engineering projects since the 1920s. Yet, having been largely neglected by architects until then, shell structures are that much more of a formal novelty. Visually, they differ markedly from the common glass-and-steel buildings in the tradition of the International Style.[122] Saarinen recognizes this: "There were new and significant things to be done in structure," he says with hindsight. "The whole science of concrete thin shell construction was developing exciting new possibilities."[123] Shell structures had opened up the possibility to defy the prevailing formal canon, explains his then employee Mark Jaroszewicz. The dome, which looks fundamentally different from the common curtain wall, ought to pay respect to MIT's demand for a "forward-looking project, even if it ends up being controversial."[124] With the MIT Auditorium, Saarinen's keen sense for architectural trends and his ambition to be the first to take these up are revealed, as architecture critic Peter Blake explains in 1981: "When people were talking about shell concrete structures," says the critic, "he was trying to get there first with the Kresge Auditorium. . . . He was enormously competitive, enormously competitive."[125] Accordingly, for the auditorium Saarinen designs a shell structure that had no equal at the time. "This auditorium does something others have not attempted," confirms *Architectural Forum* appreciatively, "it brings the graceful and fluid technology of airplane hangars and shopping centers into 'polite' architecture—recently so dominated by the rigid rectangular forms of post-and-beam construction."[126] Affinities with the thin concrete shells that engineers have already been calculating for years, however, exist only at first glance. Saarinen's dome in the form of one eighth of a sphere obeys, above all, formal criteria; its static structural behavior, by contrast, is extremely unfavorable.[127] This primacy of external appearance above structural efficiency should provide the template for the TWA Terminal building.

As explained above, for the design of the TWA airport terminal Eero Saarinen and Associates are once again faced with the demand for a novel appearance for the building that is tailored to the client's wishes—and once again a shell structure is to achieve the desired effect; a cubic building is apparently never

95 Kresge Auditorium, MIT, Boston, MA, ES&A, 1955

96 Dorton Arena, Raleigh, NC, Matthew Nowicki, 1952

under discussion, as a document from Aline Saarinen's estate suggests.[128] Yet, by the time the TWA project is being designed in 1956, shell structures have already lost the novelty they still had earlier in the decade, when Eero Saarinen designed Kresge Auditorium. On the contrary, shell structures threaten to become a "design cliché," states architect Serge Chermayeff in 1954 at the Conference on Thin Concrete Shells at MIT. Given the architectural community's propensity for copying, the construction form degenerates into an "architectural Scrabble which everybody is playing," says Chermayeff.[129] The best-known examples, in addition to Kresge Auditorium, are the Dorton Arena (1952) by Matthew Nowicki and the Berlin Congress Hall (1957) by Hugh Stubbins. **Figs 96, 97** But Saarinen feels a competitive challenge most notably from Minoru Yamasaki's 1956 St. Louis terminal, which obtains much publicity and is lauded as the "Grand Central of the air."[130] **Fig. 98** This challenges Eero Saarinen's ambition: "There was a little competition," recalls his senior employee Kevin Roche, especially since Yamasaki's studio in the Detroit suburb of Bloomfield Hills is only a stone's throw away.[131] With the TWA airport terminal, Saarinen wanted to reach new heights and eclipse the shell structures that had already been built.

2.3 New Economic Focus

97 Congress Hall, Berlin, Hugh Stubbins and Associates, 1957

98 Lambert–St. Louis International Airport, St. Louis, MO, Yamasaki and Associates, 1956

As Kevin Roche and Leon Yulkowski start designing in the spring of 1956, Eero Saarinen, as usual, has his employees explore multiple formal approaches so he can ultimately select the one best tailored to the building's function, the client, and the logic of outdoing the competition.[132] For his design decisions, predominantly formal aspects are once again decisive; the resulting curvy design of the vaults and their supports violates scores of structural principles.[133] Like Kresge Auditorium, Saarinen designs the TWA airport terminal largely without regard to the ideal static structural behavior of the vaults, but does so primarily with regard to their desired visual appearance. But at the same time, the architect increases the complexity of the design considerably, so as to distinguish it from previous shell structures. "The whole thing," he sums up, "really becomes much more a problem related to sculpture than to mathematics."[134] The slender shell structures of engineers like Eduardo Torroja, Pier Luigi Nervi, Félix Candela, and Eduardo Catalano have the objective to span spaces with a minimum of material. Torroja, for instance, developed a concrete shell with a thickness of less than 3.5 inches (85 mm) for the 180 feet long by 108 feet wide (55 m by 33 m) market hall in Algeciras

(1935). Fig. 99 However, it is not the ingenious achievement behind such constructions that fascinates Saarinen but the new design possibilities. Shell structures are, for

99 Algeciras Market Hall, Spain, Eduardo Torroja, 1935

him, first and foremost a formal impulse, as he affirms in a 1957 speech at the Royal Institute of British Architects:

> "I feel that usually there are no economic reasons for arriving at these structures—and in the end the same space could have been covered more cheaply by some conventional method. Therefore, I think, the reason why these are being built now and why we are interested is really aesthetic and not economic; and we should face that."[135]

That Saarinen is not guided in his design by the economic objectives of the engineers is evinced by the vaults of the TWA Terminal, which have cross sections ranging between 7 and 44 inches (18 and 112 centimeters).[136] Moreover, the complicated manual calculations for the vaults are tremendously expensive, as is their subsequent execution.[137] Despite these seemingly inefficient special expenditures, Saarinen's economic focus has merely shifted. Instead of minimizing costs through constructional or material efficiency, as would be the case with traditional shell construction, another kind of economy has taken its place, which aims to garner an increasingly scarce resource for the benefit of TWA: the public's attention. With the rising importance of mass media and the plethora of commercial products and services on offer in the American consumer society that prospers after the Second World War, people's limited capacity to process information necessitates attracting the consumer's attention with a striking building.[138] "Most people are blind," Saarinen thus explains, "if you get too subtle about architecture . . . , people come in and walk through it and never notice the difference. . . . I think you need the strong impact to be appreciated. But that isn't all, you also need the strong impact to really get the idea across."[139] To ensure the effect on the viewer that is called for, Saarinen relies on the means of exaggeration and repetition: "If you are going to have an overhang," he clarifies, "it has to be a hell of an overhang, if it is going to come across to people."[140] In exactly this spirit, he wants to use an extravagant style for the building's exterior to gain visual attention for TWA and thereby secure the desired competitive advantage for the company.

To this end, Saarinen first explores the opportunities presented by the building site—and comes to a surprising conclusion. "Everybody thought that's the worst site," says Kevin Roche in explanation of TWA's displeasure about the unfavorable wedge-shaped lot lying in a tight curve. "But typical of Eero, he thought it was the best site."[141] Saarinen recognizes a locational quality of the assigned property that the others involved in the project fail to notice: In the ring-shaped Terminal City, the TWA lot lies directly along the axis of the airport access road. He sees the opportunity to dramatize the TWA Flight Center as a monumental eye-catcher ("a dramatic accent") for the arriving airline passengers.[142] Against this backdrop, he develops a symmetrical building whose axis of symmetry is aligned with the access road. Furthermore, Saarinen differentiates between his airport terminal, with its incomparable wing-like barrel vaults at the sides, and the adjacent International Arrivals Building, which has a repetitive, modular curtain-wall facade. Fig. 100 The further design of the terminal is also dominated by the objective of garnering public attention for the client using the same artistic means. According to Saarinen, the exterior de-

100 TWA Flight Center as an eye-catcher at Idlewild, on the right is the International Arrivals Building, 1962

sign "has to be exaggerated and overstated and repeated in every part of its interior." And he explains, "that is why, for instance, the interior of the TWA terminal <u>had</u> to be the way it is."[143] Saarinen combines curved interior walls, sculptural columns, and sweeping staircases, as well as seating to match, finely textured vaulted ceilings, and even curved and sloped glazing that offers views of the apron, into a coherent unity. Here, like with the exterior form, the visual impression is again of primary importance, as is proven by a sectional drawing of the sculptural departures board. It merely contains a small rectangular cable duct, but it is clad in an equally elaborate and fitting manner for the sake of the intended overall impression of consistency.

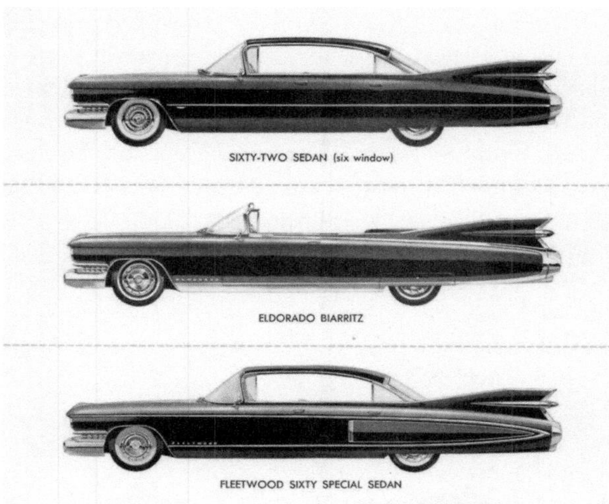

101 Page from the "1959 Cadillac Data Book"

To design the building's coherent appearance, the architect avails himself of a new method: model-making. "Eero never really used models before that. Models were for presentation, they weren't for study," describes Kevin Roche in reference to the new approach taken for design work on the departure hall.[144] A merely hand-sized working model is followed by many more; several hundred were to come together during the roughly three years of design work.[145] Saarinen's employee Helmut Borcherdt summarizes the process: "On the whole, the design process [for the terminal] is similar to the design of cars being practiced a few miles away from Saarinen's office in the studios of General Motors, Ford, and Chrysler."[146] Thus the final form of the building emerges in the way that automobile designs do, almost exclusively on the basis of models. "Then," Saarinen clarifies, "we were able to make drawings of what we actually had."[147] While the use of models is new in Saarinen's studio, the working method has already been prevalent in industrial design for a long time. One designer known for using models is Norman Bel Geddes, with whom Eero Saarinen completed an internship in 1938.[148] The chief designer of General Motors (GM), Harley Earl (1893–1969), who had hired Saarinen to design the General Motors Technical Center, also relied heavily on the use of models. The extent to which Saarinen is influenced by Earl—who can often be found visiting the architect's studio, located just a few kilometers from the GM corporate campus, during their joint project from 1948 to 1956—seems not to be conclusively evidenced.[149] What is certain is that the working method of automobile designers, which Earl exemplified ideally, impressed Saarinen. His colleague Harry Weese corroborates this on the basis of the time they spent studying together at the Cranbrook Academy, very close to numerous car factories: "[Eero Saarinen] was very influenced by the designers that surrounded the auto industry, their techniques, how they mocked up things, the nuts and bolts and all that."[150] It is also noteworthy that Saarinen hires George Spacek, who previously worked for GM as an industrial designer, and involves him in work on the TWA project (and the "Pedestal" furniture series).[151]

By using modeling to design the interior space according to formal considerations, Saarinen not only relies on the same means of production as the car designers, but the result also reminds various reviewers of the "styling" of automotive design of the time.[152] The formal parallels may be unintentional, but it is clear in any case that Saarinen's terminal, just like the car bodies, is greatly determined by the sought-after visual impact on consumers, be they flight customers or car buyers. Namely to create purchase incentives and increase sales, Harley Earl has the bodywork and decorative applications of GM car brands Buick, Cadillac, Chevrolet, Oldsmobile, and Pontiac remodeled every year, while the chassis and engines used across brands remain virtually unchanged.[153] **Fig. 101** Hence, individually designed bodies serve as attractive cladding for a far less exclusive automotive technology and construction. Similarly, the terminal has a goal of attracting the attention of airline passengers and capturing their imagination with a unique design, which Saarinen describes as follows:

> "As the passenger walked through the sequence of the building, we wanted him to be in a total environment where each part was the consequence of another and all belonged to the same form-world. It is our strong belief that only through such a consistency and such a consequential development can a building make its fullest impact and expression."[154]

As shown above, Eero Saarinen wants to maximize the impact on the (flying) public by tailoring the building silhouette to the arriving motorists, designing the interior space in an equally striking manner, and enveloping technical facilities that are also employed in other terminals with a special cladding. The same focus is also reflected by the fact that only the public areas of the building and visible building elements are designed with curved lines, while the ancillary spaces, which are accessible only to staff members, are conventional and orthogonal. The extraordinary design is reserved for the customers, while those areas where no customer contact takes place present a far more commonplace sight. Saarinen even accentuates this contrast by reflecting TWA's corporate design in the public areas of the building: Thousands upon thousands of light-colored mosaic tiles covering the walls and floor, white marble, and a similar shade on the underside of the vaults, together with burgundy carpets and upholstery, harmonize with the TWA corporate colors.

Against this backdrop, the styled terminal seems like a consumer good that, with its exceptional design, is intended to attract the attention of consumers (passengers) and aims to increase their enthusiasm for consumption (desire to travel). The underlying formula bears evidence of the attitude that characterizes American industrial design of the 1930s, with its protagonists Norman Bel Geddes, Raymond Loewy, Walter Dorwin Teague, Harley Earl, and Henry Dreyfuss The outward appearance of consumer goods thus becomes the crucial distinctive feature guiding Americans' purchasing activity.[155] This also alters the perspective of architects into the 1950s, such that the boundary between industrial design and architecture blurs noticeably: "Many of us think the two [industrial design and architecture] get closer every year. There is no question that the industrial designer has contributed a great deal to architecture," writes Dreyfuss in 1955.[156] Saarinen internalizes the principles of industrial design like no other architect of his time: "Eero Saarinen's constant search," confirms *Industrial Design* in 1963, "his probing for the appropriate specific image, rather than a general style, brings him close to the industrial designer's attitude towards contemporary products and corporate identity design."[157]

Eero Saarinen had already previously demonstrated his sense for the market value of novel forms as a successful designer working on behalf of the furniture manufacturer Knoll. The designer, explains Saarinen, must take into account not only user requirements but also the (market) developments and the external form: "He must be sensitive and adaptable to trends and needs; he must be part of and understand our society. At the same time, he is not just a mirror. He is also a co-creator and must have the strength and urge to produce form, not compromise."[158] Saarinen's finding can be understood by examining the example of his intent with the "Pedestal" furniture series: "We have four-legged chairs, we have three-legged chairs, and we have two-legged chairs," he notes, "but no one has done one-legged chairs, so we are going to do this."[159] **Fig. 102** With this product idea, Saarinen proves his understanding of the principles of the market economy twice over: Firstly, he recognizes that every customer—whether manufacturer, dealer, or consumer—desires unique products. Secondly, he seems to have originated a promising new development for extracting market share from the main competitor, as a letter to his client Hans Knoll makes clear: "I have come up with an idea that I think would wipe Herman Miller off the map!"[160] The outward appearance of the TWA Terminal bears evidence of the same economic thinking of attracting public attention through an exclusive design—and possesses that very potential.

102 "Pedestal" chairs and table, Eero Saarinen, 1958

2.4 Come Fly with Me

"TWA's concrete, wing-roofed terminal now ready for flight."[161] This headline marking the opening is representative of a seemingly endless number of comparisons of the building with the form of a giant bird. Countless reviewers from across the media landscape describe the two upwardly oriented concrete vaults as wings. Eero Saarinen plays down the similarity as "coincidental." "That was the last thing we ever thought about," he assures, only to immediately add that, when dealing with laypeople, such comparisons are however quite appropriate.[162] Whether Saarinen consciously evokes the image of a bird must remain an open question. What is clear, however, is that thanks to its symbolic power, the terminal actually provides more than just a welcome catchword for the press. In 1962, architecture critic Edgar Kaufmann, Jr. sees in the terminal building "the magnificence which belongs to the average man today."[163] His colleague Douglas Haskell formulates it more precisely in 1958: "Intentionally or not, the symbolic reference to an alighting bird is just as simple and direct as it would be in a popular building." Haskell illustrates his finding by comparing the TWA Terminal to the Sleeping Beauty Castle in Disneyland, which opened in 1955. According to Haskell, both buildings satisfy a widespread "popular need . . . for more drama: a 'good show,' symbolism, even fairy tales."[164]

Viewed from this perspective, the birdlike terminal at Idlewild Airport—also popularly referred to as "Disneyland East"—and the fairy-tale castle in the real Disneyland are alike insofar as they each present an easy-to-understand symbol to the broad general public.[165] In the same article, Haskell stylizes buildings with this capacity by using the term "googie," which, upon encountering the restaurant Googies by John Lautner, he coined in 1952 for the curvy building forms, upward-reaching or overhanging structures, and eccentric choice of materials in Californian motels, gas stations, and coffee shops.[166] **Fig. 103** Seen in this light, two architectural cultures—the architecture of an elite high culture and that of a popular mass culture—merge in the TWA Terminal.[167] Statements by Saarinen also substantiate this conclusion. The architect should not dismiss "public taste," but must instead respond to it, Cesar Pelli recalls his boss having repeatedly insisted.[168] With this focus, in the TWA Terminal Saarinen refines the design vocabulary that emerged, far from architectural high culture, in theme parks, along highways, and also in shopping malls—thereby appealing to the taste of a broad audience of professionals and laypeople, of "society as a whole," as Saarinen himself aptly demands of architecture.[169] The shift in the boundary between culture and commerce that Haskell recognizes in 1952 has, by the end of the decade, become further accentuated in Eero Saarinen's airport terminal.

103 Ship's Coffee Shop, Los Angeles, CA, Martin Stern, Jr., 1958

From this position, Saarinen designs the TWA departure building in Idlewild as a striking and highly symbolic attention-getter for the New Yorkers who flock past in droves. The potential inherent in the design is surmised by curators Arthur Drexler and Wilder Green as early as 1959, as they present a model of the building in the exhibition *Architecture and Imagery* at New York's Museum of Modern Art (MoMA). "The images such forms evoke become part of a building's ultimate value," they write in the exhibition catalog.[170] Drexler and Green rightly identify the highly symbolic building form as the real and inherent value of the terminal, as they make it out to be an exceptional and recognizable building at a major airport where all the airlines are courting attention. The Pan Am Terminal (1960), with its wide overhanging roof that is reminiscent of a UFO, is most able to compete with the TWA Terminal in terms of the uniqueness of its external appearance; the remaining airport terminals in Idlewild are, by contrast, designed far more conventionally.[171] **Figs 104, 105** A small selection of media statements leaves no doubt about this. The travel columnist for the *Dallas Morning News* writes after a visit to Idlewild: "Highlight of my visit a couple of weeks ago was the new TWA Terminal Building, an architectural stunner."[172] The Swiss architecture journal *Werk* is impressed by the "meticulous formal design of the project" and the "streamlined shape," because the terminal building "is new in many respects and has therefore created a stir even before its realization."[173] *Architectural Record* writes: "The soaring concrete sculpture of the great arches surely meets any man's criteria for distinction and drama, for excitement and dynamics."[174] Given the rivalry among the airlines in Idlewild, *Architectural Forum* sums up as follows: "There can be little doubt about who won."[175] On the loop at Idlewild, the TWA Flight Center stands out from the other terminals thanks to its special form and draws the desired attention to itself.

The economic capital of this attention exists in the ability of the terminal to favorably influence

104 Pan Am Terminal, Idlewild, Ives, Turano and Gardner Associated Architects with Walther Prokosch, 1961

105 American Airlines Terminal, Idlewild, Kahn and Jacobs Architects, 1960

TWA's corporate image in the public eye, since the building leaves the public with a highly desirable impression. With its curvy interior, which the press repeatedly associates with movement (e. g. "constant motion") and speed (e. g. "high-speed curves"), Eero Saarinen conveys the message of fast and trouble-free handling.[176] That this is equally suitable and welcome needs no further explanation in the face of widespread criticism of contemporary airport terminals. The exterior form, which resembles a bird about to take flight, refers just as directly to the building's purpose and—like a company logo—remains recognizable even as a small silhouette. Fig. 106 This message, too, is as clear as a TWA advertisement or the title of the Frank Sinatra record which the airline sponsors in 1958: *Come Fly with Me.*[177] Fig. 107 The conscious intent with which Saarinen sought this effect is attested by his own statements: the TWA Terminal should create the impression "of movement and transition" and "uplift."[178] Saarinen's frequently cited design intent—"express the drama and specialness and excitement of [air] travel"—must be understood against this backdrop.[179] Apart from enabling business on a large scale, the terminal is intended to make flying seem desirable again. With the prospect of an exciting travel experience, Saarinen promises the flight audience—beyond the base value of a smoothly functioning transfer—that emotional added value which distinguishes a brand from a mass product. Specifically, unlike the majority of the Idlewild terminals, where the customers are merely "dispatched" in the plainest sense of the word, the uniquely designed TWA building promises an exclusive travel experience. Herein lie the economic benefits and competitive advantage for TWA. From this point of view, in the final analysis the terminal ensures that people fly with TWA rather than any other airline—which, at least in the years directly after the commencement of operations, would also increasingly happen.[180] "That was what TWA wanted and what Mr. Saarinen provided," remarks President Charles C. Tillinghast, extremely satisfied after completion of construction.[181]

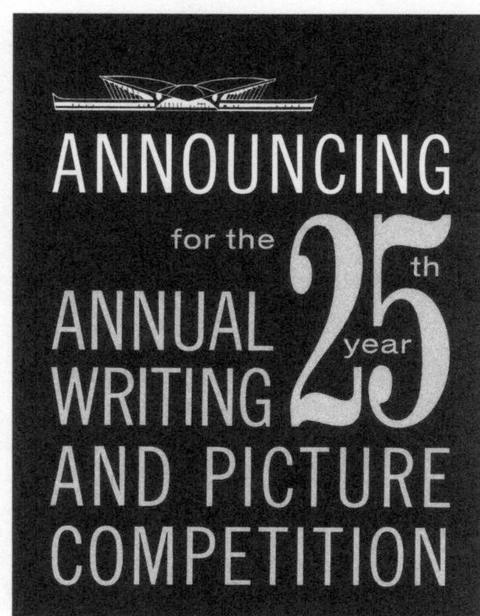

106 TWA Flight Center as silhouette, flyer, TWA, 1962

107 Vinyl album cover for *Come Fly with Me*, Frank Sinatra, 1958

Because TWA understands the unique selling point of Saarinen's design, the elaborate and costly building or, more precisely, its appearance survives all the rounds of cost cutting and changes of leadership on the part of the financially distressed client. Whereas the initial estimates in 1956 forsee construction costs of nearly $9 million, the building would ultimately cost $15 million. But none of the no less than five TWA presidents who are successively involved in the planning and realization of the terminal makes cutbacks to the elaborate design. Even the board of directors, which enacts various austerity programs and even briefly considers suspending the project, does not choose to forgo the high visibility of the building's extraordinary appearance.[182] The striking appearance of the building defies all budgetary constraints in favor of an economy of attention.

Endnotes

96 **Anonymous**: "Giant Lockheed Air Transport Makes Test Flight in California," in: *Washington Post*, January 10, 1943, pp. 1–2, p. 1.
97 See **Maxfield**, William: "TWA Standardizes Paint: New Painting Chart Guides Base and Terminal Crew," in: *Aviation*, vol. 40, no. 11 (November 1941), pp. 62–63, 168.
98 **Canty**, Donald: "Architecture for the Jet Age: New Buildings, New Problems, New Solutions," in: *Architectural Forum*, vol. 117, no. 1 (July 1962), pp. 66–83, p. 72.
99 See **Thomis**, Wayne: "Idlewild: 'Showcase Airport' Born of an Afterthought," in: *Chicago Tribune*, September 24, 1960, p. 8.
100 **Cook**, Robert H.: "Idlewild Sprawl Poses Transfer Problems," in: *Aviation Week & Space Technology*, vol. 79, no. 5 (July 29, 1963), pp. 33–34, 37, p. 33.
101 See **Anonymous**: "Fourteen Corporation Staff Designers," in: *Contract Interiors*, vol. 124, no. 12 (July 1965), pp. 85–105, p. 86. It seems that Werner is not directly involved in the subsequent project development, but increasingly exerts influence again toward the end. See **Price**, Ralph, ES&A employee 1956–1966, e-mail to the author, June 3, 2008.
102 According to Henry-Russell Hitchcock, a practice of "'shopping around' for

architects with names" becomes commonplace in the 1950s. With the commission being awarded to Saarinen, it appears that TWA also follows this trend. **Hitchcock**, Henry-Russell: "American Architecture in the Early Sixties," in: *Zodiac*, no. 10 (1962), pp. 4–17, p. 13.

103 **TWA**: "Summary of Planning Data: Proposed TWA Unit Terminal," October 3, 1956, p. 3, Trans World Airlines Collection (M-234), The Saint Louis Mercantile Library, University of Missouri-St. Louis, box 1-65.

104 The main result of the so-called "Denver Case" is the liberalization of the continental flight routes awarded in 1930. As a result, TWA receives the takeoff and landing rights in Denver, for instance, and United is granted them for Kansas City. See **Davies**, R. E. G.: *A History of the World's Airlines*, London: Oxford University Press, 1964, p. 247.

105 See **Cooper**, Michael H.; **Maynard**, Alan K.: *The Price of Air Travel* (series: "Hobard Paper," no. 53), London: Institute of Economic Affairs (IEA), 1971, pp. 15–16.

106 **Adams**, Don: "Filling Those Seats: US Airlines Try New Publicity Baits to Lure the Passenger," in: *Flight International*, vol. 80, no. 2735 (August 10, 1961), p. 190.

107 Floyd D. Hall, cited in **Johnson**, George: *The Abominable Airlines*, New York: Macmillan, 1964, pp. 246–247.

108 **Gilmore**, Gordon L.: "Public Relations Objectives: An Informal Study," July 16, 1959, [p. 1], Gordon L. Gilmore Papers, 1946–1973, Wisconsin Historical Society, Administrative Records, box 2, folder 3.

109 On the marketing strategy until that point, see **TWA**: "Three-Pronged Air Advertising Effort Helps Keep Name of TWA Before Public," in: *Skyliner*, vol. 17, no. 25 (June 24, 1954), p. 2.

110 Charles S. Thomas, cited in **TWA**: "Raymond Loewy Touch Is Added to TWA Design," in: *Skyliner*, vol. 23, no. 7 (March 31, 1960), p. 1.

111 See e.g. **TWA**: "Werner Appointed Design Director," in: *Skyliner*, vol. 22, no. 26 (December 24, 1959), p. 5; **TWA**: "By Design (Rex Werner's), TWA Projects Proud Image," in: *Skyliner*, vol. 27, no. 5 (March 2, 1964), p. 8; **TWA**: "Werner Is Named Sr. Dir. of Design," in: *Skyliner*, vol. 27, no. 3 (March 17, 1964), p. 6.

112 **Loewy**, Raymond: "Design Thoughts and Theories ..." in: *Skyliner*, vol. 23, no. 21 (October 20, 1960), pp. 1–2, p. 2. On the system of gaining higher status through Loewy's design, see also **Schönberger**, Angela (ed.): *Raymond Loewy: Pionier des amerikanischen Industriedesigns*, Munich: Prestel, 1990, p. 146. Loewy's corporate design would endure until 1975. See **TWA**: "Introducing Trans World Service and Trans World Vacations," in: *Skyliner*, vol. 38, no. 5 (March 1975), p. 1.

113 **Tillinghast**, Charles C., Jr.: "Grandeur: Trans World Flight Center," in: *Jetage Airlanes: The International In-Flight Magazine*, vol. 27, no. 6 (June 1962), pp. 9, 15, p. 9.

114 That the buildings for MIT and General Motors gain the attention of TWA is suggested by the first *Skyliner* report about the terminal, where ES&A are presented as "creators of the award-winning General Motors Research Center and the auditorium and chapel of Massachusetts Technical Institute of Technology." See **TWA**: "Modernistic New Terminal Planned to Capture Spirit of Flight During Jet Age," in: *Skyliner*, vol. 20, no. 30 (November 21, 1957), p. 3. TWA President Ralph S. Damon, who unexpectedly dies shortly after the commission is made, was supposedly also impressed by Saarinen's Auditorium for MIT, which had been inaugurated a few months before. See **Scullin**, George: *International Airport: The Story of Kennedy Airport and U.S. Commercial Aviation*, Boston: Little Brown and Co., 1968, pp. 154–155.

115 Cesar Pelli, ES&A employee, 1954–1964, cited in **Price**, Cathy (ed.): *Saarinen Swanson Reunion Proceedings*, Bloomfield Hills, MI: Cranbrook, 2001, p. 32.

116 Eero Saarinen, cited in **Jones**, Cranston; **Connery**, Donald S.: "The Maturing Modern," in: *Time*, vol. 68, no. 1 (July 2, 1956), pp. 50–57, p. 50. "Saarinen was preeminently a client's architect," observes John Jacobus, while naming "Mies and Louis Kahn [as] being, for purposes of comparison, architects' architects." **Jacobus**, John M.: "John Deere Office Building, Moline, IL, USA," in: *Architectural Review*, vol. 137, no. 5 (May 1965), pp. 364–371, p. 371.

117 Eero Saarinen, cited in **Jones**, Cranston; **Connery**, Donald S.: "The Maturing Modern," in: *Time*, vol. 68, no. 1 (July 2, 1956), pp. 50–57, p. 57.

118 See **Kieran**, Stephen: "The Architecture of Plenty: Theory and Design in a Marketing Age," in: *The Harvard Architecture Review*, vol. 6, "Patronage" (1987), pp. 102–113, p. 107.

119 **Saarinen**, Eero: "Problems Facing Architecture," lecture in the "Benjamin Franklin Lecture Series" at the University of Pennsylvania in Philadelphia, December 8, 1960, p. 1. Eero Saarinen Collection (MS 593), Manuscripts and Archives, Yale University Library, series 2, box 21, folder 77.

120 Eero Saarinen, cited in **Saarinen**, Aline B.: *Eero Saarinen on His Work: A Selection of Buildings Dating from 1947 to 1964 with Statements by the Architect*, New Haven, CT: Yale University Press, 1968 (second ed.), p. 16.

121 Ibid. p. 68.

122 The magazine *Time* describes the widespread phenomenon of curtain wall facades as "the tyranny of the grid with its curtain wall." **Anonymous**: "New World of Shells," in: *Time*, vol. 73, no. 10 (March 9, 1959), p. 50. Also frustrated on that account is Thomas Creighton, the editor of *Progressive Architecture* at the time: "No one is doing anything, except watered-down versions of Miesian architecture. Curtain walls! Curtain walls and stripped-down architecture everywhere." **Creighton**, Thomas H.: "The New Sensualism [I]," in: *Progressive Architecture*, vol. 40, no. 9 (September 1959), pp. 141–147, p. 141.

123 **Saarinen**, Eero: "What Is Architecture?," in: *Perspecta*, no. 7 (1961), pp. 29–42, p. 30. According to Saarinen, the range of solutions in American architecture is too dreary and monotonous: "What once was a great hope for a great new period of architecture has now somehow become an automatic application of the same formula over and over again." The bone of contention is mainly the prevalence of glass and steel frame construction, which fundamentally altered the appearance of the inner cities and suburbs in the country well into the 1950s. **Saarinen**, Eero: Letter to Rex Raab, Anthroposophischer Architektenkreis, Stuttgart, July 22, 1958, p. 1, Eero Saarinen Collection (MS 593), Manuscripts and Archives, Yale University Library, series I, box 14, folder 227.

124 Mark Jaroszewicz, ES&A employee, 1949–1954, cited in: **Price**, Cathy (ed.): *Saarinen Swanson Reunion Proceedings*, Bloomfield Hills, MI: Cranbrook, 2001, p. 24.

125 Peter Blake, cited in: **Dean**, Andrea O.: "Eero Saarinen in Perspective: A Generation After His Loss; A Discussion of His Work and Influence," in: *AIA Journal*, vol. 70, no. 13 (November 1981), pp. 36–51, p. 50.

126 **Anonymous**: "Saarinen Challenges the Rectangle: Designs a Domed Auditorium and a Cylindrical Chapel for MIT's Laboratory Campus," in: *Architectural Forum*, vol. 98, no. 1 (January 1953), pp. 126–133, p. 127.

127 See **Isler**, Heinz: "Moderner Schalenbau," in: **Henn**, Ursula (ed.): *Zum Werk von Felix Candela: die Kunst der leichten Schalen* (vol. 18), Cologne: Müller, 1992 (series: "Arcus"), pp. 50–66, p. 52.

128 See **Saarinen**, Aline B.: Letter to unknown recipient, n. d., Aline and Eero Saarinen Papers, 1906–1977, Archives of American Art, Smithsonian Institution, series 1, box 2, folder 45, p. 34.

129 **Chermayeff**, Serge: "History of Thin Concrete Shells," in: **Massachusetts Institute of Technology** (ed.): *Proceedings of a Conference on Thin Concrete Shells*, Cambridge, MA: MIT Press, 1954, pp. 2–4, p. 3.

130 **Anonymous**: "Grand Central of the Air," in: *Architectural Forum*, vol. 104, no. 5 (May 1956), pp. 106–115. See also **Pearman**, Hugh: *Airports: A Century of Architecture*, London: Laurence King, 2004, p. 145.

131 Author interview with Kevin Roche, August 2, 2007, Hamden, CT.

132 See **Ringli**, Kornel [interview with Abba Tor, responsible engineer at Ammann and Whitney]: "Der Ingenieur von Kahn und Saarinen: ein Gespräch mit Abba Tor," in: *archithese*, vol. 41, no. 5 (2011), pp. 54–59, p. 59.

133 An ideal shell has a continuous curve, but the upper ridges of the TWA Flight Center disrupt the curvature and create a discontinuity in the vaults (bending moments). In addition, deformations occur at the edge beams because the vaults cantilever out markedly and are held up at isolated points instead of resting optimally on a continuous linear support. The fact that each vault rests only on two supports instead of a minimum of three is also structurally disadvantageous. The imaginary third support for each vault, a central connecting plate where the four vaults meet, is also subject to unfavorable structural loading. Due to the overhang, three vaults tend outward and one vault (street side) tends inward, so that tensile and compressive forces occur simultaneously at the middle point of connection. See **Anderson**, Boyd G.; **Tor**, Abba; **Yeakel**, Ralph W., Jr.: "Design and Construction of Shell Roof for the New York International Airport TWA Flight Center," in: *Proceedings World Conference on Shell Structures, October 1–4, 1962, San Francisco, CA*, Washington, D.C.: National Academy of Sciences–National Research Council, pp. 319–328, p. 320. See also **Ringli**, Kornel [interview with Abba Tor, responsible engineer at Ammann and Whitney]: "Der Ingenieur von Kahn und Saarinen: ein Gespräch mit Abba Tor," in: *archithese*, vol. 41, no. 5 (2011), pp. 54–59, p. 55.

134 **Saarinen**, Eero: "Function, Structure, and Beauty," in: *Architectural Association Journal*, vol. 73, no. 814 (July/August 1957), pp. 40–51, p. 43.

135 Ibid. It is not shell structures that Saarinen considers to be the least-expensive construction form but glass and steel-frame structures: "The most econimcal [sic], the most practical means with our building materials is to put them into a cube. This was the big market in the U.S. and Mies found a way to solve the problem." **Saarinen**, Eero: [On Mies van der Rohe, FLW, Philip Johnson, SOM]', dictation, n. d., p. 1, Eero Saarinen Collection (MS 593), Manuscripts and Archives, Yale University Library, series II, box 28, folder 117.

136 "I admit there is a lot of concrete in that shell," concedes Saarinen in a letter to the architecture critic John Peter, "but I think you will agree if you see it that it is the least earthbound shell that has ever been built." **Saarinen**, Eero: Letter to John Peter, December 6, 1960, Eero Saarinen Collection (MS 593), Manuscripts and Archives, Yale University Library, series IV, box 273, folders 906–910.

137 The structural calculations were done without a computer, whereas the calculations for the complex concrete formwork were done with a computer. Author interview with Abba Tor, responsible engineer at Ammann and Whitney, May 4, 2008, Hastings-on-Hudson, NY. Also **Scullin**, George: *International Airport: The Story of Kennedy Airport and U.S. Commercial Aviation*, Boston: Little Brown and Co., 1968, pp. 171–187.

138 Fundamental for this argument is **Franck**, Georg: *Ökonomie der Aufmerksamkeit: ein Entwurf*, Munich: Hanser, 1998, esp. pp. 49–51, 159–160.

139 **Peter**, John [interview with Eero Saarinen]: *The Oral History of Modern Architecture: Interviews with the Greatest Architects of the Twentieth Century*, New York: Abrams, 1994, pp. 200–201.

140 Eero Saarinen, cited in **McQuade**, Walter: "Eero Saarinen: A Complete Architect," in: *Architectural Forum*, vol. 116, no. 4 (April 1962), pp. 102–127, p. 107.

141 Author interview with Kevin Roche, August 2, 2007, Hamden, CT.

142 Eero Saarinen, cited in: **Saarinen**, Aline B.: *Eero Saarinen on His Work: A Selection of Buildings Dating from 1947 to 1964 with Statements by the Architect*, New Haven, CT: Yale University Press, 1968 (second ed.), p. 68.

143 **Saarinen**, Eero: [Untitled lecture, held on the occasion of his receiving the Dickinson College Arts Award], December 1, 1959, p. 6, Eero Saarinen Collection (MS 593), Manuscripts and Archives, Yale University Library, series II, box 21, folder 73. Emphasis in original.

144 Author interview with Kevin Roche, May 5, 2008, Hamden, CT.

145 See **Borcherdt**, Helmut: "Planung des TWA-Flughafengebäudes in New York," in: *Baukunst und Werkform*, vol. 13, no. 5 (May 1960), pp. 256–263, p. 257; **Knight**, Richard: "Once upon a Time . . . ," in: **Idem**: *Saarinen's Quest: A Memoir*, San Francisco, CA: William Stout Publishers, 2008, pp. 17–64, p. 28.

146 **Borcherdt**, Helmut: "Planung des TWA-Flughafengebäudes in New York," in: *Baukunst und Werkform*, vol. 13, no. 5 (May 1960), pp. 256–263, p. 258.

147 Eero Saarinen, cited in **Anonymous**: "Shaping a Two-Acre Sculpture," in: *Architectural Forum*, vol. 113, no. 2 (August 1960), pp. 118–123, p. 119. On the construction drawings, see **Ringli**, Kornel: "Planned Myth: The Building Plans for Eero Saarinen's TWA Terminal as Marketing Tool," in: **Spiro**, Annette; **Ganzoni**, David (eds): *The Working Drawing: The Architect's Tool*, Zurich: Park Books, 2013, pp. 298–300.

148 According to a statement by Kevin Roche, the industrial designers Norman Bel Geddes and Henry Dreyfuss exert great influence on Saarinen. See **Dean**, Andrea O.: "Eero Saarinen in Perspective: A Generation After His Loss; A Discussion of His Work and Influence," in: *AIA Journal*, vol. 70, no. 13 (November 1981), pp. 36–51, p. 41. On Saarinen's work experience with Bel Geddes, see **Meikle**, Jeffrey L.: *Twentieth Century Limited: Industrial Design in America, 1925–1939*, Philadelphia, PA: Temple University Press, 1979, p. 230. For a description of Bel Geddes model-making technique, see **Houghton**, Norris: "The Designer Sets the Stage: Norman Bel Geddes and Vincente Minnelli," in: *Theatre Arts Monthly*, vol. 20, no. 10 (October 1936), reprint: *Theatre Arts*, New York: Arno Press, 1971, pp. 776–788, pp. 781–782.

149 See **Serraino**, Pierluigi: "Modernism beyond Reasonable Doubt: Model Making and Photography in Eero Saarinen and Associates," in: **Knight**, Richard: *Saarinen's Quest: A Memoir*, San Francisco, CA: William Stout Publishers, 2008, pp. 151–159, p. 155.

150 Harry Weese, cited in **Dean**, Andrea O.: "Eero Saarinen in Perspective: A Generation after His Loss; A Discussion of His Work and Influence," in: *AIA Journal*, vol. 70, no. 13 (November 1981), pp. 36–51, p. 43.

151 See **Serraino**, Pierluigi: "Modernism beyond Reasonable Doubt: Model Making and Photography in Eero Saarinen and Associates," in: **Knight**, Richard: *Saarinen's Quest: A Memoir*, San Francisco, CA: William Stout Publishers, 2008, pp. 151–159, p. 157 (image caption).

152 See **Colquhoun**, Alan: "TWA Terminal Building, Idlewild, New York," in: *Architectural Design*, vol. 32, no. 10 (October 1962), pp. 465–469, p. 465; **Blake**, Peter: "Modern Architecture: Its Many Faces," in: *Architectural Forum*, vol. 108, no. 3 (March 1958), pp. 76–81, p. 78; **Knight**, Richard: "Once upon a Time . . . ," in: **idem**: *Saarinen's Quest: A Memoir*, San Francisco, CA: William Stout Publishers, 2008, pp. 17–64, p. 53.

153 For Harley Earl's design process, see **Bayley**, Stephen: *Harley Earl and the Dream Machine* (series: "Design Heroes"), London: Trefoil Publications, 1990, pp. 88–89.

154 Eero Saarinen, cited in **Saarinen**, Aline B.: *Eero Saarinen on His Work: A Selection of Buildings Dating from 1947 to 1964 with Statements by the Architect*, New Haven, CT: Yale University Press, 1968 (second ed.), p. 68.

155 See **Riesman**, David; **Larrabee**, Eric: "Autos in Amerika," in: **Riesman**, David (ed.): *Wohlstand wofür? Essays*, Frankfurt a. M.: Suhrkamp, 1966, pp. 202–238, p. 213; Engl. original title: "Autos in America," in *Abundance for What? And Other Essays*, New York: Doubleday, 1964.

156 **Dreyfuss**, Henry: *Designing for People*, New York: Simon and Schuster, 1955, pp. 217, 218. Saarinen concurs and sees similarities, especially with regard to design, between both disciplines: "The problem of forms, of structure and so on, is really exactly the same in furniture as in architecture," he is convinced. **Saarinen**, Eero: "Function, Structure, and Beauty," in: *Architectural Association Journal*, vol. 73, no. 814 (July/August 1957), pp. 40–51, p. 44.

157 **Dorr**, Maude: "Portraits in Architecture: A Review of the Most Recent Buildings of the Late Eero Saarinen," in: *Industrial Design*, vol. 10, no. 5 (May 1963), pp. 62–71, p. 63.

158 **Saarinen**, Eero: "The Challenge to the Arts Today," in: *Yale Daily News*, 1953, pp. 112–113, 191, p. 191.

159 Eero Saarinen, cited according to Gunnar Birkerts, ES&A employee 1951–1955, in **Price**, Cathy (ed.): *Saarinen Swanson Reunion Proceedings*, Bloomfield Hills, MI: Cranbrook, 2001, p. 38.

160 **Saarinen**, Eero: Letter to Hans Knoll, November 22, 1954, Eero Saarinen Collection (MS 593), Manuscripts and Archives, Yale University Library, series IV, box 83, folder 151.

161 **Anonymous**: "TWA's Concrete, Wing-Roofed Terminal Now Ready for Flight," in: *Engineering News-Record*, vol. 168, no. 22 (May 31, 1962), pp. 48–50.

162 Eero Saarinen, cited in **Saarinen**, Aline B.: *Eero Saarinen on His Work: A Selection of Buildings Dating from 1947 to 1964 with Statements by the Architect*, New Haven, CT: Yale University Press, 1968 (second ed.), p. 68.

163 **Kaufmann**, Edgar, Jr.: "Inside Eero Saarinen's TWA Building," in: *Interiors*, vol. 121, no. 7 (July 1962), pp. 86–93, p. 92.

164 **Haskell**, Douglas: "Architecture and Popular Taste," in: *Architectural Forum*, vol. 109, no. 2 (August 1958), pp. 104–109, pp. 106, 108.

165 On the term "Disneyland East," see **Johnson**, George: *The Abominable Airlines*, New York: Macmillan, 1964, p. 102. The notion of Idlewild as a flashy theme park is also shared by Ada Louise Huxtable. See **Huxtable**, Ada Louise: "Idlewild: Distressing Monument to Air Age," in: *New York Times*, November 25, 1962, p. 25.

166 **Haskell**, Douglas: "Architecture and Popular Taste," in: *Architectural Forum*, vol. 109, no. 2 (August 1958), pp. 104–109, p. 106. For Robin Boyd, however, it is clear that only an inattentive viewer would identify the TWA Terminal as representing the "Googie Style." See **Boyd**, Robin: "The Counter-Revolution in Architecture," in: *Harper's Magazine*, vol. 219, no. 10 (September 1959), pp. 40–48, p. 48. On the origin of the term, see **Haskell**, Douglas: "Googie Architecture: Los Angeles Does Its Bit," in: *House and Home*, vol. 1, no. 2 (February 1952), pp. 86–88.

167 This dichotomy between art and commerce presents architectural criticism with problems: "You can't write like Theodore Dreiser and Thomas Mann at the same time," criticizes Walter McQuade in reference to Saarinen's ambivalent stance. **McQuade**, Walter: "The Exploded Landscape," in: *Perspecta*, no. 7 (1961), pp. 83–90, p. 86.

168 **Yamashita**, Tsukasa [interview with Cesar Pelli]: "Eero Saarinen and His Works," in: **Hozumi**, Nobuo (ed.): *Eero Saarinen* (series: "A&U Extra Edition"), Tokyo: A&U Publishing Co., 1984, pp. 226–230, p. 228.

169 **Saarinen**, Eero: "The Challenge to the Arts Today," in: *Yale Daily News*, 1953, pp. 112–113, 191, p. 191. That Saarinen's architecture addresses the broad masses is condemned sharply by some contemporary critics: "Saarinen's buildings are the most popular packages of their time and a revealing image of it. Through them runs the insistent American instinct for simplistic and, in this case, spectacular solutions," writes Vincent Scully in 1969. **Scully**, Vincent J.: *American Architecture and Urbanism*, London: Thames and Hudson, 1969, p. 198. Various other contemporaries note Saarinen's penchant for simple, at times banal forms. See **Jacobus**, John M.: "Reviewed Work(s): Eero Saarinen on His Work by Aline B. Saarinen; Eero Saarinen . . . ," in: *Journal of the Society of Architectural Historians*, vol. 22, no. 4 (December 1963), pp. 237–239, p. 238; **Larrabee**, Eric; **Vignelli**, Massimo (eds): *Knoll Design*, New York: Abrams, 1981, p. 50 (quote from Charles Eames).

170 **Drexler**, Arthur; **Green**, Wilder: "Architecture and Imagery: Four New Buildings," in: *Museum of Modern Art Bulletin*, vol. 26, no. 2 (1959), p. 1. The other buildings are the Sydney Opera House (Jørn Utzon), Eglise Notre-Dame de Royan (Guillaume Gillet), and the First Presbyterian Church of Stamford (Wallace K. Harrison).

171 See **Blacklock**, Mark: *Recapturing the Dream: A Design History of New York's JFK Airport*, London: M. Blacklock, 2005, p. 82.

172 **Simmons**, Jean: "A New Look for Playland," in: *Dallas Morning News*, October 28, 1962, p. 6.

173 **Huber**, Benedikt: "Projekt für den TWA Terminal in Idlewild, New York," in: *Werk*, vol. 47, no. 2 (February 1960), pp. 53–54, p. 53.

174 **Anonymous**: "Saarinen's TWA Flight Center," in: *Architectural Record*, vol. 132, no. 7 (July 1962), pp. 129–134, p. 129.

175 **Canty**, Donald: "Architecture for the Jet Age: New Buildings, New Problems, New Solutions," in: *Architectural Forum*, vol. 117, no. 1 (July 1962), pp. 66–83, p. 72.

176 Ibid., pp. 72, 73.

177 On the back of the album: "Cover produced in cooperation with Trans World Airlines and featuring the TWA Jetstream Super Constellation." Frank Sinatra is not at all pleased about the deal his record company made with TWA. See **Martin**, George; **Hornsby**, Jeremy: *All You Need Is Ears*, New York: St. Martin's Press, 1994, pp. 144–145. The interpretation of the terminal as an architectural translation of the invitation "come fly with me" is also found in **Dunlap**, David W.: "A Move to Make a Silent Air Terminal Hum Again," November 16, 2006, http://www.nytimes.com/2006/11/16/nyregion/16blocks.html (accessed February 3, 2015).

178 See Eero Saarinen, cited in **Saarinen**, Aline B.: *Eero Saarinen on His Work: A Selection of Buildings Dating from 1947 to 1964 with Statements by the Architect*, New Haven, CT: Yale University Press, 1968 (second ed.), p. 68.

179 Eero Saarinen, cited in ibid.

180 Author interview with Abba Tor, responsible engineer at Ammann and Whitney, May 4, 2008, Hastings-on-Hudson, NY.

181 **Tillinghast**, Charles C., Jr.: "Grandeur: Trans World Flight Center," in: *Jetage Airlanes: The International In-Flight Magazine*, vol. 27, no. 6 (June 1962), pp. 9, 15, p. 9.

182 According to Ralph Price, a former employee of ES&A, Saarinen's airport terminal receives the moniker "five chairmen terminal" because of the many leadership changes. Price, Ralph, ES&A employee 1956–1966: e-mail to the author, June 3, 2008.

3 Universal Press Acclaim

Before Eero Saarinen ascends to become one of the best-known American architects of his time, he makes himself a name as a furniture designer. In 1940, working together with Charles Eames, he wins two categories in the competition "Organic Design in Home Furnishing." In 1943 he wins the competition "Designs for Postwar Living," together with Oliver Lundquist, and in 1948 the furniture manufacturer Knoll brings his "womb" chair to market, which receives a thrilled reception by the mainstream press.[183] But Saarinen, whose psychological assessment attests "strong status concerns about his own greatness," is not satisfied by such success.[184] He seeks more. Saarinen makes no secret of his wish to be remembered by history as a great architect: "I would frankly like to leave a place for myself in architectural history," he declares in a 1953 letter to an unknown recipient.[185]

After a failed first marriage to sculptor Lilian Swann he actually gives high priority to choosing a new partner. The person he seeks is a woman who can aid him in his professional ambitions.[186] He uses a chart to record his evaluation of various potential partners according to aspects such as "work integrity," "own work," "sex," and "representation quality," and one candidate does particularly well: the art historian and journalist Aline B. Louchheim.[187] The two first met in 1953 during the interview for her article "Now Saarinen the Son," which appeared in the *New York Times*. Less than a year later they marry, and the successful art critic resigns from her position at the prestigious daily newspaper, because she has a new job: Aline Saarinen becomes the head of communications at Eero Saarinen and Associates. Thus she fills a new post in the architectural firm and from that point on actively promotes the publication of Saarinen's works. Along with Eero Saarinen, Trans World Airlines will also reap the benefits.

108 In Aline B. Louchheim, Eero Saarinen finds a wife who can aid him in his professional ambitions. She becomes the head of communications at ES&A.

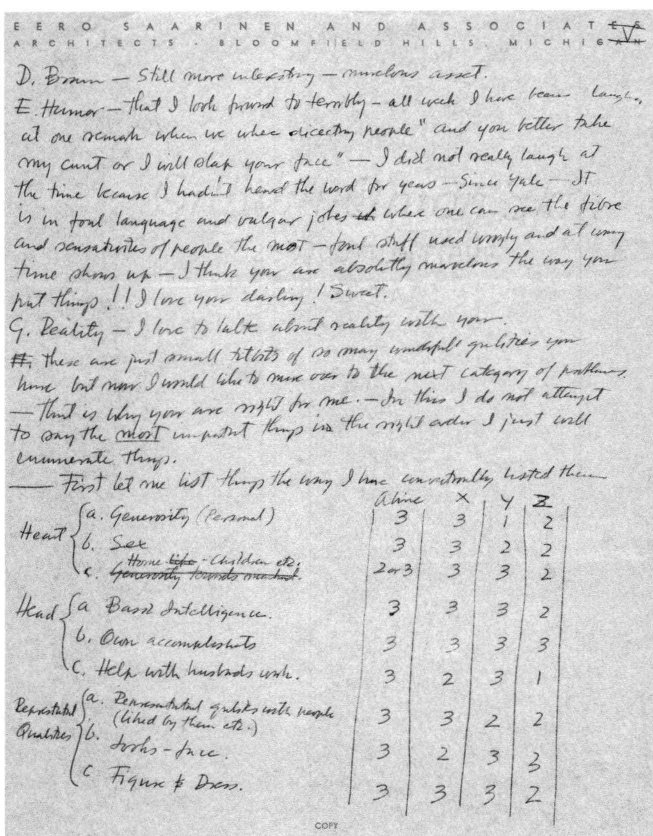

EERO SAARINEN AND ASSOCIATES
ARCHITECTS · BLOOMFIELD HILLS, MICHIGAN

D. Brains — Still more interesting — marvelous asset.
E. Humor — that I look forward to terribly — all week I have been laughing at one remark when we were discussing people" and you better take my cunt or I will slap your face" — I did not really laugh at the time because I hadn't heard the word for years — Since Yale — It is in foul language and vulgar jokes ~~th~~ where one can see the fibre and sensitivities of people the most — foul stuff used wrongly and at wrong time shows up — I think you are absolutely marvelous the way you put things!! I love you darling! Sweet.
G. Reality — I love to talk about reality with you.
~~H.~~ these are just small bits of so many wonderful qualities you have but now I would like to move over to the next category of problems. — that is why you are right for me. — In this I do not attempt to say the most important things in the right order I just will enumerate things.
— First let me list things the way I have conventionally listed them

		Aline	X	Y	Z
Heart	a. Generosity (Personal)	3	3	1	2
	b. Sex	3	3	2	2
	c. ~~Generosity towards mankind.~~ Home ~~life~~ - Children etc.	2 or 3	3	3	2
Head	a. Basic Intelligence.	3	3	3	2
	b. Own accomplishments	3	3	3	3
	c. Help with husbands work.	3	2	3	1
Representational Qualities	a. Representational qualities with people (liked by them etc.)	3	3	2	2
	b. Looks - face.	3	2	3	3
	c. Figure & Dress.	3	3	3	2

COPY

109 The architect even subordinates his choice of a partner to his craving for recognition. Eero Saarinen uses a chart to record his assessment of various potential wives.

110 Aline Saarinen arranges public engagements for her husband and also orchestrates the publication of his works. The couple even chooses their attendance at social events to serve their purposes.

111 Eero Saarinen wants to be remembered by history as a great architect. With her excellent network in the media sector, Aline Saarinen can ideally support him.

112 While Aline Saarinen gives the architect a voice, he perfects the visualization of his projects.

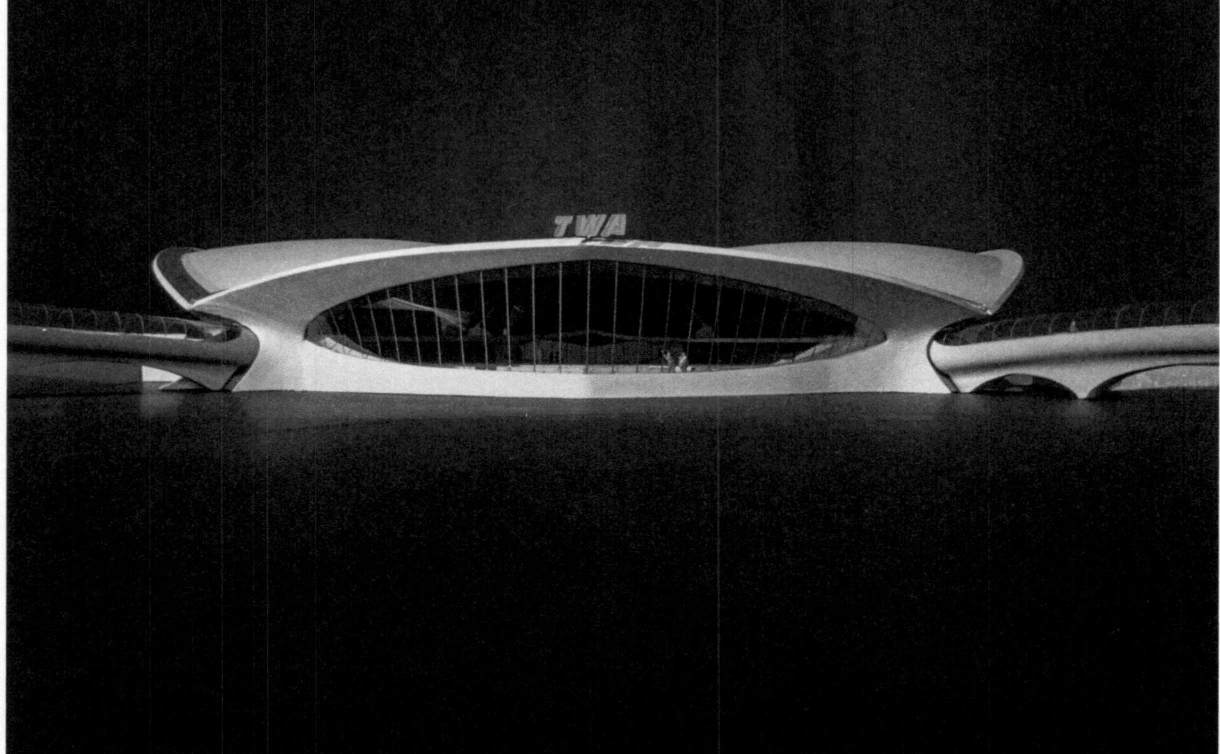

113 ES&A produce elaborate presentation models. They not only serve as a means of communication with TWA but are also widely publicized.

114 When making presentations to his clients, Eero Saarinen favors showing extremely realistic photomontages of models.

115 For Eero Saarinen, photographs of models are also a design tool that is used to check the visual impact of the future building.

116 Eero Saarinen elevates pictorial impact—here we see a multiple-exposure photograph by employee Balthazar Korab—to a design-determining aspect. Thus even at the design stage, he takes into account the terminal's ability to be disseminated in the media.

117 In marketing the terminal, Aline Saarinen and TWA work together as a team. From the groundbreaking ceremony to the grand opening, they intensively use the three-year period of construction for their goals.

118 The communication construes a relationship between the building's constructional complexity and the ground handling efficiency of the completed terminal.

119 Thanks to numerous press releases, the elaborate construction of the vaults and the photogenic building shell elicit broad coverage in the media.

120 For this photograph TWA has dressed the workers in matching numbered T-shirts in the company colors and positioned a jet aircraft in the distance. The press photo is intended to veil TWA's delayed entry into the jet age.

ARCHITECT EERO SAARINEN points to the entrance on the artist's drawing of the new terminal, as Mrs. Saarinen and TWA vice president George Clay stand by.

ASSEMBLED PRESS REPRESENTATIVES, and officials of the Port of New York Authority and TWA, listen as President Burgess outlines plans for the new terminal.

THE SCENE as President Charles C. Tillinghast, Jr., spoke at the dedication of the Trans World Flight Center May 28 at New York International Airport. The program climaxed a week of festive events in connection with the Center's formal opening.

THE FIRST SPADES OF EARTH are turned, signifying the start of construction of TWA's new passenger terminal at Idlewild. Doing the honors (left to right) are Horace K. Corbin, vice chairman of the Port of New York Authority; President Charles S. Thomas; architect Eero Saarinen and E. W. Shepherd of Grove Shepherd Wilson and Kruge, Inc., New York construction firm which will build the terminal. At a luncheon following the ceremony, President Thomas commented that with the new terminal "TWA becomes a real part of the greatest airport in the world." In reply, Corbin reminded the group that 29 years ago—on October 25, 1930—TWA inaugurated the first transcontinental air service from Newark airport, which then served New York City.

"MY HUSBAND would have been both humble and proud at this moment," Mrs. Eero Saarinen said as she unveiled the dedication plaque for the Trans World Flight Center. Tribute to the famed architect, who died September 1, 1961, was paid by Arthur Drexler (behind Mrs. Saarinen), director of architecture and design for the New York Museum of Modern Art. TWA President Charles C. Tillinghast, Jr., officiated. The plaque reads: *Trans World Flight Center; Dedicated May the Twenty-eighth, 1962; Eero Saarinen, Architect.*

TWA Backs Area Idea

121 Beginning with the announcement of the project in 1957 and continuing from the groundbreaking ceremony in 1959 to the terminal's opening in 1962, TWA and Aline Saarinen jointly orchestrate a series of elaborate media events. Here we see the coverage in the employee magazine.

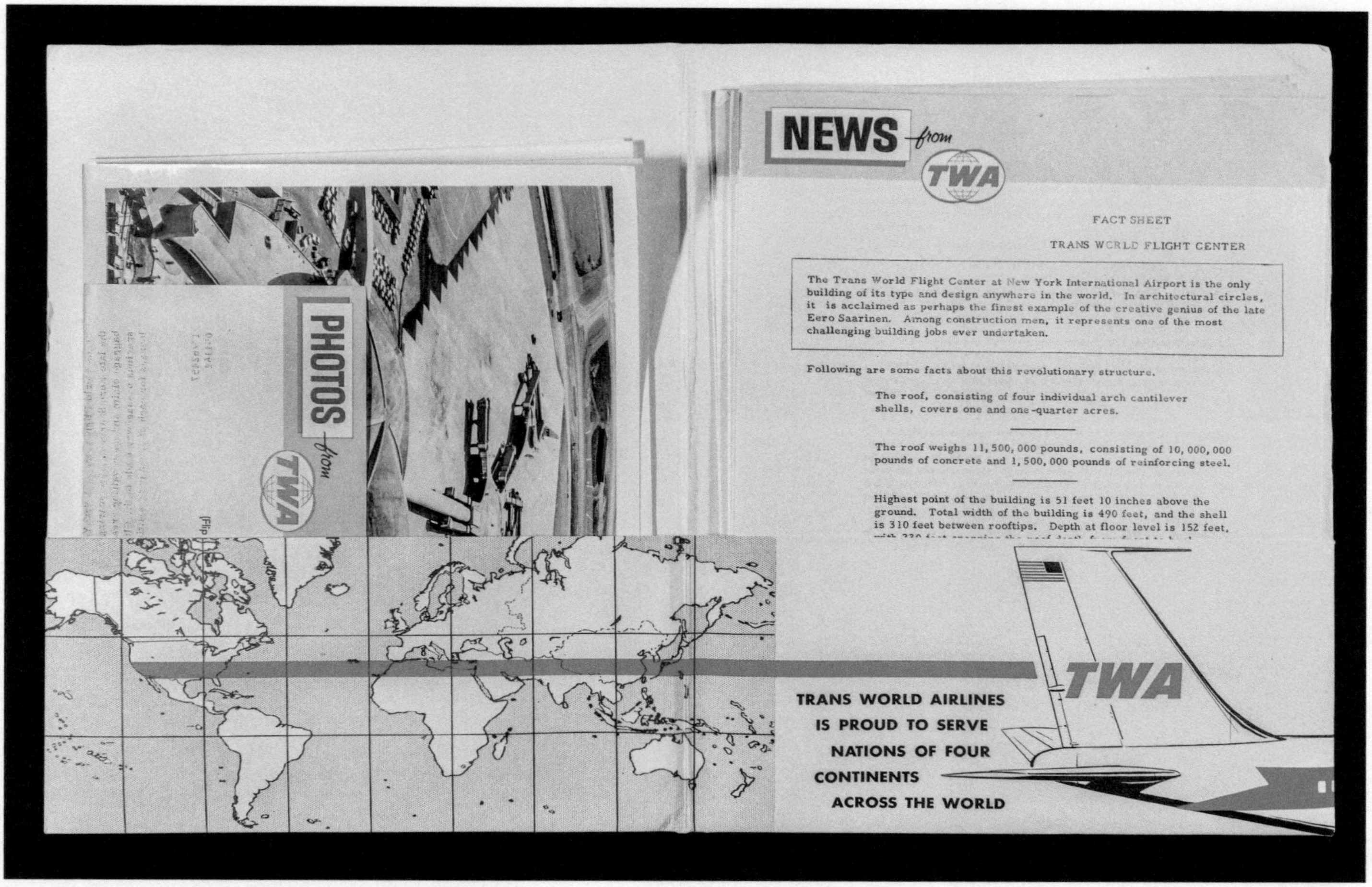

PHOTOS from TWA
NEWS from TWA
FACT SHEET
TRANS WORLD FLIGHT CENTER
The Trans World Flight Center at New York International Airport is the only building of its type and design anywhere in the world. In architectural circles, it is acclaimed as perhaps the finest example of the creative genius of the late Eero Saarinen. Among construction men, it represents one of the most challenging building jobs ever undertaken.
Following are some facts about this revolutionary structure.
The roof, consisting of four individual arch cantilever shells, covers one and one-quarter acres.
The roof weighs 11,500,000 pounds, consisting of 10,000,000 pounds of concrete and 1,500,000 pounds of reinforcing steel.
Highest point of the building is 51 feet 10 inches above the ground. Total width of the building is 490 feet, and the shell is 310 feet between rooftips. Depth at floor level is 152 feet,
TRANS WORLD AIRLINES
IS PROUD TO SERVE
NATIONS OF FOUR
CONTINENTS
ACROSS THE WORLD
TWA

122 **Press releases and photos are distributed in portfolio folders like this one, which is dated May 17, 1962, shortly before the grand opening.**

LE NOUVEAU CENTRE DES LIGNES MONDIALES TWA

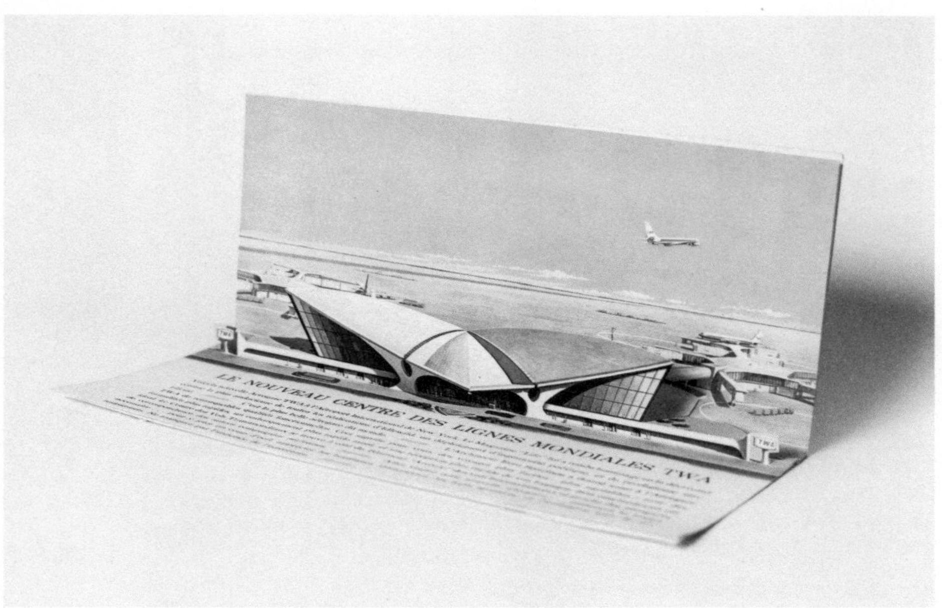

123 **During the time surrounding the opening, TWA produces a variety of promotional materials in several languages, such as this pop-up TWA Terminal with French text.**

Il nuovo Centro Aereo TWA all'Aeroporto Internazionale di New York

"Il mondo sotto un solo tetto"

Questa è la nuova Stazione Aerea TWA dell'Aeroporto di New York. Le sue arditissime linee, concepite dall'architetto Saarinen, sembrano esprimere la esaltante esperienza del volo. Sotto il suo tetto ad ala e le immense vetrate hanno trovato applicazione centinaia di nuove idee per rendere più spedite le operazioni aeroportuali, quali il controllo biglietti, l'imbarco, la consegna automatica dei bagagli. Nella nuova stazione aerea trovano posto negozi di classe, comode sale d'attesa, ristoranti di lusso. Una particolare caratteristica rende inoltre la Stazione Aerea TWA unica al mondo; quella di essere il solo punto di incontro tra le rotte dall'Europa, dall'Africa e dall'Asia e quelle che collegano 70 città negli Stati Uniti. Il mondo sotto un solo tetto.

Volate SuperJet TWA - Roma-New York senza scalo, partenze alle ore 12.00, 13.00, 17.15
Consultate il vostro Agente di Viaggio o la TWA,
Roma : Via Barberini 67 - Tel. 471.141,
Milano : Corso Omenoni 2 - Tel. 794.650.

8

124 This full-page, Italian-language advertisement (ca. 1962) illustrates that TWA uses the terminal for marketing worldwide.

**StarStream and DynaFan are service marks owned exclusively by Trans World Airlines, Inc.*

Compare what your TWA ticket buys today:

Wherever you fly within the United States or overseas, all fares on major airlines are the same. The big difference is in what you get for your ticket, whether you travel First Class or Coach. Today, TWA makes flying more of a pleasure than ever. A great new network of TWA terminals offers conveniences like fast "carousel" baggage delivery and instantaneous flight information. A great new fleet of StarStream* jetliners with DynaFan* power adds to TWA's reputation for on-time dependability. And you enjoy food with an international touch—because only TWA flies throughout the United States and to Europe, Africa and Asia.

Compare what all airlines offer. Compare ... and you'll fly TWA.

125 With regard to the TWA Terminal, this advertisement (1962) promises that flying is more comfortable than ever before, thanks to the most up-to-date infrastructure.

THE NEW TWA TRANS WORLD FLIGHT CENTER AT NEW YORK INTERNATIONAL AIRPORT, IDLEWILD

Most Beautiful
In All the World—
So Functional, Too!

Eero Saarinen's Marvel

"To express the excitement of flight" was the architect's purpose . . . and every step you take in the new Trans World Flight Center spells excitement. You sense it in the sweeps and curves, the *contrasts*, of the Center. The main concourse, with its soaring soft-toned ceiling, flowing into the quiet, restful waiting area with its panoramic view of the airfield. The graceful stairways that lead gently to the upper level with its restaurant and lounge areas, linked by a slender bridge. In these views, and all around you, Saarinen's art is revealed. This new building has a simple unity, a compelling beauty, that set it apart from all other air terminals.

Above: For fine dining in the international manner: one of the three restaurants on the upper level.

Left: A view across the main concourse; the bridge links the two sections of the upper level.

A Passenger's Dream

In the midst of all this beauty . . . the crisp efficiency that results from painstaking planning. Thoughtful arrangement of facilities to speed you, the passenger, through the Center and on your way. All the details connected with your trip are taken care of in a matter of moments . . . yet without the slightest suggestion of haste. TWA seeks to provide the same ease and comfort at the airports that it assures you in SuperJet flight. Electronic aids work unseen toward this end: the waiting area, the fine restaurants and shops, the comfortable boarding lounges, are visible evidences. Everything here is designed to add pleasure to all your journeys.

Above: The main waiting area, with its electronic flight information board and sweeping airfield view.

Right: Colorful lounges in the flight wing, reached from the main building by a spacious passageway.

126 This double-page spread from the pamphlet "Winged Gateway to the World of Flight" (1962) also celebrates the putative progressiveness of the terminal.

127 The communication efforts do not miss their mark. The terminal is widely publicized and often appears on the covers of magazines, as seen here.

128 This caricature-like illustration suggests the comparison with a bird taking flight. It exaggerates a characteristic of the building, evoked inside the magazine, which purports to transfix those who behold the terminal.

129 Marking its completion, the terminal appears on the cover of *Engineering News-Record,* which celebrates the concrete vaults as a constructional masterpiece.

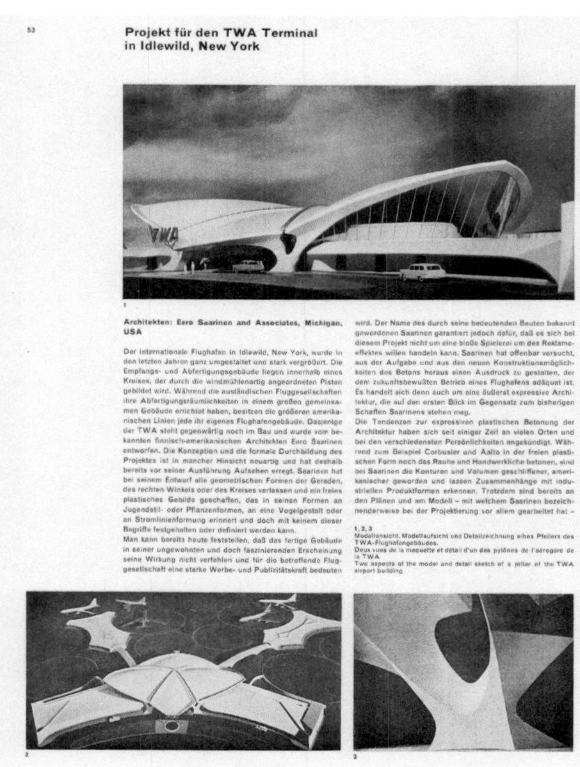

53

Projekt für den TWA Terminal in Idlewild, New York

1

Architekten: Eero Saarinen and Associates, Michigan, USA

Der internationale Flughafen in Idlewild, New York, wurde in den letzten Jahren ganz umgestaltet und stark vergrößert. Die Empfangs- und Abfertigungsgebäude liegen innerhalb eines Kreises, der durch die windmühlenartig angeordneten Pisten gebildet wird. Während die ausländischen Fluggesellschaften ihre Abfertigungsräumlichkeiten in einem großen gemeinsamen Gebäude errichtet haben, besitzen die größeren amerikanischen Linien jede ihr eigenes Flughafengebäude. Dasjenige der TWA steht gegenwärtig noch im Bau und wurde vom bekannten finnisch-amerikanischen Architekten Eero Saarinen entworfen. Die Konzeption und die formale Durchbildung des Projektes ist in mancher Hinsicht neuartig und hat deshalb bereits vor seiner Ausführung Aufsehen erregt. Saarinen hat bei seinem Entwurf alle geometrischen Formen der Geraden, des rechten Winkels oder des Kreises verlassen und ein freies plastisches Gebilde geschaffen, das in seinen Formen an Jugendstil- oder Pflanzenformen, an eine Vogelgestalt oder an Stromlinienformung erinnert und doch mit keinem dieser Begriffe festgehalten oder definiert werden kann.

Man kann bereits heute feststellen, daß das fertige Gebäude in seiner ungewohnten und doch faszinierenden Erscheinung seine Wirkung nicht verfehlen und für die betreffende Fluggesellschaft eine starke Werbe- und Publizitätskraft bedeuten wird. Der Name des durch seine bedeutenden Bauten bekannt gewordenen Saarinen garantiert jedoch dafür, daß es sich bei diesem Projekt nicht um eine bloße Spielerei um des Reklameeffektes willen handeln kann. Saarinen hat offenbar versucht, aus der Aufgabe und aus den neuen Konstruktionsmöglichkeiten des Betons heraus einen Ausdruck zu gestalten, der dem zukunftsbewußten Betrieb eines Flughafens adäquat ist. Es handelt sich denn auch um eine äußerst expressive Architektur, die auf den ersten Blick im Gegensatz zum bisherigen Schaffen Saarinens stehen mag.

Die Tendenzen zur expressiven plastischen Betonung der Architektur haben sich seit einiger Zeit an vielen Orten und bei den verschiedensten Persönlichkeiten angekündigt. Während zum Beispiel Corbusier und Aalto in der freien plastischen Form noch das Rauhe und Handwerkliche betonen, sind bei Saarinen die Konturen und Volumen geschliffener, amerikanischer geworden und lassen Zusammenhänge mit industriellen Produktformen erkennen. Trotzdem sind bereits an den Plänen und am Modell – mit welchem Saarinen bezeichnenderweise bei der Projektierung vor allem gearbeitet hat –

1, 2, 3
Modellansicht, Modellaufsicht und Detailzeichnung eines Pfeilers des TWA-Flughafengebäudes.
Deux vues de la maquette et détail d'un des pylônes de l'aérogare de la TWA
Two aspects of the model and detail sketch of a pillar of the TWA airport building

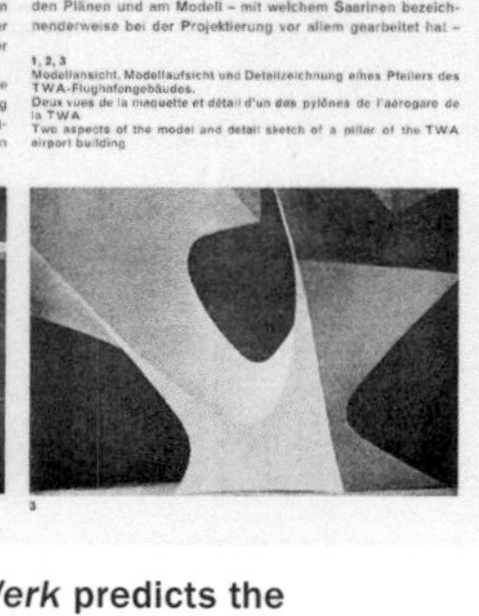

2 3

130 The German-language journal *Werk* predicts the building will have a "strong advertising and publicity effect," a full two years prior to its completion.

Changes

New form for an air terminal that looks like nothing on earth: for TWA in New York.

OPERA HOUSE CURTAIN AT SPOLETO WHERE A NEW FESTIVAL BEGINS IN JUNE.

This extraordinary air terminal, designed by Eero Saarinen & Associates for Trans World Airlines, will be built at New York's Idlewild Airport. Those two jutting structures, shaped rather like violins, are connected with the main building by long, sheltered passageways, equipped with both moving and stationary sidewalks; no one will get wet boarding or leaving a plane.
The new music festival, for a month, at Spoleto, Italy, is called "Festival of Two Worlds," will have known and unknown American and European artists, and is under the special protection of Gian-Carlo Menotti, president of the Festival Foundation. (Menotti, the composer-librettist of *The Consul, The Medium,* and *The Saint of Bleecker Street,* is just the librettist of the new opera, *Vanessa.*)
Tessalon, developed by Ciba of Canada, gives promise, after experiments in Nova Scotia at Point Edward Hospital, of being more effective as a cough remedy than codeine, for years the standard medication.
Twelve-metre boats will fight it out for the first time internationally when the America's Cup race is held off Newport, in September, 1958. To meet the British challenger, "Sceptre," the defending sloop will be chosen by the New York Yacht Club after preliminary trials.
Pinhole spectacles, always famous nerve calmers, framed now in brave new colours. Stenopeic Glare Guards. $10.50.

Twelve-metre boats will race for the first time in international competition, next September.

100 Perles IN EACH PERLE OF TESSALON, A NEW NON-NARCOTIC COUGH REMEDY, 100 M.G.

Glasses without glass, vision without glare—new use of the pinhole principle

New plastic, Porelon, holds almost any liquid (from medicine to ink) tightly in its straight-laced molecular structure, releases it, on pressure—at a controlled rate, over extended periods.

60 VOGUE, JANUARY 1, 1958

131 *Vogue* acknowledges the terminal's unique appearance and declares it a sensation of the year 1958.

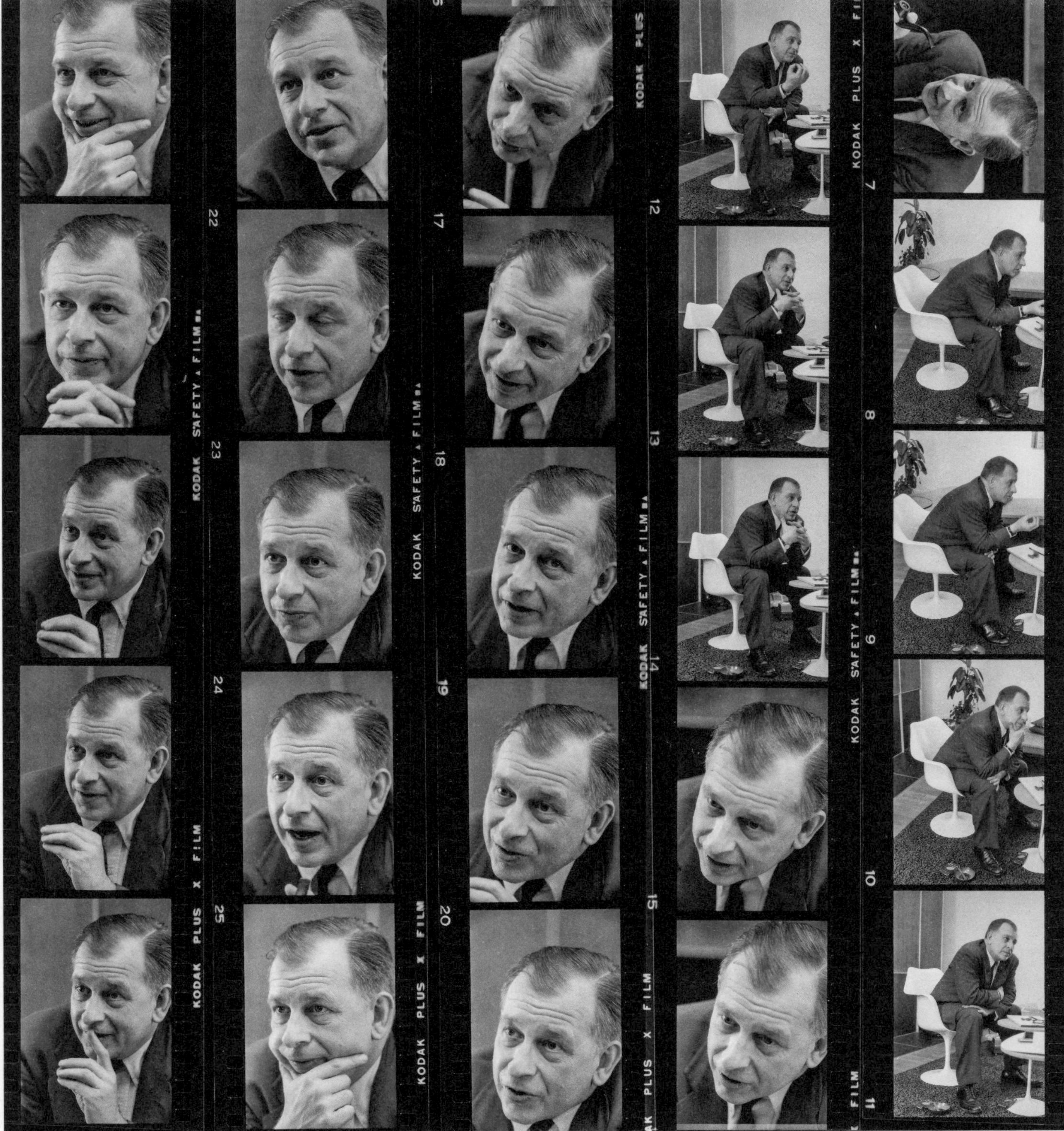

132 The terminal's strong publicity is of use not only to TWA. It also supports Aline Saarinen's mission to portray her husband in the public as a great architect.

3.1 Legend of Eero Saarinen

Aline Saarinen pursues her new job with equal amounts of professionalism and commitment. Fig. 133 She hires an assistant, Pat Burley, who organizes and maintains the office's own photo collection and also manages general press inquiries and correspondence. Aline Saarinen arranges engagements, lectures, and publications for her husband and tries to demonstrate his professional

133 Aline Saarinen, year unknown

skills to potential clients.[188] In so doing, she can draw on excellent relationships in the media and art sector, which she built up as a journalist. The Saarinens cultivate their network carefully: they choose social events purposefully, give advance thought to who the guests will be, and contemplate which people to speak with and what topics to discuss.[189]

Aline Saarinen also uses the contacts for her media relations. For instance, she encourages Peter Blake to discuss Yale University's Morse and Stiles

134 Simulation of grapefruit anecdote, 2008

Colleges (1961) in sympathetic terms after they had been savaged by the architectural critic Reyner Banham in the *New Statesman*.[190] An early highlight of their work is a lead article in a 1956 issue of *Time* magazine. At the age of just 46, Saarinen is the youngest of only 15 architects to have thus far appeared on the cover of the weekly news magazine.[191] In addition, Aline Saarinen writes texts herself, such as articles like the one in 1955 for *Vogue* with the title "Four Architects Helping to Change the Look of America," in which she stylizes Saarinen, along with Mies van der Rohe, Philip Johnson, and Gordon Bunshaft as the figureheads of American architecture.[192] And there are sessions in which Aline Saarinen or a secretary records

135 Aline and Eero Saarinen, year unknown

with a typewriter what Eero Saarinen openly soliloquizes.[193] Such dictated thoughts are passed along to the media by Aline Saarinen and later emerge in articles, sometimes as excerpts and sometimes word for word. For the attention of the *Time* author, she writes a seven-page manuscript, entitled "Homey Stuff," that does not skimp on private, even intimate details from the personal life of the married couple. As evidenced by the much-quoted grapefruit anecdote, which purports that Eero Saarinen developed the design idea for the TWA Terminal while eating a grapefruit, she supplied the media with well-exploitable stories. What in its published version seems like the creative stroke of genius of a workaholic is in reality Saarinen's attempt to explain his design for the terminal to his wife.[194] Fig. 134 Despite this, the embellished media-genic anecdote has been repeated umpteen times since first being published in *Time* magazine.[195] Given his ambitious career goals, Eero Saarinen finds the ideal skills and character in his second wife, as Glen Paulsen, a former employee at ES&A, explains:

> "She became his greatest supporter and could put into words what Eero couldn't about himself and his work. He was not a great speaker, and he wrote very little. But she more than made up for that when she married Eero."[196]

The two complement each other almost perfectly with their skills. While she gives the architect a voice, he perfects the visualization of his projects. Fig. 135 "We have been most backward," Eero Saarinen writes in an internal memo, "in having decent publishable plans of various jobs that need to be published, presented or submitted for awards."[197] For client presentations he likes to choose photographic images. "Very often we didn't show the models to the clients," says Balthazar Korab (1926–2013), "we would show them a slide show."[198] What was shown were primarily extremely realistic photomontages of models. The clients could imagine the project more easily that way, recalls another employee.[199] Thus, Eero Saarinen intentionally selects the method. "When he sat at a table with a group of executives," recalls Kevin Roche, "he didn't make a fool of himself, he talked to them about things that they wanted to talk about, that he knew they would listen to."[200]

For the TWA project, in the summer of 1956 Saarinen has a brochure prepared as a presentation aid. The cover references one of the design features which would later make the building so unique: the image of a bird. Across the front and back of the booklet designed by Balthazar Korab, which Saarinen hands out at the first project presentation as an easy-to-understand explanation of his ideas, flutters an entire flock of birds. **Fig. 136** "Saarinen was happy with it, which means that for him the image was there," says Cesar Pelli, describing the equally conscious and deliberate use of the bird motif in dealing with the client, "at least as an image that he could sell to TWA."[201] Photographs are not only a communication tool, however, but also a design tool—and even during the design of the TWA Terminal they are used to check the visual impact of the future building. "We developed a routine where the camera and the photographer became an integral part of the design process," explains Balthazar Korab. "The photograph became a visual test for the designer. We were intrigued by the extent Eero grew dependent on the images, particularly during the TWA studies."[202] By elevating pictorial impact to a design-determining aspect, Saarinen accounts, even in an early design stage, for the terminal's impact in the

136 Cover of a brochure for the attention of TWA, ES&A, 1956

media and its capacity for being publicized—he shapes the building with respect to its two-dimensional impact on paper, a projection screen, or a monitor.

The success of the communication measures promoted by the combined efforts of the Saarinens does not fail to materialize. Within a decade, Eero Saarinen becomes one of the most published architects of the 1950s in professional as well as in popular magazines, and as a result of radio and television appearances he attains wide renown.[203] In the emerging architectural star system, which architecture critic Allan Temko compares in 1962 with that of Hollywood, he takes on a leading role.[204] Moreover, he becomes a famous name within America's upper class, as demonstrated by the fact that the Saarinens are invited to John F. Kennedy's inauguration in January 1961. As Saarinen dies a few months later, at the age of only fifty-one and at the peak of his career, "the most famous young architect in America, perhaps in the world" has a legendary status, as shown by the commentary made by Walter McQuade as Saarinen is posthumously bestowed the AIA Gold Medal in 1962:

> "Many people were reminiscent about Eero Saarinen this month, before he began to slide away from personal memory into myth. It was already evident that there was going to be an Eero Saarinen legend; it had begun even in his lifetime."[205]

The opinion is precisely in line with the thoughts of Aline Saarinen; she had striven for this very same creation of a legend, as she states in a 1958 letter to her mentor, the art critic Bernard Berenson:

> "Now I observe myself ardently promulgating the Eero-myth. All of us around create situations to reveal him as we understand him. He creates situations to reveal himself as he understands himself and as he wishes to be understood. Reporters and photographers create situations to satisfy editorial demands. He is all of this and none of this. But recorded, it becomes truth for the future."[206]

The resolution with which the PR specialist shapes the Eero Saarinen legend is demonstrated by three articles in established popular newspapers. Starting with Eero Saarinen's outward appearance, in particular his ubiquitous pipe **Fig. 137**, and continuing with his manner of speech (he has a Finnish accent), his famous father—Eliel Saarinen, his enthusiasm for work, his formal diversity and creativity, and his architectural laurels—these attributes are brought to bear in each of the articles: Eero Saarinen is once described as looking "like an old-fashioned family doctor" (*New York Times*), then he "looks like a country family doctor, [who] dresses with the casualness of a young college prof" (*Time*), and finally we are told he has "somewhat of a college-professor character" (*Vogue*). Once there is a statement that he "works at the office until at least midnight," then "spends most evenings ... at his draughting table," or that he is "a round-the-clock-worker." Once he is characterized as a "form giver," then he is attributed "a wide vocabulary" or "imagination, versatility and good sense." Once he is "the most widely known and respected architect of his generation" and "a great architect," then "a consistent winner," or his "record number of medals at the Yale School of Architecture" are stressed.[207]

Until her own death in 1972, Aline Saarinen continues working on the legend of an aspiring, passionate, and successful architect. In the year directly after his death, she publishes the monograph *Eero Saarinen on His Work*, which appears in a revised version with twenty-three new photographs in 1968. Given its large size, the numerous full-page or even double-page photographs, and the comparatively small amount of text, Reyner Banham denounces the book as "coffee-table literature."[208] There is no question that the publication is tailored to the broad general public that has now come to know Eero Saarinen as—to use the words found in the popular magazine *Look*—"a leading architect of his time."[209] The great fame of the architect would, if nothing else, benefit the ability of the TWA Flight Center to be disseminated in the media.

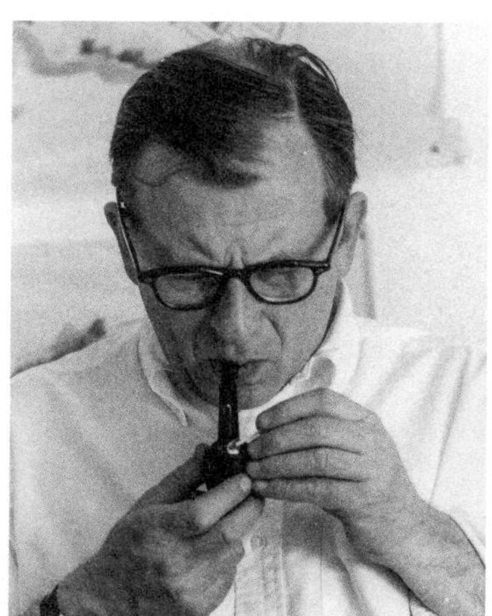

137 Eero Saarinen tamps his pipe, year unknown

3.2 Joint Marketing Tool

With thirty million flight customers, the American companies in the aviation industry, unlike their European counterparts, are able to spend substantial sums on advertising. The British magazine *Flight International* writes accordingly in 1955: "Every new development is publicized to the fullest extent. T.W.A.'s latest 'Super-G' Constellation, for example, was the subject of whole-page advertisements in the New York dailies."[210] **Fig. 138** It is significant that the aviation magazine mentions a Constellation advertisement. Until well into the 1950s, images of airplanes dominate the ads; other resources such as airport buildings are meanwhile sought in vain. *Business Week* fathoms the phenomenon as follows in 1960: "In the days when airlines were still struggling for passengers and revenues, it was smarter to sell flying itself, and let ground facilities go."[211] However, toward the end of the 1950s this begins to change. Because confidence rises in the airplane as a means of personal transport and, conversely, flight safety decreases as an advertising factor, a new message is needed. Additionally, jet aircraft are less suitable for being featured in advertising because of their prevalence and outward similarity to each other. While the jets fill entire advertising pages until the early 1960s, over the course of the decade they shrink to small silhouettes and later disappear entirely. Another reason for the growing promotional value of the ground infrastructure lies in the inadequate standard of the existing airport terminals. Alongside the potential for improving operations, this also offers the new marketing theme being sought: efficiently functioning airports with a welcoming atmosphere. The ground infrastructure thus attains importance for the airlines, not only as an operational and visual differentiator but also as a communicative one. The expression of this, along with the Pan Am Terminal in Idlewild, for which its owner receives a fair amount of media attention, is most notably the TWA Flight Center.[212]

138 TWA advertisement with Constellation, *Time* (Atlantic), 1954

The foundation for the marketing of the terminal is laid by TWA on November 12, 1957 at an elaborately staged presentation to the press in a New York luxury hotel known at the time as the Barbizon Plaza.[213] The very first statements by the airline leave no doubt as to its marketing ambitions. Not one but two detailed press releases are issued, each of which comprise several pages that emphasize the procedural and architectural advantages of Eero Saarinen's terminal. The press conference does not miss its mark. Numerous articles are subsequently published in prestigious periodicals, covering a broad journalistic spectrum: from the *Washington Post* and the *New York Times*, which devotes two articles to the terminal in the following week, to the professional journals *Progressive Architecture* and *Architectural Forum,* as well as the aviation magazines *Flight International* and *Aviation Week*.[214] Behind the successful launch is TWA's communications department, which holds a special status within the company in the postwar years and enjoys an

139 Gordon L. Gilmore (right), TWA Head of Public Relations, 1960

excellent reputation in professional circles. It can rely on one of the largest advertising budgets in the industry and has a presence not only nationally but also worldwide, with six overseas locations. Their boss, Gordon L. Gilmore, holds the rank of vice president, which was unparalleled in the airline industry at that time. Fig. 139 Characteristic of the importance of the communications activities for the air carrier is a statement by President Charles C. Tillinghast, Jr., made shortly after his inauguration in 1961. Based on an in-house investigation, he claims that TWA trusts its advertising more than the performance of its aircraft.[215] Public relations is a priority for TWA. With the terminal project, however, the air carrier receives significant support in the person of Aline Saarinen. Her recipe for success includes close cooperation with the client's communications department.

Aline Saarinen's communication efforts are carried out according to a procedure that remains consistent across various projects and envisions "four target moments for publicity": at the time the commission is made, upon submitting the final design, as the construction progresses, and finally upon inauguration of the building.[216] These stages can be reconstructed in detail in the TWA project. Extrapolating from a letter to another client, Aline Saarinen believes that when, as with the terminal, the first marketing phase (commissioning) coincides with the second (final design), this has the advantage that model photos and plans are already available. Pictorial material, she says explaining its importance, is responsible for ensuring that a message addresses not only the local but also the national media. Even though the TWA model is "castigated" by some critics, much to the annoyance of the client, this procedure succeeds ideally with the TWA Terminal.[217] Model photos illustrate numerous articles in trade and consumer magazines; in fact, two important exhibitions held in 1959—*Form Givers at Mid-Century* and *Architecture and Imagery*—rely on model photos. Fig. 140 Even before the first shovel of earth is dug, TWA can realize with satisfaction that "a scale model of the structure which has been on exhibition at the New York Museum of Modern Art has attracted much attention."[218]

As the construction work begins with a groundbreaking ceremony on June 9, 1959 and a banquet for selected guests, the third phase begins. It can be marketed in a likewise manner, at least in the case of the TWA Terminal, which has "some spectacular

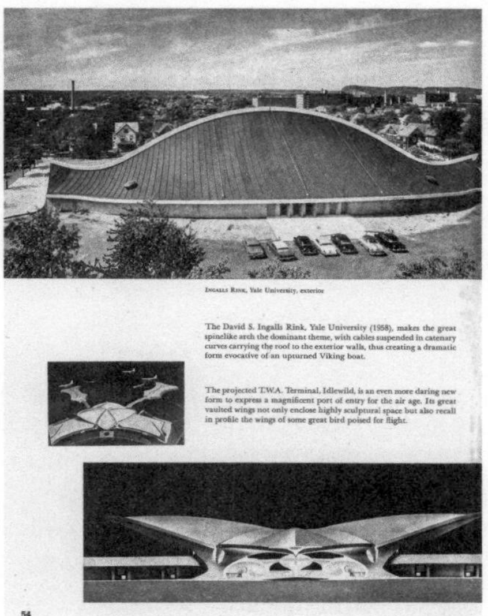

Ingalls Rink, Yale University, exterior

The David S. Ingalls Rink, Yale University (1958), makes the great spinelike arch the dominant theme, with cables suspended in catenary curves carrying the roof to the exterior walls, thus creating a dramatic form evocative of an upturned Viking boat.

The projected T.W.A. Terminal, Idlewild, is an even more daring new form to express a magnificent port of entry for the air age. Its great vaulted wings not only enclose highly sculptural space but also recall in profile the wings of some great bird poised for flight.

54

140 Page from *Form Givers at Mid-Century*, TWA Flight Center and David S. Ingalls Hockey Rink (above), 1959

technological innovation which is photogenic," explains Aline Saarinen with reference to the vaults.[219] Fig. 141 During construction, the company magazine (eleven articles) and press releases (at least ten), as well as articles in the trade and general press (at least twenty-four) regularly inform about the progress of construction. As in the first phase of the project, too, a main theme of these publications centers around the suitability of the terminal for jet aircraft. Shortly before the start of construction, for example, TWA wholeheartedly stresses in a communiqué that its new airport terminal will not only be able to handle the current generation of jet aircraft but also the future generation of supersonic aircraft.[220] This is supposedly attested by descriptions of the complex process of erecting the vaults and by staged press photos. The client dresses all the workers who are concreting the vaults in matching numbered T-shirts in the company colors; in the background, a TWA jet can be seen.[221] The photos, one concludes, are intended to evoke the impression of meticulous, complex planning and, in this way, establish a reference to the jet age. In an advanced stage of construction, a brochure entitled "Jet Age Air Terminals," which also introduces other TWA terminal buildings alongside

141 TWA Flight Center under construction, ca. 1961

Eero Saarinen's, underscores the promise of a jet-proven ground infrastructure. Fig. 142 After having mainly introduced procedural and technical (constructive) building features as evidence, TWA now also recognizes a correspondence with the jet age in the external appearance of the building. The unusual vaults, it says in the brochure, uphold the motto "to design buildings that match, in scale and visual excitement, the jet aircraft that make them necessary."[222] The claim that Saarinen has taken into account the requirements of the jet age is furthermore attested by the brochure with a reference to the spacious passageways, gently rising stairs, and logically arranged areas of the building.[223]

The marketing of the Trans World Flight Center as an airport terminal that is suitable for jets initially corresponds to a widespread trend. The term "jet" appears at that time in highly varied terms, such as the magazine of the same name, the cartoon series

142 Front page of the pamphlet "Jet Age Air Terminals," TWA, 1961

The Jetsons, the Jetstream transistor radio, and the New York Jets football team. The fascination can still be felt in 1968 as the sound of a jet airplane is repeatedly heard in the Beatles song Back in the *U.S.S.R.* So on the surface, the marketing of the building as a jet-capable terminal comes as no surprise. A look at the company's history, however, casts a different light on the marketing goal. After TWA fails to place an order for jet aircraft in good time, President Ralph S. Damon must declare in 1955 the following to his board of directors: "Every airplane TWA now owns or has on order or option will be either totally obsolete or heavily outclassed in speed, comfort, passenger acceptability, and economics on competitive routes."[224] Although TWA ultimately orders 33 Boeing 707s in March of 1956, delivery times are long because the order is at the bottom of a long list. Now TWA can at least begin to design the flight schedule for their future jet aircraft, mocks a trade journal.[225] The airline is at risk of losing its reputation as a technologically advanced airline, which it has built up since the early 1930s, thanks in part to its majority shareholder, Howard Hughes, who is highly enthusiastic about aviation.[226]

As a Pan Am jet takes off on the first scheduled transatlantic flight on October 26, 1958, and other competitors rapidly follow, TWA's image is tarnished. Even as the airline finally makes its move into the jet age on March 20, 1959, the problems are far from resolved. As a result of outstanding deliveries, TWA starts into the jet age with a single jet airplane, which poses high operational risks and only permits operation of a single route (New York–San Francisco). On the prestigious transtlantic route, TWA winds up with a delay of more than one year—which in the face of the trailblazing technological milestone equals an eternity. Further adversity threatens TWA in its ground handling. United and Eastern start using their new Idlewild terminals in 1959, and American and Pan Am do so in 1960, while Eero Saarinen's building is still midway through construction. Fig. 143 TWA's backlog in comparison with its fiercest business rivals is an additional burden for the airline. So as not to have to operate with the existing, outdated infrastructure, a

143 Eastern Airlines Terminal, Idlewild, Chester Lindsay Churchill, 1959

terminal building from 1951, and in order to avert the worst damage to its operations and its reputation, beginning in August 1960, TWA operates a temporary terminal in Idlewild. Nevertheless, the construction delays weigh heavily. A customer survey informs the board of directors that the lack of a modern terminal building in Idlewild is increasingly doing harm to the airline's business, and 12 percent of the air passengers criticize the temporary terminal.[227]

Ultimately, the approaching jet age also makes the planning of the Saarinen terminal more difficult. That's because although the planning committee that TWA appoints in 1957 to implement deployment of the jets does indeed have extensive knowledge of the new generation of aircraft, this pertains mainly to the planes' flight characteristics; with respect to the requirements for the ground infrastructure, there are still wide gaps in knowledge. A guideline for jet flights revealingly ends with the touchdown of the airplane—the steps that follow in the process are not explained in the expert report due to insufficient information.[228] In 1957 *Business Week* runs the headline "Dream of Jet Age Airports Still Far from Reality."[229] ES&A cannot escape this reality.

3.3 Jet Propaganda

In the TWA Flight Center the departing and arriving air travelers do not circulate systematically, each exclusively on their own level, but instead mix in most areas of the building, with the exception of the two side wings, where the check-in and baggage claim respectively take place. This particularly diminishes the performance and thereby the terminal's suitability for jets, because the newly introduced jet aircraft carry many more passengers than do propeller aircraft like the Constellation. In addition, on their way from ground transportation to the airplane (and vice versa), air travelers in the TWA Terminal are forced to negotiate stairs, which, although flat, not only decrease the flow of people but also reduce passenger comfort.[230] Even though ES&A take into account the essential operational criteria for success, in spatial terms alone their design does not conform to the textbook ideal of one-way paths with no steps. Above all, however, as they conceive the main features of the terminal in 1956, the architects do not know the specific requirements that the next generation of aircraft demand for the ground infrastructure, especially in regard to the passenger and baggage facilities as well as noise protection. Key knowledge about ground handling would only be available beginning in 1958, after jet aircraft are introduced in the US. As *Progressive Architecture* aptly states in 1961: "The recent establishment and constant expansion of commercial jet service has profoundly affected air terminal design."[231]

This is confirmed by ES&A employees who were involved in the design. According to their own testimony, they knew very little about the requirements of jet aircraft with respect to the terminal being designed, and hardly no reliable information was provided by the client.[232] Kevin Roche recalls that the information boiled down to generalized statements: "You had to accommodate a jet."[233] Except for dimensions of the aircraft itself, ES&A obtained no reliable information from the client about ground handling requirements for the recently ordered Boeing 707-320. Hence the architects' level of knowledge is merely sufficient to indicate on their plans the safety area of the wings—a circle with a radius of 110 feet (33.5 m).[234] In line with this, in a status report TWA solely points out that the terminal offers space for 14 Boeing 707 planes.[235] One searches in vain for additional evidence that the jets on order somehow influenced the planning. Even before the building goes into service, Eero Saarinen himself expresses skepticism about the TWA Terminal functioning properly, as the current rate of development in civil aviation is so high. "Now," he writes in 1958 while working on Washington, D.C.'s Dulles International Airport (1958–1962), "we are in the process of making a really fundamental analysis of how the jet really differs, what people really do at the airport, and how all this can be best put together into a building."[236] **Fig. 144**

As if wanting to increase Saarinen's doubts even more, in early 1961 TWA implements cost-cutting measures that further reduce the operating capacity of the terminal building. The client forgoes the moving walkways in the 310-foot-long (95 m) connecting tunnels. This means of conveyance would have mitigated the long distances to be covered on foot within the satellite arrangement and especially those within the decentralized Terminal City, which *Time* magazine would later call "a nightmare to travelers who have to change airlines."[237] As if abandoning the moving walkways does not already do enough to endanger the progressiveness of the terminal, the board of directors also postpones construction of one of the satellites. For cost reasons, "Flight Wing Two" is to be built first, and it would not be followed until years later by its counter-

144 Mobile Lounges, Dulles International Airport, Chantilly, VA, ES&A, ca. 1962

part. This decision further reduces the operational suitability of the flight terminal, which even the board of directors is subsequently forced to admit internally.[238] Planned in the Constellation era, the terminal building is impaired by the lack of knowledge about the new generation of aircraft as well as by cost-cutting measures, with the consequence that as operations commence, it is neither up-to-date for operational needs nor specifically tailored to the new generation of aircraft as the client had suggested.

145 Parking lot at Idlewild, with TWA Flight Center, year unknown

In spite of this, TWA continues to present the terminal as suitable for jets. And more: the communication measures respond specifically to the deficits that become increasingly known over the course of the planning, selectively glossing over them. For instance, the PR department stresses that the drop-off area for passengers arriving by car and the check-in and ticket counters are on the same level, directly behind electronically controlled doors, but neglects to mention that many vehicles arrive at the central parking lot. Fig. 145 It likewise conceals how air travelers reach the waiting room after checking in: up twelve steps with a height difference of roughly 5 feet (1.5 m). Fig. 146 By contrast, they do not fail to mention that once they are there, those waiting will find every desirable amenity. Also, the restaurants, which are located a full story above, are euphemistically described as "slightly elevated areas."[239] Figs 147, 148 The PR department also gladly refers to the various technological facilities in order to feign the terminal building's operational capacity, and it repeatedly emphasizes that the airline passengers are protected from the weather while on the ground. TWA takes advantage of the fact that the passenger boarding bridges used ease a fundamental problem that has preoccupied airport planners since the early days of civil aviation: "The days of dashing across windswept ramps . . . are past history at TWA's Idlewild installation."[240] But irrespective of that, travelers are still exposed to the weather on the street side, be it on the way from the main parking lot at the center of Terminal City or along the passenger drop-off, where the canopy that extends lengthwise along the building does not—unlike that of the neighboring Pan Am Terminal—extend out far enough to cover the arriving cars. According to the same formula, TWA promises that the terminal offers "the speediest baggage delivery available in any terminal in the world," and in another press release the luggage conveyor belts are celebrated as an innovation.[241] However, the facts paint a different picture. For one thing, such baggage handling systems were already being used in Montreal, San Francisco, and Los Angeles, and for another, the conveyor belts do not return the bags to their owners faster, as verified by contemporary studies.[242]

Despite all the inconsistencies, the PR measures bear fruit. A brief review of the press coverage shows that the contemporary media professionals adopt TWA's portrayal—of optimal passenger and baggage handling on par with the needs of the jet age—and do so largely without changes, sometimes even using text verbatim from the press releases. The *Boston Globe* sweepingly proclaims: "T.W.A.'s Flight Center dramatizes Jet Age."[243] The *New York Times* praises: "Passengers arriving . . . will enter one wing at street level through electronic doors and deposit their baggage at a long counter immediately inside."[244] Like the underlying communiqué, the newspaper also refrains from mentioning the difference in height between the arrival and waiting areas. In contrast, although *Progressive Architecture* notes the level changes in the arrival hall, it euphemistically writes of "gentle-rise steps" that "ascend to the lobby level."[245] The German journal *Baukunst und Werkform* describes the layout, in equally approving and incorrect terms, as representing the "best possible traffic management."[246] Also with regard to the automation of ground handling, the press substantially repeats the descriptions provided by TWA. One journalist believes, for example, that the jetways would allow boarding "without going up or down stairs."[247] And the baggage carousels are erroneously described by the *Neue Zürcher Zeitung* as "one of the most stiking features" of the new terminal, because they enable "the

146 Departure hall with stair, TWA Flight Center, 1969

147 Lisbon Lounge, TWA Flight Center, Raymond Loewy and William Snaith, Inc., 1962

148 Paris Cafe, TWA Flight Center, Raymond Loewy and William Snaith, Inc., 1962

fastest baggage handling . . . hitherto available on an airfield."[248] Thus, the TWA Terminal helps its owner to restore its tarnished image as a technologically advanced airline. As the project progresses, the building would take on yet another promotional task.

3.4 Glamourous Gala

As the project partners jointly make known, the communication measures cooperatively implemented by TWA and Aline Saarinen reach a climax with the opening of the terminal."[249] TWA should treat this not as simply the opening of a new terminal belatedly catching up with competition," communication chief Gordon L. Gilmore tells his colleagues in 1961, almost a year before the opening, "but as something grand, unique, and a giant step leapfrogging TWA over all others into the future."[250] Accordingly, marketing of the TWA Flight Center enjoys high priority for TWA's corporate communications in 1962, the building's opening year, and TWA intensifies its marketing efforts with support from Aline Saarinen. The preparatory work for the opening takes up a full year and aims "to develop a series of events which would arouse public interest and curiosity to the point where passengers will buy tickets on TWA to pass through the new flight center," according to Gilmore.[251] "If this is well done," it says in a statement to all employees about the opening of the terminal, "then a great step forward will have been made in making the investment pay the dividends it must if our Company is to be successful."[252] In the months leading up to and following the opening, TWA has various promotional materials prepared and publishes a variety of advertisements, arranges for Ezra Stoller to photograph the terminal on emphatic recommendation of Aline Saarinen, and sends out a whole series of press releases.[253] Of at least twenty-four press releases that TWA disseminates between the announcement and the opening of the Saarinen terminal, a dozen are issued in the three months before operations commence. "We advertised it as though it were a national monument," avows Henry C. Riegner, TWA's advertising manager.[254]

The communication measures are part of a company-wide campaign designed to strengthen TWA's reputation as the "airline of the stars."[255] Faced with a high-volume business, this is increasingly jeopardized, since TWA attracts a particularly large number of first-time flyers and tourists precisely because of their glamorous image.[256] In light of the aim "to create an impression of quality and sophistication in our services and strengthen TWA's identification as a United States airline with international tastes and standards," the airline revises the substance of how the terminal is promoted. Promises of trouble-free, rapid ground handling take a backseat in favor of a new message.[257] Instead of focusing on procedural and technical sophistication on par with the needs of the jet age, TWA now puts its emphasis on a refined, indeed, luxurious and multicultural travel experience within the terminal. According to mastermind Gordon L. Gilmore, the campaign aims "to perpetuate the [Trans World Flight] Center as the most stylish crossroads of world travel."[258] The measures clearly express this goal: A promotional brochure with the title "Winged Gateway to the World of Flight" applauds "a passenger's dream" and extols "everything here is designed to add pleasure to all your journeys."[259] TWA thereby gives thought to both international restaurant offerings (Lisbon Lounge, Paris Cafe, Italian Snack Bar, London Club) and architectural attractions like the connecting corridors between the departure lounge and satellite: "The tubelike connection, bathed in soft indirect lighting, stirs an anticipation that it leads to an enjoyable experience."[260] "Like the tunnel Alice followed to Wonderland," it says at another point, "the Flight Center walkway leads to the excitement of air travel and distant lands."[261] **Fig. 149** An art gallery called "Galerie des Deux Mondes" (the name is a reference to the two hemispheres of Loewy's TWA logo) that presents temporary exhibitions by international artists can also be understood in terms of the intended cultivated, international travel experience, just like the building's moniker "Trans World Flight Center," which was evaluated and chosen in an elaborate selection procedure. According to the jury, it is the most suitable name "to clearly relate TWA as a world airline with the purpose of the building."[262]

As a continuation of the campaign, numerous, sometimes exclusive events that are peppered with international connections take place in conjunction with the opening: At the "Around the World Charity

149 Connecting corridor between main building and satellite, TWA Flight Center, 1962

Ball," the PR department stages multicultural performances (Spanish flamenco dancers, an Egyptian belly dancer, a British folk singer, a French chanteuse), enjoins the speakers to discuss "a global theme," dresses the hostesses in traditional national costumes, distributes mock front pages of newspapers from London, Rome, Cairo, and Paris, hoists the national flags of the route network, and invites chefs from around the world to cook as well as a chorus to intone a vocal piece called *Wings over the World.*[263] The array of events, which is meant to culminate with the ceremonial start of operations, begins one and a half weeks earlier: On May 17, 1962 the official press tour takes place, for which TWA flies in 150 to 200 media professionals from all across the country.[264] On May 22 "the glitterati of New York society, business community and news media" are invited to a "Grand Opening Charity Ball."[265] The agenda for the next day includes a viewing for invited guests, and on May 26 there is an open house for the general public. Because the latter is a great success and, according to TWA information, attracts as many as 16,000 onlookers, the airline schedules additional official viewings for the public in the following months. And on June 6 TWA President Charles C. Tillinghast receives selected representatives of other airlines in the terminal.[266]

The undisputed culmination of the opening activities is the inauguration gala on May 28, 1962, which is broadcast live by the NBC television network.[267] This, too, is planned jointly by Aline Saarinen and TWA, and in addition to the members of the TWA board of directors, numerous exponents from business, media, and culture, as well as two members of the US Senate, are placed on the guest list. The 400 invited guests are greeted by President Tillinghast, who serves as the master of ceremonies for the gala, which, according to the employee magazine *Skyliner*, culminates "with the unveiling of the dedicatory plaque by Mrs. Aline B. Saarinen, widow of the Center's designer, Eero Saarinen." Thus, in addition to celebrating the terminal itself, its builder—who had passed away nine months earlier—is also honored. The importance of this point in the program is underscored by a large photo adorning the cover of TWA's employee magazine, which also points out that the keynote speakers (including Arthur Drexler, Director of New York's Museum of Modern Art) are full of praise for the master architect (a "genius").[268] Even though the inscription originally intended to appear on the commemorative plaque—"As a memorial to its great architect Eero Saarinen, 1910–1961"—was more pretentious than the one that was ultimately used—"Trans World Flight Center / Dedicated May the Twenty-eighth, 1962 / Eero Saarinen, Architect"—the dedication once again illustrates Aline Saarinen's effort to secure her deceased husband's fame.[269] **Fig. 150** She turns the terminal into a memorial to the architect, who died at the young age of fifty-one.

TWA supports the PR specialist much earlier in her efforts to cultivate a legend for the architect, however.

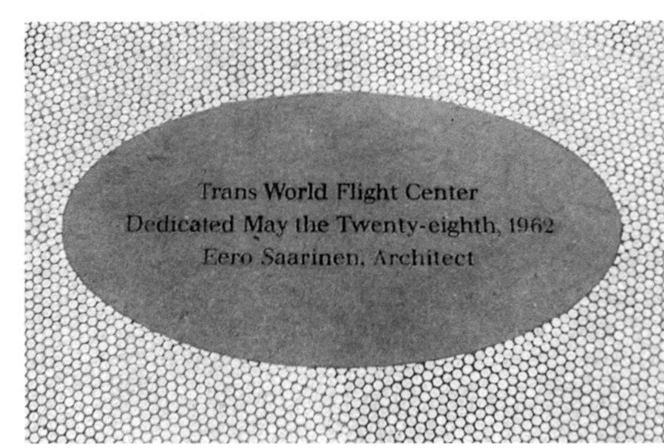

150 Commemorative plaque for Eero Saarinen, TWA Flight Center, 1962, photo from 2007

"New TWA Terminal to Feature Unique Saarinen Design," was the headline used by the airline as early as 1957, as the terminal was first announced, and on the same occasion *Skyliner* presented Saarinen to its readership as a "world-famous architect."[270] The marketing of the architect subsequently continues unabated—not a single publication about the TWA Trans World Flight Center appears without mention of Eero Saarinen. Approaching the opening day, TWA even publishes a promotional brochure entitled "Eero Saarinen and the Trans World Flight Center," in which the introductory greeting by President Tillinghast refers to the airport terminal as "a monument to the bold and prophetic architectural genius of the late Eero Saarinen."[271] These quotations show more than merely how the name Eero Saarinen serves as an architectural

151 Actresses Jane Russell, Linda Cristal, Martha Hyer, and Ann Miller, Idlewild, 1959

152 Actor Cary Grant, Idlewild, 1958

seal of approval for TWA. Just like the countless movie stars, politicians, musicians, and other celebrities who the airline has photographed in front of its planes, the famous architect is expected to attract additional attention from the media and the public. **Figs 151, 152** And precisely like the terminal's architecture, he should convey the exclusive image of an "airline of the stars." Thus, Eero Saarinen's growing fame offers a promotional benefit for TWA as well.

Inasmuch as the airline evokes the celebrity, genius, and daring spirit of the prematurely deceased VIP, it fosters the Eero Saarinen legend that Aline Saarinen tirelessly encourages. This is a significant expression for the great mutual benefit gained by the PR measures. Thanks to TWA, Aline Saarinen is given the opportunity to promote the reputation of the architect, from which the airline can also profit. Conversely, the Saarinen terminal also proves to be a suitable communication tool for TWA to restore its reputation as a technologically advanced and glamorous airline. Evidence that the partnership benefits both parties comes from mutual statements of gratitude made after the project reaches completion. PR chief Gordon L. Gilmore and even President Charles C. Tillinghast duly thank Aline Saarinen for her services.[272] And Aline Saarinen likewise expresses great praise of the client and its communications department. In her many years as a journalist and as the person responsible for Eero Saarinen's PR she has never before experienced such an agreeable and productive collaboration.[273] The success of this collaboration is described by TWA in a letter to Aline Saarinen some months after the terminal has been put into service: "The wonderful publicity about the Saarinen legend and the terminal continues to flow in from all over the world."[274] Indeed, the marketing activities before and after the inauguration bring about countless positive, sometimes enthusiastic articles in newspapers, professional journals, and illustrated magazines, as well as television and movie documentaries.[275] The employee magazine summarizes the yield harvested from the joint marketing with a simple formula: "universal press acclaim."[276]

Endnotes

183 See **Anonymous**: "New Furniture: Top American Designers Make It Simple, Slim and Comfortable," in: *Life*, vol. 25, no. 20 (November 15, 1948), pp. 115–118; **Anonymous**: "Country Salute to Modern Design," in: *House Beautiful*, vol. 83, no. 10 (October 1941), pp. 50–51.

184 Interview by Neil J. Smelser with Eero Saarinen: "Personal History and Professional Field Interview File," p. 2, April 25, 1959, University of California, Berkeley, Institute of Personality and Social Research.

185 **Saarinen**, Eero: Letter to "Dr. B." [Bartemayer], n. d. [1952–1953], Aline and Eero Saarinen Papers, 1906–1977, Archives of American Art, Smithsonian Institution, series 1, box 2, folder 49, sheet 13.

186 See ibid., sheet 16.

187 See **Knight**, Richard: "Once upon a Time … ," in: **Idem**: *Saarinen's Quest: A Memoir*, San Francisco, CA: William Stout Publishers, 2008, pp. 17–64, p. 35. The marriage chart is found here: **Saarinen**, Eero: sketch, n. d. [1953], Aline and Eero Saarinen Papers, 1953–1977, Archives of American Art, Smithsonian Institution, series 1, box 2, folder 20, p. 2.

188 Examples can, for instance, be found in the correspondence of the new couple. Aline suggests that a talk which Eero Saarinen held in Cleveland could be published in *Architectural Forum*. See **Louchheim** [Saarinen], Aline B.: Letter to Eero Saarinen, n. d. [1953], Aline and Eero Saarinen Papers, 1906–1977, Archives of American Art, Smithsonian Institution, series 1, Correspondence: Aline Saarinen to Eero Saarinen, box 2, folder 15. On another occasion, she draws the attention of New York publishing house Charles Scribner's Sons to the just-completed ice hockey rink at Yale University. See **Louchheim** [Saarinen], Aline B.: Letter to Eero Saarinen, n. d. [1953], Aline and Eero Saarinen Papers, 1906–1977, Archives of American Art, Smithsonian Institution, series 1, Correspondence: Aline Saarinen to Eero Saarinen, box 2, folder 40. For the mediation effort in the construction of an opera house for Pittsburgh, see **Louchheim** [Saarinen], Aline B.: Letter to Eero Saarinen, n.d. [1953], Aline and Eero Saarinen Papers, 1906–1977, Archives of American Art, Smithsonian Institution, series 1, Correspondence: Aline Saarinen to Eero Saarinen, box 2, folder 17.

189 See interview by Marc Guberman with Robert and Pat Burley, ES&A employees 1956–1963, December 13, 2004, Waitsfield, VT, unpublished (conducted as part of the research project "Eero Saarinen: Shaping the Future" for the book publication and traveling exhibition of the same name).

190 See **Blake**, Peter: Letter to Aline Saarinen, August 6, 1962, Eero Saarinen Collection (MS 593), Manuscripts and Archives, Yale University Library, series I, box 14, folder 228.

191 Although Charles Luckman is just thirty-seven when the cover story is written, its appearance is attributable to his success as a businessman at Lever Brothers. He does not begin the architectural partnership Pereira and Luckman until four years later. See **Drummond**, Alanya: "Architects on the Cover of *Time* magazine," in: *The International Journal of the Image*, vol. 2, no. 1 (2012), pp. 83–98, p. 86.

192 See **Saarinen**, Aline B.: "Four Architects Helping to Change the Look of America," in: *Vogue* [US edition], vol. 126, no. 8 (August 1955), pp. 118–121, 149–150, 152.

193 See **Knight**, Richard: "Once upon a Time . . . ," in: **Idem**: *Saarinen's Quest: A Memoir*, San Francisco, CA: William Stout Publishers, 2008, pp. 17–64, p. 35 (FN 40, p. 165).

194 See **Saarinen**, Aline B.: "Homey Stuff," unpublished, n.d. [1956], Aline and Eero Saarinen Papers, 1906–1977, Archives of American Art, Smithsonian Institution, series 1, box 2, folder 7, sheets 7–13.

195 See **Jones**, Cranston; **Connery**, Donald S.: "The Maturing Modern," in: *Time*, vol. 68, no. 1 (July 2, 1956), pp. 50–57, p. 50.

196 Interview by Ed Moore and Bill Kubota with Glen Paulsen, ES&A employee 1949–1951 and 1953–1957, August 11, 2004, Chelsea, MI, unpublished (conducted as part of the research project "Eero Saarinen: Shaping the Future" for the book publication and traveling exhibition of the same name).

197 **Saarinen**, Eero: "Presentation Plans" [internal memo to Joe Lacy, Kevin Roche, "Mo" and Aline Saarinen], October 26, 1959, Eero Saarinen Collection (MS 593), Manuscripts and Archives, Yale University Library, series II, box 18, folder 39.

198 Balthazar Korab, ES&A employee 1955–1958, cited in **Makowsky**, Paul; **Pedersen**, Martin C.; **Lanks**, Belinda; **LaBarre**, Suzanne: "Team Eero," in: *Metropolis*, vol. 28, no. 4 (November 2008), pp. 70–79, p. 76.

199 See **Knight**, Richard: "Once upon a Time . . . ," in: **Idem**: *Saarinen's Quest: A Memoir*, San Francisco, CA: William Stout Publishers, 2008, pp. 17–64, p. 45; **Borcherdt**, Helmut: *Architekten: Begegnungen 1956–1986*, Munich: Langen Müller, 1988, p. 93. Robert and Pat Burley, both longtime employees at ES&A, recall that the model photos were mistaken for photographs of the actual building. See interview by Marc Guberman with Robert and Pat Burley, ES&A employees 1956–1963, December 13, 2004, Waitsfield, VT, unpublished (conducted as part of the research project "Eero Saarinen: Shaping the Future" for the book publication and traveling exhibition of the same name).

200 **Yamashita**, Tsukasa [interview with Kevin Roche]: "Eero Saarinen and His Works," in: **Hozumi**, Nobuo (ed.): *Eero Saarinen* (series: "A&U Extra Edition"), Tokyo: A&U Publishing Co., 1984, pp. 20–24, p. 23.

201 Author interview with Cesar Pelli, June 24, 2009, New Haven, CT. Aline Saarinen doubtlessly contributed to the decision to include the bird comparison in TWA's first press release. See **ES&A**: "Draft of Description of the Trans-World Flight Center for Press Release," May 1962, Eero Saarinen Collection (MS 593), Manuscripts and Archives, Yale University Library, series IV, box 330, folder 935.

202 **Korab**, Balthazar: "Remembering Eero Saarinen: the Bloomfield Hills Office, 1955–58," in: **De Long**, David G.; **idem** (eds): *Eero Saarinen: Buildings From the Balthazar Korab Archive*, New York: W. W. Norton, 2008, pp. 410–411, p. 410.

203 His buildings appear in all the major American popular magazines such as *Harper's Magazine*, *House Beautiful*, *Life* (seven articles), *Look*, *Sports Illustrated*, *Time* (ten articles), *Playboy*, *Vogue*, and *Holiday*. See **Colomina**, Beatriz: "Saarinen's Use of the Media" [lecture at the conference "Eero Saarinen: Beyond the Measly ABC"], October 11, 2008, Walker Art Center, Minneapolis, MN, http://channel.walkerart.org/play/eero-saarinen-symposium-beatriz-colomina/ (accessed December 2, 2011). After SOM and the firm Harrison and Abramovitz, Saarinen is the third-most-published architect, appearing in the dominant American architecture magazines. See **Dixon**, John Morris: "Star-chitects of the 1950s," in: *Docomomo New York/Tri-State Newsletter*, Winter 2007, pp. 4–5.

204 See **Temko**, Allan: *Eero Saarinen* (series: "Makers of Contemporary Architecture"), New York: Braziller, 1962, p. 33.

205 **McQuade**, Walter: "Eero Saarinen: A Complete Architect," in: *Architectural Forum*, vol. 116, no. 4 (April 1962), pp. 102–127, p. 103.

206 **Saarinen**, Aline B.: Letter to B. B. [Bernard Berenson], May 24, 1958, pp. 1, 2. Aline and Eero Saarinen Papers, 1906–1977, Archives of American Art, Smithsonian Institution, series 2, box 6, folder 18, page 3. Aline Saarinen writes these lines nostalgically, after she and Eero Saarinen had, over a period of ten days, made themselves available to two reporters doing up-close and personal stories. Contrary to what one might suspect, she is averse to the methods of the media and its impact on their private life. Resignedly, in the rest of the letter Aline Saarinen deplores the lack of privacy along with the superficiality and lack of reality of the media portrayal.

207 **Louchheim**, Aline B.: "Now Saarinen the Son," in: *New York Times*, April 26, 1953, pp. 26–27, 44–45; **Saarinen**, Aline B.: "Four Architects Helping to Change the Look of America," in: *Vogue* [US edition], vol. 126, no. 8 (August 1955), pp. 118–121, 149–150, 152; **Jones**, Cranston; **Connery**, Donald S.: "The Maturing Modern," in: *Time*, vol. 68, no. 1 (July 2, 1956), pp. 50–57, p. 50.

208 **Banham**, Reyner: "The Trouble with Eero," in: *New Statesman*, vol. 64, no. 1654 (November 23, 1962), pp. 745–746, p. 745.

209 **Peter**, John: "Eero Saarinen: Second-Generation Genius," in: *Look*, vol. 22, no. 20 (September 30, 1958), pp. 66–68, p. 67.

210 **R.J.B.**: "T.C.A. and the Viscount," in: *Flight International*, vol. 67, no. 2412 (April 15, 1955), pp. 502–503, p. 502.

211 **Anonymous**: "Terminal City Rises at Idlewild," in: *Business Week*, no. 1610 (July 9, 1960), pp. 86–89, 90, 92, p. 89.

212 On the public reception of the Pan Am Terminal, see **Leslie**, Thomas: "The Pan Am Terminal at Idlewild/Kennedy Airport and the Transition from Jet Age to Space Age," in: *Design Issues*, vol. 21, no. 1 (Winter 2005), pp. 63–80, p. 68.

213 See **TWA**: "New Idlewild Terminal Designed by Saarinen Previewed in New York," in: *Skyliner*, vol. 20, no. 30 (November 21, 1957), p. 1.

214 See **Hudson**, Edward: "Bold Design is Set for Air Terminal: Trans World Airlines Plan a Terminal at Idlewild," in: *New York Times*, November 13, 1957, p. 37; **Hudson**, Edward: "Unusual Terminal for Idlewild: Startling Effect," in: *New York Times*, November 17, 1957, p. 37; **Anonymous**: "TWA Unveils Terminal Plans," in: *The Washington Post*, December 22, 1957, p. E19; **Anonymous**: "New for Idlewild Airport," in: *Chicago Tribune*, December 8, 1957, p. D16.

215 See **Serling**, Robert J.: *Howard Hughes' Airline: An Informal History of TWA*, New York: St. Martin's Press, 1983, pp. 176, 257.

216 See **Saarinen**, Aline B.: Letter to William A. Hewitt [President of Deere and Company], March 26, 1962, p. 1. Eero Saarinen Collection (MS 593), Manuscripts and Archives, Yale University Library, series I, box 14, folder 228.

217 Aline Saarinen later warns against the use of model photos. Normally she would not want to publicize a building before completion, because with the TWA project, photos of models would have also provoked criticism. Ibid., p. 3.

218 **TWA**: "Work to Begin Soon on New TWA Terminal at Idlewild Airport" [press

release], April 15, 1959, Trans World Airlines Collection (M-234), The Saint Louis Mercantile Library, University of Missouri-St. Louis, box 1-65.
219 **Saarinen**, Aline B.: Letter to William A. Hewitt [President of Deere and Company], March 26, 1962, p. 1. Eero Saarinen Collection (MS 593), Manuscripts and Archives, Yale University Library, series I, box 14, folder 228.
220 See **TWA**: "Work to Begin Soon on New TWA Terminal at Idlewild Airport" [press release], April 15, 1959, Trans World Airlines Collection (M-234), The Saint Louis Mercantile Library, University of Missouri-St. Louis, box 1-65. In the fall of 1963, TWA orders four Concorde supersonic aircraft. In 1973, after years of back and forth, they finally announce that they would not exercise their purchase option. See **Serling**, Robert J.: *Howard Hughes' Airline: An Informal History of TWA*, New York: St. Martin's Press, 1983, p. 314.
221 See **TWA**: "Fact Sheet" [press release], May 2, 1962, esp. pp. 1–2, Trans World Airlines Collection (M-234), The Saint Louis Mercantile Library, University of Missouri-St. Louis, box 1-30. According to Kenneth P. Morris, site manager for the construction company Grove Shepherd Wilson and Kruge, in order to distinguish the sixty to seventy building laborers who worked in several shifts, they (as well as the construction cranes) were actually identified with different colors, albeit not in the company colors. The numbering, too, was a PR idea that came from TWA. See **[TWA]**: [Untitled document, questions posed by TWA with answers from Kenneth P. Morris, n. d., ca. 1960], p. 2, Trans World Airlines Collection (M-234), The Saint Louis Mercantile Library, University of Missouri-St. Louis, box 1-65.
222 **TWA**: "Jet Age Air Terminals" [advertising brochure], [1961], p. 1, Trans World Airlines Collection (M-234), The Saint Louis Mercantile Library, University of Missouri-St. Louis, box 1-65.
223 Ibid., pp. 3, 4.
224 **Damon**, Ralph S.: "To the Directors" [internal notice], December 6, 1955, p. 5, Trans World Airlines (TWA) Records (KC0453), WHMC-KC, University of Missouri, box 236. Emphasis in original. See also **Rummel**, Robert: *Howard Hughes and TWA*, Washington, D.C.: Smithsonian Institution Press, 1991, p. 300.
225 See **Anonymous**: [Untitled news item], in: *Flight International*, vol. 70, no. 2489 (October 5, 1956), p. 596.
226 See **Davies**, R. E. G.: *TWA: An Airline and Its Aircraft*, McLean, VA: Paladwr Press, 2000, p. 7.
227 See **TWA**: [Untitled Board of Directors report], August 1961, pp. 1–2, Floyd D. Hall Papers (RG 488), Auburn University Special Collections and Archives, series I, box 2, folder "Meetings, Agendas & Reports, August 1961."
228 See **Garrison**, Glenn: "TWA Forecasts Jet Costs, Operations," in: *Aviation Week*, vol. 67, no. 15 (October 14, 1957), pp. 38–40, p. 39, p. 40 (quote).
229 **Anonymous**: "Dream of Jet Age Airports Still Far from Reality," in: *Business Week*, no. 1474 (November 30, 1957), pp. 90–92, 94, 96.
230 It is surely no coincidence that TWA reservedly characterizes the selected split-level solution in an early internal report as "the best compromise of the various factors to be reconciled in the planning." **TWA**: "Summary of Planning Data: Proposed TWA Unit Terminal," October 3, 1956, p. 2, Trans World Airlines Collection (M-234), The Saint Louis Mercantile Library, University of Missouri-St. Louis, box 1-65.
231 **Anonymous**: "Air Terminal for Jet Travel: Choosing a Terminal Plan," in: *Progressive Architecture*, vol. 42, no. 11 (November 1961), pp. 128–129, p. 128.
232 See Roger Johnson, ES&A employee 1953–1956, cited in **Price**, Cathy (ed.): *Saarinen Swanson Reunion Proceedings*, Bloomfield Hills, MI: Cranbrook, 2001, p. 32.
233 Author interview with Kevin Roche, May 5, 2008, Hamden, CT.
234 See **ES&A**: "Plane Position Plan" [construction drawing], 1963, Eero Saarinen Collection (MS 593), Manuscripts and Archives, Yale University Library, series IV, box 274.
235 See **TWA**: "Summary of Planning Data: Proposed TWA Unit Terminal," October 3, 1956, p. 2, Trans World Airlines Collection (M-234), The Saint Louis Mercantile Library, University of Missouri-St. Louis, box 1-65.
236 **Saarinen**, Eero: Letter to Rex Raab, Anthroposophischer Architektenkreis, Stuttgart, July 22, 1958, pp. 1–2, Eero Saarinen Collection (MS 593), Manuscripts and Archives, Yale University Library, series I, box 14, folder 227.
237 **Anonymous**: "Design for the Jet Age," in: *Time*, vol. 80, no. 22 (November 30, 1962), pp. 50–51, 53, p. 50. See also **Cook**, Robert H.: "Idlewild Sprawl Poses Transfer Problems," in: *Aviation Week and Space Technology*, vol. 79, no. 5 (July 29, 1963), pp. 33–34, 37, p. 33. On the routes at various airports, see **Tough**, John M.; **O'Flaherty**, Coleman A.: *Passenger Conveyors: An Innovatory Form of Communal Transport*, London: Allan, 1971, p. 106. Given the fact that the connecting corridor exceeds 300 feet (90 m) in length and must be traversed on foot, a TWA employee confesses at the opening: "It makes a long walk." **Anonymous**, cited in **Davenport**, Tony: "TWA to Open Unique N.Y. Terminal," in: *Hartford Times*, May 22, 1962, n. p.; newspaper clipping from Raymond Loewy Collections (Accession 2251), Hagley Museum and Library, series II, subseries B, vol. 12. According to *Architectural Record*, moving walkways do not accelerate passenger circulation, but increase customer satisfaction. See **Gusrae**, G. B.: "Moving Sidewalks," in: *Architectural Record*, vol. 119, no. 7 (June 1956), pp. 220–222, 233.
238 See **TWA**: "Amendment of Agreements Covering Construction of Unit Terminal at New York International Airport to Provide Increased Facilities" [meeting minutes of the board of directors], November 1961, p. 1. Floyd D. Hall Papers (RG 488), Auburn University Special Collections and Archives, series I, box 2, folder "Meetings, Agendas & Reports, November 1961."
239 See **TWA**: "New Idlewild Terminal Designed by Saarinen Previewed in New York," in: *Skyliner*, vol. 20, no. 30 (November 21, 1957), p. 1; **TWA**: "New TWA Terminal to Feature Unique Saarinen Design" [press release], November 13, 1957, Trans World Airlines Collection (M-234), The Saint Louis Mercantile Library, University of Missouri-St. Louis, box 1-66. Also **ES&A**: "Longitudinal Section thru Building" [construction drawing], [1963], Eero Saarinen Collection (MS 593), Manuscripts and Archives, Yale University Library, series IV, folder 274.
240 **TWA**: "The Story of the Trans World Flight Center" [internal communiqué], May 28, 1962, Trans World Airlines Collection (M-234), The Saint Louis Mercantile Library, University of Missouri-St. Louis, box 1-65.
241 **TWA**: "Fact Sheet" [press release], May 2, 1962, p. 3; **TWA**: "New Innovations Improve Services at Idlewild's Trans World Flight Center" [press release], May 1, 1962, pp. 2–3, Trans World Airlines Collection (M-234), The Saint Louis Mercantile Library, University of Missouri-St. Louis, box 1-30.
242 See **Hake**, Bruno H.: "Baggage Handling: Passenger and Baggage Processing at Air Terminals," in: *Journal of the Aero-Space Transport Division* (series: "Proceedings of the American Society of Civil Engineers"), vol. 39, no. 3677, AT (October 1963), pp. 29–44, p. 42; **Canty**, Donald: "Architecture for the Jet Age: New Buildings, New Problems, New Solutions," in: *Architectural Forum*, vol. 117, no. 1 (July 1962), pp. 66–83, p. 77.
243 **Anonymous**: "New York's Modern Wonder: T.W.A.'s Flight Center Dramatizes Jet Age," in: *The Boston Globe*, May 13, 1962, p. 59.
244 **Hudson**, Edward: "Unusual Terminal for Idlewild: Startling Effect," in: *New York Times*, November 17, 1957, p. 37.
245 **Anonymous**: "Saarinen Designs Terminal for TWA," in: *Progressive Architecture*, vol. 38, no. 12 (December 1957), pp. 66–67, p. 66.
246 **Borcherdt**, Helmut: "Planung des TWA-Flughafengebäudes in New York," in: *Baukunst und Werkform*, vol. 13, no. 5 (May 1960), pp. 256–263, p. 256.
247 **Hudson**, Edward: "Unfinished T.W.A. Terminal Is an Elegant Causeway," in: *New York Times*, April 22, 1962, p. 14.
248 **Anonymous**: "Neues Flight Center in New York-Idlewild," in: *Neue Zürcher Zeitung*, June 22, 1962 (evening edition), no. 2491, p. 6. TWA's own characterization of the vault as a "thin shell" is also widespread. Even professional journals adopt the description for the roof construction, which measures 7 inches (18 cm) at the thinnest point and 44 inches (112 cm) at the thickest. See e.g. **Anonymous**: "Sculpture

in Concrete," in: *Concrete Construction*, vol. 6, no. 10 (October 1961), pp. 282–284, p. 282.
249 See **Saarinen**, Aline B.: Letter to William A. Hewitt [President of Deere and Company], March 26, 1962, p. 1. Eero Saarinen Collection (MS 593), Manuscripts and Archives, Yale University Library, series I, box 14, folder 228.
250 **Gilmore**, Gordon L.: "Public Relations Planning for 1961–62" [file memo], July 25, 1961, p. 2. Gordon L. Gilmore Papers, 1946–1973, Wisconsin Historical Society, Administrative Records, box 2, folder 3. For further evidence, see **TWA**: "Public Relations Planning for 1961–62," July 25, 1961, p. 2. Gordon L. Gilmore Papers, 1946–1973, Wisconsin Historical Society, Administrative Records, box 2, folder 3.
251 Gordon L. Gilmore, cited in **TWA**: "World's News Media Cover Flight Center," in: *Skyliner*, vol. 25, no. 12 (June 4, 1962), p. 3.
252 **TWA**: [Untitled internal memo to the employees in Idlewild], May 5, 1962, p. 1, Trans World Airlines Collection (M-234), The Saint Louis Mercantile Library, University of Missouri-St. Louis, box 1-65.
253 On the commission given to Ezra Stoller, see **Saarinen**, Aline B.: "T.W.A." [internal memo to Joe Lacy, John Dinkeloo, and Kevin Roche], April 5, 1962, Eero Saarinen Collection (MS 593), Manuscripts and Archives, Yale University Library, series IV, box 273, folders 906–910.
254 Henry C. Riegner, cited in: **Carlson**, Walter: "Advertising: How T.W.A. Got off the Ground; Ailing Airline Found Key to Recovery in Research," in: *New York Times*, June 4, 1965, p. F12.
255 See **Davies**, R. E. G.: *TWA: An Airline and Its Aircrafts*, McLean, VA: Paladwr Press, 2000, p. 109; also **TWA**: "Airline of the Stars," in: *TWA Ambassador* [in-flight magazine], July 2000, pp. 38–43. TWA never uses this label for its advertising. The reason for this is likely that National Airlines began making this claim first, using it in the 1950s and 1960s.
256 See **Serling**, Robert J.: *Howard Hughes' Airline: An Informal History of TWA*, New York: St. Martin's Press, 1983, p. 258.
257 **TWA**: "TWA Ads Featured in Top National Magazines," in: *Skyliner*, vol. 25, no. 2 (January 15, 1962), p. 1.
258 **TWA**: "TWA Public Relations 1963/1964" [internal report], [1964], part 1, p. 5, Gordon L. Gilmore Papers, 1946–1973, Wisconsin Historical Society, Administrative Records, subseries 2, box 3.
259 **TWA**: "Winged Gateway to the World of Flight" [advertising brochure], 1962, n. p., Eero Saarinen Collection (MS 593), Manuscripts and Archives, Yale University Library, series IV, box 330, folder 936.
260 **TWA**: "TWA Welcomes You to the Trans World Flight Center" [advertising brochure], n. d. [1962], Trans World Airlines Collection (M-234), The Saint Louis Mercantile Library, University of Missouri-St. Louis, box 1-66. The connecting corridor is indeed suited as a backdrop for dramatic moments, as attested by the film showdowns in *The April Fools* and *Catch Me If You Can*. Ezra Stoller depicts a farewell from his father in the same style. See **Stoller**, Ezra: "Preface," in: **idem** (ed.): *The TWA Terminal* (series: "Building Blocks"), New York: Princeton Architectural Press, 1999, pp. VII–VIII, p. VIII.
261 **TWA**: "The Story of the Trans World Flight Center" [internal communiqué], May 28, 1962, Trans World Airlines Collection (M-234), The Saint Louis Mercantile Library, University of Missouri-St. Louis, box 1-65.
262 **TWA**: "Name Chosen for Terminal," in: *Skyliner*, vol. 25, no. 1 (January 1, 1962), pp. 1–2, p. 2. See also **TWA**: "'Trans World Flight Center' Is Name for TWA's New Terminal" [press release], February 21, 1962, Gordon L. Gilmore Papers, 1946–1973, Wisconsin Historical Society, Publicity, box 4, folder 1; also **TWA**: "Public Relations Planning for 1961–62," July 25, 1961, p. 2. Gordon L. Gilmore Papers, 1946–1973, Wisconsin Historical Society, Administrative Records, box 2, folder 3; letter from Robert W. Rummel to Gordon L. Gilmore, August 7, 1961, p. 1. Gordon L. Gilmore Papers, 1946–1973, Wisconsin Historical Society, Administrative Records, box 2, folder 3.
263 See **TWA**: "Eero Saarinen and the Trans World Flight Center" [advertising brochure about the opening], [1962], n. p., Gordon L. Gilmore Papers, 1946–1973, Wisconsin Historical Society, Publicity, box 4, folder 1; **Cosley**, Jerry W. [former employee of TWA Public Relations]: "What Be Shakin', Nagwa?," TWA Seniors Club, January 3, 2004, http://twa-seniorsclub.org/memories/contrails/shakin.htm (accessed February 3, 2015); **TWA**: "Trans World Flight Center Dedication: Progress Report III," April 17, 1962, p. 3, Trans World Airlines Collection (M-234), The Saint Louis Mercantile Library, University of Missouri-St. Louis, boxes 1–7.
264 See **TWA**: "'Scenario' for the Trans World Flight Center Press Review" [internal planning document], May 17, 1962, Gordon L. Gilmore Papers, 1946–1973, Wisconsin Historical Society, Publicity, box 4, folder 1.
265 **Cosley**, Jerry W. [former employee of TWA Public Relations]: "What Be Shakin', Nagwa?," TWA Seniors Club, January 3, 2004, http://twaseniorsclub.org/memories/contrails/shakin.htm (accessed February 3, 2015). See also **Gilmore**, Gordon L.: "Trans World Flight Center Dedication: Progress Report III" [file memo], April 17, 1962, Trans World Airlines Collection (M-234), The Saint Louis Mercantile Library, University of Missouri-St. Louis, boxes 1–7.
266 See **TWA**: "Eero Saarinen and the Trans World Flight Center" [advertising brochure about the opening], [1962], n. p., Gordon L. Gilmore Papers, 1946–1973, Wisconsin Historical Society, Publicity, box 4, folder 1.
267 As early as March 19, 1962, "Flight Wing Two" begins operation, remaining connected to the existing reception building until the entire complex opens. See **TWA**: "Trans World Flight Center Opens at Idlewild May 28," in: *Skyliner*, vol. 25, no. 7 (March 26, 1962), p. 1.
268 **TWA**: "Saarinen's Genius, TWA's Bold Vision Are Cited at Flight Center Dedication," in: *Skyliner*, vol. 25, no. 12 (June 4, 1962), pp. 1, 5, p. 1.
269 For the originally intended inscription, see **Saarinen**, Aline B.: [Div. sketches, untitled], n. d., Eero Saarinen Collection (MS 593), Manuscripts and Archives, Yale University Library, series IV, box 329, folder 917. A memo indicates that Aline is the author of the idea. See **Saarinen**, Aline B.: "TWA Plaque" [memo to Kevin Roche], March 12, 1962, Eero Saarinen Collection (MS 593), Manuscripts and Archives, Yale University Library, series IV, box 329, folder 919.
270 **TWA**: "Meet the Architect," in: *Skyliner*, vol. 20, no. 30 (November 21, 1957), p. 3.
271 **Tillinghast**, Charles C., Jr.: "A Message from Mr. Charles C. Tillinghast, Jr.," in: TWA: "Eero Saarinen and the Trans World Flight Center" [advertising brochure about the opening], [1962], n. p., Gordon L. Gilmore Papers, 1946–1973, Wisconsin Historical Society, Publicity, box 4, folder 1.
272 See **Gilmore**, Gordon L.: Letter to Aline B. Saarinen, June 5, 1962, Eero Saarinen Collection (MS 593), Manuscripts and Archives, Yale University Library, series IV, box 273, folder 906–910; **Tillinghast**, Charles C., Jr.: Letter to Aline B. Saarinen, May 31, 1962, Eero Saarinen Collection (MS 593), Manuscripts and Archives, Yale University Library, series IV, box 273, folders 906–910.
273 **Saarinen**, Aline B.: Letter to Gordon L. Gilmore, June 4, 1962, Eero Saarinen Collection (MS 593), Manuscripts and Archives, Yale University Library, series IV, box 273, folders 906–910.
274 **Riordan**, Emmet [TWA]: Letter to Aline B. Saarinen, November 12, 1962, Eero Saarinen Collection (MS 593), Manuscripts and Archives, Yale University Library, series IV, box 273, folders 906–910.
275 For example, even prior to completion of the building, a television station slates the terminal for a program about art and society. See **Granada TV Network Ltd.**: Letter to ES&A, August 24, 1961, Eero Saarinen Collection (MS 593), Manuscripts and Archives, Yale University Library, series IV, box 273, folders 906–910. A British production company also films a movie about Saarinen in the terminal. See **Moyer**, Donald B. [public relations, TWA]: Letter to D'Arnold Davis, Cleveland, OH, October 17 and 31, 1962, TWA, Eero Saarinen Collection (MS 593), Manuscripts and Archives, Yale University Library, series IV, box 273, folders 906–910.
276 **TWA**: "World's News Media Cover Flight Center," in: *Skyliner*, vol. 25, no. 12 (June 4, 1962), p. 3.

TWA Designed

153 Check-in area, TWA Flight Center, ca. 1964

Eero Saarinen's TWA Flight Center is, to begin with, based on organizational logic. It is created in the second half of the 1950s, in the face of growing mass tourism in civil aviation. The terminal building is intended to ensure efficient and thus cost-effective ground handling processes for its financially troubled operator. Conceived in the fading Constellation era, however, when the terminal opens in 1962 it is not ready for the jet aircraft that are meanwhile used, which becomes noticeable all too quickly during operations. Within a short time it reaches the limits of its capacity. Instead of the predicted seven million airline passengers, almost eleven million pour through the terminal in the first five years of operation. Fig. 153 Soon the available parking positions no longer suffice, especially since the decision to not build one satellite has reduced the original number by half.[277] Although the operator does repeatedly try to adapt the airport building to the ever-greater operational requirements—alongside passenger growth there are also additional security needs—only middling success is achieved. In 1966 Trans World Airlines considers adding an underground car and taxi drop-off area with ticket counter, baggage check-in, and connecting passage into the main building.[278] At the end of the 1960s, TWA does, in fact, build the second satellite, which was originally delayed for reasons of cost, and simultaneously enlarges the existing south wing. But even this and other increases in capacity are not able to deal with the growth in civil aviation. Fig. 154 By the time TWA goes bankrupt and merges with American Airlines in 2001, the Port Authority judges the terminal as "inadequate to meet passenger, baggage and security standards required for contemporary aviation operations."[279] The low-cost carrier Jet Blue comes to the same conclusion. The two satellites of the Saarinen terminal must give way to a new terminal building, designed by the architectural firm Gensler and opened in 2008. Fig. 155 The main building, the actual departure hall, meanwhile remains standing. Discussions about its use by Jet Blue as an arrival hall end without success, so it currently stands empty, and its fate is unclear.

At first glance, the TWA Terminal seems to be no exception. All terminal buildings of its time have undergone scores of modifications over the years to meet new requirements, often enough only to be replaced in the end. The same is also true for the Pan Am Terminal, which began operations in 1960 at today's John F. Kennedy Airport in New York. After demolition plans become a pressing threat in 2010, a civil movement forms and the building is identified by the National Trust for Historic Preservation as one of the eleven most endangered historic places in the country. Yet in 2013, after fifty-three years of operation, the "Worldport" is torn down. In the case of the Pan Am Terminal, business concerns prevailed over those of historic preservation. This is different for the TWA Terminal. Aware of the impending demolition, a heated debate flares up between the Port Authority, the architectural community, and landmark preservationists in

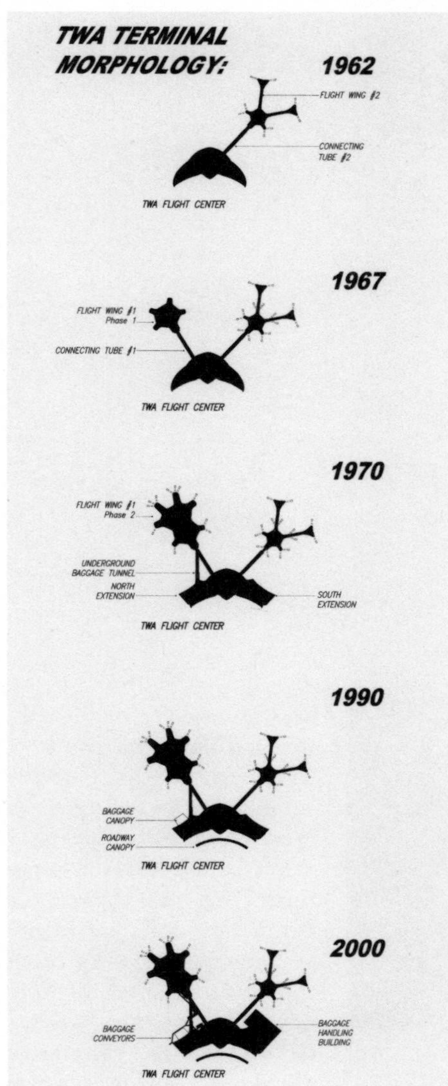

154 Structural alterations to TWA Flight Center, schematic 2004–2005

2001—with a weighty difference. New York's Landmarks Preservation Commission had already entered Saarinen's building in the National Register of Historic Places in 1994, but had not considered the Pan Am Terminal to be sufficiently worthy of preservation in 2001.[280] While both departure buildings have admittedly become unfit for normal use, the memorable rotunda of the Pan Am Terminal seems to lack that formal uniqueness that saves the TWA Terminal from demolition and which prompts the landmark commission to grant it protected status:

> "Saarinen's firm revolutionized air terminal design through its use of daring concrete and glass forms and technological advances, producing a distinctive and highly-acclaimed work of expressionistic architecture with the TWA Terminal."[281]

Much like a wide variety of reviewers from its nascent period to the present day, the landmarks preservation authority asserts that Saarinen has revolutionized airport architecture both from a design stand-

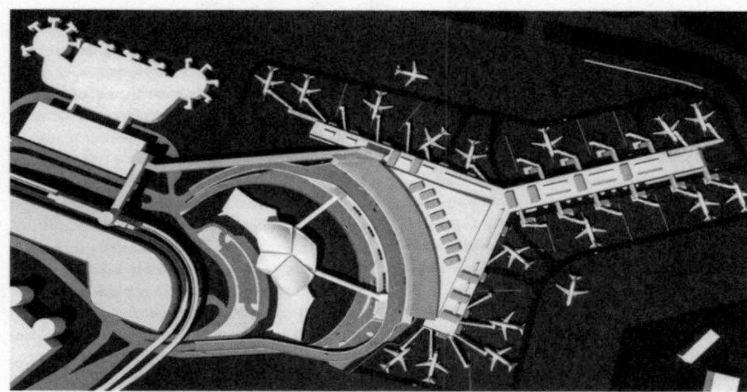

155 Site plan, Jet Blue Terminal and TWA Flight Center, 2007

point and operationally—and thereby supports a legend. By disregarding that the TWA Terminal was obsolete practically from day one, it turns a blind eye on the operational and economical requirements set out at the time, and with the dysfunctional terminal's protected status also on today's needs. When the authority denies the operating function and simultaneously preserves the building's appearance, it cultivates an idealized image of the real building, whose origin dates back to the early marketing of it as a jet-compatible terminal. With dwindling functional capacity, media attention thus increasingly constituted the true value of the terminal, while the operational importance shifted more and more into the background, until ultimately becoming irrelevant upon its closure. Its reproduction in the media became more important than the building itself. In this era of mass media, the TWA Flight Center is increasingly monumentalized by publications that are richly illustrated and documented.[282]

The foundation for this development is laid by TWA and Aline Saarinen with an extremely successful PR campaign. From the announcement of the project to its construction to the opening and thereafter: Eero Saarinen's terminal generates enormous media publicity. Accordingly, the owner benefits greatly from the public impact which exceeds that of all the other terminals at Idlewild.[283] Doubtlessly without exaggeration, TWA can summarize as follows in the year after the opening: "Publicity-wise, the Flight Center has earned for TWA more favorable comment in magazines and newspapers, and on television and radio, than ever received by any other airline facility."[284] Not least because of its presence in the media, the terminal becomes a magnet for visitors: 1.5 million flight customers—250,000 more than projected—pour through the terminal building in the first year of operation, followed by 3000 visitors each month thereafter.[285] The terminal consequently soon becomes general knowledge, which is underscored by exam questions from a high school in 1963. The students are asked to identify two other buildings by Eero Saarinen, the "feeling" that he tried to express with the TWA Terminal, and the primary building materials.[286]

Encouraged by the decidedly large public impact, TWA tries to continue profiting from its buildings after the terminal has gone into service: "TWA's facilities . . . lend themselves to 'show case' treatment," it says in the PR strategy report for the years 1963 and 1964.[287] Another example for the subsequent measures, in addition to the TWA Flight Center, is a new Hostess Training Center in Kansas City. Given the maxim "To attract the caliber of young women we want we are creating a quality atmosphere," the architecture of the Breech Academy appears to represent a competitive advantage in the battle for the ablest young talent.[288] The airline has a less specific goal in mind as it announces in 1967 that a hangar with concrete shell roof is to be built in Kansas City for the Boeing 747 and supersonic transport (SST). However, even the title of a later press release—"Concrete and Steel Etch Outline of New Home for TWA's Super-Jets"—and the reference to "the spectacular design of the structure" demonstrate how TWA continues trying to gain benefit from the architectural appearance for its public image.[289] **Fig. 156** Nonetheless, the buildings do not attain nearly the same resonance as the TWA Terminal. Moreover, the hostess uniforms are now temporarily advancing to become eye-catchers and the airlines' favorite marketing tool. Whereas previously the uniforms were styled to complement the cabin design and were to attract as little attention as possible, they now seek to outdo each other with ever more extravagant designs. **Fig. 157** Between 1965 and 1974, TWA replaces the workwear of its hostesses no less than five times.[290]

156 Rendering of Technical Services Center for Boeing 747 and SST, TWA, Kansas City, MO, 1967

Typical for the lower marketing potential of airport terminals, a 1968 TWA advertisement says: "Nobody likes to hang around airports."[291] It is significant that the advertisement does not identify the TWA Terminal, even though it was photographed there (its mosaic tiles can be discerned in the background). Its reputation should not be damaged, because contrary to the trend, the building and the architect continue to serve communication purposes for TWA: The Boeing 747 and SST hangar in Kansas City, with its shell roof, is described as "a striking reminder of the TWA Flight Center designed by the late Eero Saarinen."[292] According to the *Skyliner*, the TWA World Travel Center, a ticket office in Manhattan that opened in 1968, heralds the "spirit of flight caught by the late Eero Saarinen's design for the JFK terminal."[293] As the airline announces the construction of the second satellite

157 TWA hostesses in "Foreign Accent" uniforms, TWA Flight Center, ca. 1968

158 TWA Flight Center as computer-generated imagery (CGI), Happy Finish (agency for digital images), 2009

in 1967, a five-page press release highlights the architecture of the terminal and its architect, whereas the annex by Kevin Roche John Dinkeloo and Associates is given just a few lines.[294] As the satellite is put into service in 1970, we are told: "The TWA Flight Center, designed by the late Eero Saarinen, is considered one of the most beautiful examples of 20th-century architecture in the U.S.A."[295] Although the terminal is used less and less for advertising purposes beginning in the 1960s, TWA nevertheless unswervingly contends its historical importance for architecture.[296] Even as late as the year of its bankruptcy the airline still refers to "Eero Saarinen's award-winning terminal."[297]

Even though the terminal is increasingly unable to fulfill its essential purpose of ensuring rapid passenger and cargo handling, it maintains media value for its operator. And more: articles in the trade and popular press as well as in the tabloids, advertisements by companies and suppliers involved in the construction, and educational brochures and publications—such as a German children's book from 1961 depicting major achievements of engineering—as well as general surveys of the architecture of the twentieth century and monographs on Saarinen's work all cultivate the image of a well-engineered airport terminal, which TWA has previously shaped with the assistance of Aline Saarinen.[298] The myth of a jet-age airport terminal emerges. This is additionally reinforced by a wealth of illustrations that also ignore the original mission of the building and evoke its original appearance. Starting with illustrations and including photographs—just think of the meticulously composed photos by Ezra Stoller—and computer-generated imagery, countless reproductions isolate the TWA Terminal from the temporal decomposition process. Fig. 158 They celebrate the original architecture of the terminal, which is in reality increasingly disfigured by modifications.[299] Operationally obsolete and architecturally defaced, reproductions in the media, instead of passenger and baggage handling, now constitute the building's intrinsic value.

159 Miniature model of TWA Flight Center, Minidomm theme park near Düsseldorf, year unknown

This shift is all the more pronounced as the terminal becomes exposed to ever-wider commercialization. Whereas initially only TWA and Aline Saarinen and later also those who where involved with its construction attempted to benefit from the terminal, the circle of beneficiaries increases more and more—the monumentalization takes its course. First there are postcards and movies, then the first edition of the Michelin Guide to New York (1968), which presents the building as a main attraction of the city.[300] Overseas, the Minidomm theme park near Düsseldorf introduces a model of the terminal in 1967.[301] Fig. 159 Even after being decommissioned in 2001, the TWA Terminal's significance as an attraction has been substantiated by its appearance in the feature film *Catch Me If You Can* (2002), its inclusion in the stamp series "Masterworks of Modern American Architecture" (2005), its use in the logo for the event marking the opening of the Jet Blue Terminal (2008) Fig. 160, the replica of the terminal, made of branches, leaves, and bark, in the New York Botanical Garden (2010), a commercial for financial services provider Capital One, filmed in the building with actor Alec Baldwin (2013), and fashion photographs (e. g. for Longchamp, 2013, and *Harper's Bazaar,* 2014), as well as the collector value of vintage advertisements and photos on Internet marketplaces. As an attraction, Saarinen's building advances to become the architectural epitome of an airport terminal, even a monument to buildings for the aviation industry as such.

160 Logo for an event marking the opening of the Jet Blue Terminal, 2008

This finds its architectural expression in scores of airport buildings—the TWA Terminal serves as a "pacesetter of the 'soaring' design," as *Time* writes in 1963.[302] The terminal in Las Vegas, which was completed in the same year, has a sweeping roof like its prototype, "looking for all the world as though it had been sired by TWA's Trans World Flight Center," notes the *Skyliner*.[303] Fig. 161 In Atlanta, a sequence of barrel vaults form an undulating silhouette; in Newark, clustered columns support a series of vaults; in Memphis, the roof consists of a group of hyperbolic paraboloids; and in Austin, not only the roof but also the unusually shaped control tower serve as eye-catchers.[304] For the sales office they opened in 1963 inside the Pan Am Building, even TWA's arch rival, Pan Am, relies on "the same sculptural, flight-evoking quality so evident in recent U.S. airport design," reckons *Architectural Forum*.[305] One can also see more recent works, such as the airports by Kisho Kurokawa in Kuala Lumpur (1998), Richard Rogers in Madrid (2006), and Norman Foster in Beijing (2008), as part of the same development. [306] In any event, unmistakable copies of Saarinen's terminal exist in the oval departures boards at Paris-Charles de Gaulle, Ankara, and Marrakech. Fig. 162

161 Postcard of McCarran International Airport, Las Vegas, NV, Welton Becket and Associates, 1963

With its considerable reproductive value, the TWA Flight Center represents a fundamental paradigm shift in the thinking of architecture and urban design in the 1950s and 1960s. Its suitability for presentation in the media is the central characteristic of a tradition of signature buildings—which starts with the Trans World Flight Center, along with the Guggenheim Museum (1959) by Frank Lloyd Wright and the Sydney Opera House (1959–1973)—and which is also discussed today using catchwords like "iconic architecture" and "landmark architecture."[307] That's because—for companies as well as for cities like, for instance, Bilbao, where Frank O. Gehry's Guggenheim Museum triggered a tourist boom in 1997 ("Bilbao effect")—media attention has developed a benefit that economic players use to create cultural, social, and economic

162 Departures board at Aéroport Marrakech-Ménara, 2010

value.[308] But in contrast to the Guggenheim museums and the Sydney Opera House, Eero Saarinen's airport building—which is located far outside the city center, wedged in amidst new airport buildings, the Air Train, and the much larger Jet Blue Terminal—is not suitable as a tourist attraction. **Fig. 163** There have been many ideas for new ways to use it: as a museum, restaurant, spa, shopping center, or conference center, or even as office space or a hotel.[309] Since 2001, the Port Authority has been seeking a suitable use for the disused air-

163 TWA Flight Center between the Jet Blue Terminal (above) and a parking garage (below), 2008

port terminal, which underwent a landmark restoration by Beyer Blinder Belle for $20 million in 2012 but remains empty today. In the recent past, it has opened the terminal's doors one day each year for a few hours, which is an event that regularly attracts hordes of visitors—accompanied by euphoric blog posts and news reports. This reflects the significance of Saarinen's terminal for architectural history. The Trans World Flight Center is the epitome of an architecture that is less about serving as an environment for a specific operational event, such as passenger handling, and more about representing an event in itself.

Endnotes

277 For a description of the operational deficiencies, see **Duncan**, Ian: "TWA's 'Terminal of Tomorrow': An Architectural Showpiece," in: *Airliners*, no. 75 (May/June 2002), pp. 40–49, p. 46.
278 See **ES&A**: "Lower Level Plan of Entrance Facility" [Baggage systems diagrams], Eero Saarinen Collection (MS 593), Manuscripts and Archives, Yale University Library, series IV, box 324.
279 **Dunlap**, David W.: "Unusual Planning Duel Over Kennedy Terminal," November 28, 2002, http://www.nytimes.com/2002/11/28/nyregion/blocks-unusual-planning-duel-over-kennedy-terminal.html (February 3, 2015).
280 See **Dixon**, John Morris: "Can JFK's Terminal 3 Be Saved?" May 19, 2013, http://www.docomomo-nytri.org/2013/05/19/can-jfks-terminal-3-be-saved (accessed February 3, 2015).
281 **New York Landmarks Preservation Commission**: "Trans World Airlines Flight Center at New York International Airport," in: **idem**: *New York Landmarks Preservation Commission: Designation List*; 259, LP-1916, New York: The Commission, 1994, p. 2.
282 As Mark Wigley points out in his essay "The Architectural Cult of Synchronisation," which is fundamental to the following argument, John McHale of the Independent Group understood the link between landmark cult and reproduction as early as 1966. In the essay "The Plastic Parthenon" he underscores the role of mass media and the consumer products industry in the creation of monuments. See **Wigley**, Mark: "The Architectural Cult of Synchronisation," in: *The Journal of Architecture*, vol. 4, no. 4 (1999), pp. 409–435; **McHale**, John: "Der Plastik-Parthenon," in: **Dorfles**, Gillo (ed.): *Der Kitsch*, Tübingen: Wasmuth, 1969, pp. 97–110; originally published as "The Plastic Parthenon," in: *Dot Zero Magazine*, no. 3 (spring 1967), pp. 4–11; also **Stalder**, Laurent: "Monumente der unmittelbaren Zukunft," in: **Ruhl**, Carsten (ed.): *Mythos Monument: Urbane Strategien in Architektur und Kunst seit 1945*, Bielefeld: Transcript, 2011 (series: "Urban Studies"), pp. 63–75.
283 For Rupert Spade, at that time only the Sydney Opera House gained similarly broad attention. See **Spade**, Rupert: "Introduction," in: **Futagawa**, Yukio (ed.): *Eero Saarinen* (series: "Library of Contemporary Architects"), New York: Simon and Schuster, 1971, pp. 7–20, p. 18; Japanese original edition in the series: "Gendai Kenchikuka Shirizu," 1968.
284 **TWA**: [Untitled news item], in: *Skyliner*, vol. 26, no. 11 (May 27, 1963), p. 6.

285 For the planning, TWA proceeds on the premise that there will be twice as many visitors as passengers in the terminal. See **TWA**: "Summary of Planning Data: Proposed TWA Unit Terminal," October 3, 1956, appendix A, Trans World Airlines Collection (M-234), The Saint Louis Mercantile Library, University of Missouri-St. Louis, box 1-65.
286 **TWA**: "Editor's Notes," in: *Skyliner*, vol. 26, no. 13 (June 24, 1963), p. 2.
287 **TWA**: "TWA Public Relations 1963/1964" [internal report], [1964], part 2, p. 7. Gordon L. Gilmore Papers, 1946–1973, Wisconsin Historical Society, Administrative Records, subseries 2, box 3.
288 **TWA**: "TWA Plans Flight Hostess Academy: Suburb of Kansas City Chosen for 34-Acre Campus," in: *Skyliner*, vol. 30, no. 16 (July 31, 1967), pp. 1, 9, p. 9.
289 TWA: "Concrete and Steel Etch Outline of New Home for TWA's SuperJets" [press release], December 23, 1969, p. 3, Trans World Airlines Collection (M-234), Saint Louis Mercantile Library, University of Missouri-St. Louis, box 1-8.
290 Pierre Balmain's uniform (1965) is followed by a fashionable work coat designed by Dalton of America (1968). Less than a year later, TWA clothes its hostesses in various provocative wrap dresses made of paper. Finally, new uniforms for the TWA flight attendants are designed again in 1971, this time by Valentino, only to be replaced in 1974. In so doing, TWA follows a trend that the fashion designer Emilio Pucci initiated with his unusually fashionable and colorful hostess uniforms for Braniff. According to the motto "the air strip," the ladies shed one of their garments after each stopover. On the emergence of the marketing campaign, see **Lawrence**, Mary Wells: *A Big Life in Advertising*, New York: Touchstone, 2003, pp. 34–37.
291 See **TWA**: "Sigmund Has the Brains We Look for, But Somehow ..." [advertisement], e.g. in: *Business Week*, no. 2010 (March 9, 1968), back cover.
292 **TWA**: "Concrete and Steel Etch Outline of New Home for TWA's SuperJets" [press release], December 23, 1969, p. 3, Trans World Airlines Collection (M-234), Saint Louis Mercantile Library, University of Missouri-St. Louis, boxes 1–8.
293 **TWA**: "Travel Center, Flight Center Pair Off as Three-Stars," in: *Skyliner*, vol. 31, no. 17 (August 12, 1970), p. 1.
294 **TWA**: "TWA Flight Wing One to Fulfill Destiny of Saarinen Design" [press release], June 4, 1967, Trans World Airlines Collection (M-234), The Saint Louis Mercantile Library, University of Missouri-St. Louis, box 1-66.
295 **TWA**: "Something No Other Airline Can Give You" [advertising brochure], n. d. [circa 1970], p. 12. Private collection of the author. At the same time, and in a manner very similar to how the opening of Saarinen's terminal was marked, TWA again stresses the jet suitability of the annex building—this time for the Boeing 747. See e.g. **TWA**: "TWA's Flight Wing I," in: *TWA Ambassador* [in-flight magazine], January/February 1970, pp. 32–33, p. 32.
296 The waning marketing functions of the terminal are, on the one hand, likely related to its lack of novelty. Since the Second World War, all the components of TWA's corporate image have been exploited for marketing purposes: from the airplane and the passenger cabin to the terminals and ticket offices to the uniforms of the hostesses. As if to prove that the company has exhausted its own marketing potential, the TWA logo no longer embellishes the Valentino uniform, which is instead adorned with that of the designer. On the other hand, from about 1970 onward, a certain skepticism about the past marketing strategy can be discerned. Evidence of this change of conviction is, for instance, the announcement of a completely new flight experience: "It is not just a collection of frills and changes for the sake of change—but rather a total travel experience which begins before you leave, continues in-flight and doesn't end until you leave the terminal." "What makes an airline different is not aeroplanes, booze or food," proclaims a TWA manager in 1969, "but the way it treats its customers." **TWA**: "TWA's Got a Whole New Way to Fly," in: *TWA Today* [successor magazine to *Skyliner*], vol. 33, no. 20 (October 19, 1970), pp. 1, 4; Anonymous TWA manager, cited in **Bacon**, Roger: "Straight and Level," in: *Flight International*, vol. 95, no. 3138 (May 1, 1969), p. 736a; **Hughes**, Lawrence W.: "It's Happiness Time," in: *Airline Management and Marketing*, vol. 3, no. 6 (June 1969), pp. 73–75, p. 73.
297 Such references to Saarinen's terminal appear in the airline's in-flight magazine. See e.g. **TWA**: "The Terminals at Our Flight Hubs," in: *TWA Ambassador* [in-flight magazine], July 2000, p. 68. The TWA Flight Center is awarded various distinctions, such as an AIA Award in 1963, and in the previous year the title "Building of the Year" from the New York Concrete Institute and the "Excellence in Design" award from the Queens Chamber of Commerce. The *New York Times* reports on the latter on its front page. See **Anonymous**: "Queens Chamber Cites Air Center," in: *New York Times*, December 2, 1962, pp. 1, 4.
298 A full-page advertisement for the Sloan Valve Company compares the efficiency of the terminal with the durability of the flush valves used in building. See **Sloan Valve Company**: "Performance Records of Millions of Sloan Flush Valves Indicate ..." [draft advertisement], n. d., n. p., Eero Saarinen Collection (MS 593), Manuscripts and Archives, Yale University Library, series IV, box 273, folders 906–910. See **Dietrich**, Fred; **Cieszynski**, Horst: *Große Leistungen der Technik*, Gütersloh: Bertelsmann, 1961, p. 81. The general surveys include, for example, **Gössel**, Peter; **Leuthäuser**, Gabriele: *Architecture in the 20th Century* (2 vols), Cologne: Taschen, 2005; **Podrecca**, Boris: *Almanac of Architecture: Spatial Analysis*, Salzburg: Anton Pustet, 2009.
299 Many original parts of the building fall victim to the modifications. Critics speak of TWA defacing the building. See **Fisher**, Thomas: "Landmarks: TWA Terminal," in: *Progressive Architecture*, vol. 73, no. 5 (May 1992), pp. 96–101, p. 96.
300 The terminal is slated to serve as the kick-off for a new documentary series about "the great buildings done by man." See **Barnstone**, Howard [Howard Barnstone and Partners]: Letter to Aline Saarinen, September 28, 1962, Eero Saarinen Collection (MS 593), Manuscripts and Archives, Yale University Library, series IV, box 273, folders 906–910. Over time, the terminal serves as the setting for various feature films, such as *The April Fools* (1969), *Baby Boom* (1987), *The Wedding Banquet* (1993), *Catch Me If You Can* (2002), and *Old Dogs* (2009). See **Pneu Michelin**: *Les guides verts: New York*, Paris: Michelin, 1968, p. 134. Other travel guides also list the terminal, see e.g. **Kruse-Etzbach**, Dirk: *New York*, Dormagen: Iwanowski, 2010 (sixth ed.), p. 552.
301 **TWA**: "Miniature Flight Center Is Minidomm's Aerodrome," in: *Skyliner*, vol. 30, no. 10 (May 8, 1967), p. 4.
302 **Anonymous**: "The Word Is Soar," in: *Time*, vol. 81, no. 13 (March 29, 1963), p. 48.
303 **TWA**: "Las Vegas Opens New Air Terminal," in: *Skyliner*, vol. 26, no. 7 (April 1, 1963), p. 8.
304 See **Gordon**, Alastair: *Naked Airport: A Cultural History of the World's Most Revolutionary Structure*, New York: Metropolitan Books, 2004, p. 202.
305 **Anonymous**: "Pan Am Ticket Office: An Airy Sweep of Sculptured Space," in: *Architectural Forum*, vol. 119, no. 2 (August 1963), pp. 98–101, pp. 99. See also **Clausen**, Meredith L.: *The Pan Am Building and the Shattering of the Modernist Dream*, Cambridge, MA: MIT Press, 2005, pp. 139–141.
306 See **Angélil**, Marc: "Terminal Space: Gedanken zur zeitgenössischen Flughafenarchitektur," in: *archithese*, vol. 32, no. 5 (2002), pp. 8–13, p. 11.
307 See **Jencks**, Charles: *The Iconic Building: The Power of Enigma*, London: Frances Lincoln, 2005; **Love**, Tim; **Schindler**, Susanne: "Von Museum bis Condominium: Das Phänomen *signature building* in den USA," in: *Bauwelt*, vol. 96, no. 46 (December 2, 2005), pp. 12–15.
308 On city marketing using architecture, see **Kovári**, Thomas: "Die Stadt als Marke: Planung und Architektur im Dienst des City Branding," in: *archithese*, vol. 35, no. 6 (2005), pp. 44–49.
309 See **Dunlap**, David W.: "A Move to Make a Silent Air Terminal Hum Again," November 16, 2006, http://www.nytimes.com/2006/11/16/nyregion/16blocks.html (accessed February 3, 2015).

ST. LOUIS
MILAN-ROM
LONDON
non stop
TICKET LOBBY

COCKTAIL BAR
UPSTAIRS

WA

TWA

CLEARANCE
10'

FLIGHT
ARRIVES
TWA
TWA
TWA

FLIGHT DEPARTS
7 10:30
TW

Appendix

164 Eero Saarinen at work, surrounded by Kevin Roche (on the right, standing) and other employees, probably in Bloomfield Hills, MI, year unknown

Eero was very interested in the fundamentals of why a building was being built. He was a frequent flyer. When he got involved in this particular project ... he had a stopwatch. He would record how long it took to get to the gate, because then one didn't have to go to a ticket counter. One had a ticket, went to the gate, got on the plane, and flew away.

Interview with Kevin Roche
Former Associate at ES&A

August 2, 2007
Kevin Roche John Dinkeloo and Associates
20 Davis Street, Hamden, CT

Ringli Why did TWA ask Eero Saarinen and Associates to do a design for their new terminal?

Roche At that moment in time Eero was beginning to become very well-known. He was one of the exponents of cutting-edge architecture, and the vice president, whose name I cannot remember at the moment and who was charged with this building project, looked at several different architects. Then came the interview with Eero. And I have to say that, in general, TWA as a company didn't really know much about it. I think it was all this individual. The only person we ever saw was this one vice president.

Ringli Was his name Rex Werner?

Roche No. You should be able to find his name in the correspondence.

Ringli I checked already, but Laura [Tatum, former archivist of the Eero Saarinen Collection at Yale University] told me that at one point in time all the correspondence was disposed of. Although I did find some letters exchanged by Aline Saarinen and TWA executives after the inauguration of the building. Was it Gordon L. Gilmore, the head of marketing?

Roche No. And only when we got to the more pragmatic aspects, such as the mechanics of ticketing and baggage handling, more people became involved. But as far as the concept of the building is concerned, TWA as a company had no input at all. The presentation was made to this vice president, he approved it, and that was it. It was very simple.

Ringli I read that you actually went to other airports with stopwatches.

Roche We traveled around everywhere, and Eero was very interested in the fundamentals of why a building was being built. He was a frequent flyer. When he got involved in this particular project—and I was traveling with him almost everywhere he went—he had a stopwatch. He would record how long it took to get to the gate, because then one didn't have to go to a ticket counter. One had a ticket, went to the gate, got on the plane, and flew away.

Ringli So he actually did it himself?

Roche He did. He was taking the time when we sat on the plane. He was waiting for the plane to start moving, until we got to the end of the runway, he took that, and then we took off. When we touched the ground, he was checking how long it took to taxi, to go to the gate, to go through the line, and all that kind of stuff.

Ringli Did he do that even before TWA started?

Roche I think he started it when TWA started, but he followed through with it more exhaustively and more thoroughly when we were doing Dulles Airport. At the time when TWA was designed, there were no jets operating yet. They were just being introduced at that moment.

Ringli TWA was the last of the large US airlines to have jets.

Roche We were on the first 707 test flight, but that was for Dulles. The general concept of the terminal—except for the shape of it—was very much influenced by the United Terminal in San Francisco. Up to that point, when one entered the terminal, there were the ticket counters and a line of planes pulled into four or five gate positions. So one went from the ticket counter into the plane. As they got more and more planes, United developed the idea of the "finger." That was the first terminal we went to look at, and it was working very well. The first real breakthrough was to have the ticketing on the right-hand side and the baggage on the left-hand side; the fingers were pointed outwards, which created the possibility to surround the central finger element with the planes. That was sort of the evolution of terminal planning. The second aspect is that initially one would walk out across the tarmac and get on the plane. The baggage handling happened at the same level. O'Hare Terminal in Chicago had three or four gates at that time and showed the first efforts to separate baggage and passengers—the first two-story effort. Along with that came the loading bridge. One would get up to the second floor, go out to the satellite, and there would be a loading bridge that let you board the plane under cover. The baggage was brought out at the lower level. So all the mechanics of baggage handling were at the lower level, while the passengers were all on the upper level. All of these things were happening at that moment in time.

> **When Eero died... I went out to the TWA building, and only the concrete was poured. ... We then had to deal with the problem of finishing the building.**

Ringli TWA had only just started to acquire jets but were already trying to see their terminal as the first jet terminal. As I understand, jets were never in the picture up to then? The terminal was not specifically designed for jets?

Roche No. We knew they were coming, but we didn't know what the requirements were. That was public relations.

Ringli Were there any requirements for jets at all?

Roche No, although this vice president had been very much involved in the planning of other airports and offered a lot of guidance and directions. It wasn't the chairman of the company or the president of the company; the task was handed to someone else. So this man could have picked any architect and it could have been any building. Howard Hughes didn't have a desire to build a statement by Eero, so it was really by accident that it got to be so important.

Ringli Did the General Motors Technical Center and other earlier buildings influence TWA in their decision to commission Eero Saarinen?

Roche This person in charge knew about it, but he was pretty much operating by himself.

Ringli If not for jets, were there any requirements regarding the corporate design?

Roche It was Eero's interpretation. We have done many corporate headquarters and worked with the respective chairman or the president. He's the one you meet with, he's the one who decides, he's the one who tells you what his vision for the company is. For TWA there really wasn't that kind of exchange at all.

Ringli Maybe this lack of exchange had to do with the fact that Ralph Damon, the president of TWA at that time, had passed away just around the time when Eero Saarinen got the commission.

Roche The man I remember was a vice president of, probably, construction. The terminal, at that time, that everybody knew was the one in St. Louis, the one [Minoru] Yamasaki did. And you know, when we lived in Birmingham, Michigan, Yamasaki was just down the road. So there was a little competition.

Ringli Eero Saarinen thought the St. Louis shells were not soaring, but very much on the ground.

Roche They were good friends, but they were also competitors. Birmingham was absolutely nowhere culturally, but that has probably changed a lot. We were all kind of desperate living there.

Ringli In 1960 Raymond Loewy designed a new corporate design for the airline. Did that have any influence on your design?

Roche No, no. When Eero died, I happened to be in the TWA building. I had gone to New York for a meeting for CBS, and I got a call telling me that Eero had just died. I went out to the TWA building, and only the concrete was poured. There were no windows. We then had to deal with the problem of finishing the building. Raymond Loewy's company was only involved in the furnishings. I don't think their participation was significant.

Ringli I would like to talk about the design and how it developed. How did you start?

Roche First we had done some programming, and then Eero went to Sydney for the Opera House competition. When he returned, he was very interested in the Norse helmet. The shell at Sydney Opera House is not a vault, it's not a Roman arch, it's a broken arch, which technically you're not supposed to do. He was very interested in that concept, and that influenced TWA.

Ringli There are quite a few stories surrounding the TWA building.

Roche That thing with the grapefruit, that really happened [the story goes that Eero Saarinen got the idea for the shape of the building while eating a grapefruit for breakfast one morning]. If you take a grapefruit and bend it in a certain way, it gives you the two flare-ups. One morning Eero came into the office and did something very unusual, something he almost never did. Normally we would have a program and labor through it for months. But in this case he came in with Plasticine—like sculptors use it. This was very unusual because normally he would work at the drafting board. But now he built this form.

> **Howard Hughes didn't have a desire to build a statement by Eero, so it was really an accident that it got to be so important.**

Ringli That was after he came back from Sydney?

Roche Yes, he actually built a model by himself of the first arches, about this size [indicates size, approx. 6 inch / 15 cm]. It really came from the grapefruit. And then we began building larger models. The next one was about this size [indicates size, approx. 15 inch / 38 cm]. Then we realized that we needed to build at a much bigger scale, because you couldn't draw these forms. There were no computers. It had to be done as a sculpture. So we rented a place down the street above a gas station.

Ringli So that model was huge!

Roche It was very big. TWA really was designed at a larger scale. We had a group of maybe six or seven people working on this during that stage. It kept changing and developing further.

Ringli How did the design evolve?

Roche In Idlewild TWA ended up with the worst site. It was at one of the curves. Everybody thought that was the worst site. But, typical of Eero, he thought it was the best site, because it was in line with the incoming highway. He exploited that axial view, which really contributed to the impression of this symmetrical, focused building with its expression of flight. The grapefruit, Sydney, and all those things all fed into it.

Ringli The form of the building suggests various interpretations. Some people see a bird in flight, some see wings. But according to Eero Saarinen's own statement, this was not intended at all.

Roche That's right. All of that came afterwards; that's all public relations. They were talking about the spirit of flight. Maybe it is a part of it, but I think more of it was imagined than real. But, you know, Aline [Saarinen] may have promoted those kinds of ideas. She was good, she was very good.

Ringli She was kind of the office's PR department?

Roche Yes, she was the PR person.

Ringli What was Pat Burley's role?

Roche Pat Burley came later; she was an assistant. Aline, of course, came from the *New York Times* and had been on radio and television. She had all the connections and could get things published. She knew all the people at the *Times*, the *New Yorker*, at *Time* magazine.

Ringli Did Eero Saarinen want to become famous?

Roche He was human; most people like that idea. But he was not a publicist himself. He was a very, very serious, focused architect in a very pragmatic sort of way. He had this sculptural ability and was a fabulous draftsman. But he was a true architect in the sense of not promoting himself but being responsible. How do you create the absolutely perfect building in this moment of time, which responds to a specific need? That was exactly the way he thought. He never thought of himself "I am a great person." He didn't—like Frank O. Gehry—make a sketch and hand it over to somebody. I am not criticizing Frank, he does a great job, but it wasn't like that with Eero. He was fully, fully responsible. Very serious. He came from that Finnish tradition. The Finns are very serious people.

Everybody thought that was the worst site. But, typical of Eero, he thought it was the best site, because it was in line with the incoming highway.

Ringli It's an interesting comparison you make with Frank O. Gehry. He is one of the contemporary star architects who fly around the globe. Were there people of this sort in Eero Saarinen's times?

Roche No, that didn't exist at all. Design was a very serious religion. People were willing to die for design. It was passion, it was real passion. You almost worshipped the people in the design community—people like Charles Eames. But it was not the idea of promotion or fame or anything. It was separate from all of that. I think it's important to make that distinction.

Ringli It would be interesting to find out when this change happened, because today's architecture has a lot to do with branding. For companies like TWA it's the brand value that counts. It was not like that back then?

Roche No, not at all. Those people would be appalled by what's happening today.

Ringli In Idlewild there was a lot of competition. There was the Pan Am Terminal, the SOM International Arrivals Building. Was this competition between airlines exaggerated by the media?

Roche I would say there was a little bit of that. In the case of the Pan Am Terminal it was not thought of as a branding or a public-relations exercise. It was thought of as a process for handling people and planes, all the technical aspects of it. Don't forget that Mies van der Rohe was the most famous architect in the world at that time and was having this tremendous impact on many aspects of architecture in the United States. Frank Lloyd Wright's influence had come and gone and was coming back again. He was a great self-promoter and maybe the forerunner of some of the star architects today. He was really revered but on a different level. The key guy in the 1950s was really Mies. He was having the most influence. So Eero was, of course, influenced by Mies, but then he began to look at these other directions. He did it in several different projects, for instance in the project for the Concordia [Senior] College which was completely out of the norm. There was a whole series of buildings that were completely out of the norm. Because everybody was beginning to accept the Mies thing, everything had to follow a grid, a rectangle, proportions five and seven, all the classic proportions.

My first memories and reactions, I would say, are a certain level of bewilderment. . . . I didn't actually know how to make sense of what I saw. I felt like a veterinarian who tries to define a unique animal. Is it more like a horse, or maybe a camel? . . . The second reaction was: OK, we are all in this together. We are all kind of trying to do something new.

Interview with Abba Tor
Structural engineer and project leader at Ammann and Whitney for the TWA Terminal

May 4, 2008
48 Cochrane Avenue,
Hastings-on-Hudson, NY

Ringli What is the first thing that comes to your mind when you think of the TWA terminal?

Tor My first memories and reactions, I would say, are a certain level of bewilderment. Because as a structural engineer I like to think in terms of interaction of forces, a logical definition of problems and solutions. I divide architects as far as their cooperation with structural engineers is concerned into three categories: first, the architects who try to understand exactly how best to integrate the structural and mechanical systems with the architecture. Louis Kahn, with whom I worked, wanted to understand and really try to go out of his way to integrate the major components of the project. Saarinen was in the middle. He tried to understand and to integrate up to a point, after which he wanted to express his formal and aesthetic considerations. And there are the others, most of them. Sometimes they come to the structural engineer as if they come to a gas station and ask him to "fill her up with structure." As far as the TWA building is concerned, on my first encounter I didn't know what I was looking at. I mean, the whole thing started with looking at models in Saarinen's office—big models of free-flowing undulating sculptural shapes. I didn't actually know how to make sense of what I saw. I felt like a veterinarian who tries to define a unique animal. Is it more like a horse, or maybe a camel? How am I going to treat it? It's not a shell, it's not an arch. And don't forget, we're talking about the pre-computer age. So you couldn't model it using a computer. You had to model it in your head somehow. The first reaction was that of a certain bewilderment. The second reaction was: OK, we are all in this together. We are all kind of trying to do something new. I was new at Ammann and Whitney, and I got this project because I managed to successfully complete a smaller bewildering project before. You know, fear of failure is a great motivator.

Ringli You didn't have a computer? Some sources mention one.

Tor There was one computer in use, but not by us. It was used by the contractor during the design of the formwork. The geometry of the formwork was checked by a computer to make sure that all the transitions were smooth and there were no negative curvatures. This was a relatively simple computer application. But we did not have sufficient computer tools and skills for this complex structure.

Ringli Tell me about the design process.

Tor Sometimes architects—excuse me—take structural courses seriously. But many of them treat it as a chore. For example in the case of TWA, these ridges [on the roof top, on the axis of symmetry of each vault] were a structural impediment. I argued for a smoothly transitioned continuity so that one could apply shell design theories and rely on membrane action. But Saarinen wanted these.

Ringli He wanted the ridges as sharp lines?

Tor Yes. I asked him, "Why? Do you want to see them looking up from the floor?" He said, "No, I don't need them inside." Because he had this acoustical insulation [a mixture of asbestos and mineral wool] sprayed on. He further explained, "When the plane descends, I want

The structure was really more of a sculpture. Not structure follows function, it was structure follows form.

the passengers to see those lines." I thought to myself, when I am about to land I don't look at lines, I look at my papers, passport, this, that. That is kind of an architectural way of thinking. I said, "Fine, it's gonna cost four more inches [10 cm] of concrete throughout the area, just because this discontinuity creates additional stresses." When you have a smoothly transitioned dome or an arch, usually the membrane stresses are within the thickness. But in a situation like this, there are local bending moments because of the abrupt change in shape. And these bending moments became sufficiently grave to add both concrete and steel. The

There was a kind of—I would say—tension between the architect and the engineer.

structure was really more of a sculpture. Not structure follows function, it was structure follows form. When I gave this talk in San Francisco [at the World Conference on Shell Structures, October 1–4, 1962], my old professor, Mario Salvadori, who was a consultant to Ammann and Whitney and introduced me to them, said to me, "A 15-inches-thick shell!" Not a thin shell, a thick shell!

Ringli Are there other examples for Saarinen's "sculptural" approach?

Tor The edge beams were in most instances larger than needed. I said: "I don't need such beams." He reminded me that Ammann and Whitney also did the Kresge Auditorium at MIT: "You guys complained you didn't have enough edge beams there, so I give them to you here." Sometimes, however, I had to stand my ground. For example, originally Saarinen's office wanted all of this to be one big roof. 55,000 square feet [5100 m^2], that's about one and a third acres, uninterrupted by any joints. At that stage it was nicknamed "the flying brassiere." I insisted, "You cannot do that without joints." Sometimes the architect doesn't trust the engineer. He thinks the engineer is too conservative, not daring enough, and starts bargaining. At one point I got a little upset about it and told Mr. Dinkeloo, who was the partner in charge of the technical aspects of the building, "John [Dinkeloo], concrete is dumb. It doesn't know for whom it is being poured. Even if it's poured for you, it cracks. It doesn't respect names." So that's how these skylights between the vaults developed.

Ringli The original idea was not to bring in light and to create lightness?

Tor That was an added benefit. Once they were told that they have to make joints, because the structure cannot be poured all at once, they said let's use this requirement to let some light in. There was a kind of—I would say—tension between the architect and the engineer. But it was a beneficial tension. This also became obvious when we designed the buttresses. The architects had first come up with these eight vertical stilts. It looked more like a cockroach. It didn't express the idea of flight. Very static. After the supports had been reduced to four buttresses, we talked about how best to contain the horizontal forces "kicking out." So it made sense to slope the buttresses to follow the line of the reaction of the horizontal kicks. Here again, Saarinen wanted a very specific look, a thin waist.

Ringli In order to achieve this "slimming down," you had to push the building code, which was a cause of concern for the Port of New York Authority. You mentioned this in your presentation at the National Building Museum [in Washington, D.C., Dec. 16, 2007].

Tor We had to prove to them logically that even though it's not within the code, it's still OK—because the code does allow exceptions if they can be justified.

Ringli Why did you have to convince the Port Authority and not the engineering authorities in the first place?

Tor In short: because the Port Authority is in charge of all buildings at Idlewild, now JFK, their engineers had to approve. Normally they didn't go very deep. They would just have a discussion with the structural engineer about this and that. However, for TWA it was different because in the adjacent Pan Am Terminal, now it's Delta, some of the steel bearings had cracked. So the Port Authority got nervous when they saw the TWA design. But it was too late to turn around, the building was already in the construction stage. They accepted my solution. However, we had to put in wires, attach them to the reinforcing steel and have leads come out. After the forms came down, they had this professor from NYU [New York University] come out with a black box. He attached some kind of instrument to check the stress in the reinforcing bars, ensuring it was not overstressed. The Port Authority would call me up every day and give me the readings.

Ringli The four Y-shaped buttresses carry the entire weight of the roof, approximately 6000 tons, and a lot of concrete was used for them. Did that influence the pouring?

Tor When they poured the buttresses they did it in sections going

The Port Authority got nervous when they saw the TWA design. But it was too late to turn around.

up. They had to stop the pouring at one point before they went further. I insisted that the stops would be zigzag rather than a straight line. Mr. Dinkeloo didn't like the idea and said there would be a visible joint. "Abba," he said, "if you don't do it straight the way he [Eero Saarinen] wants it, he'll have your head on his platter." I told him, "My head will not do him any good on the platter. My head has to stay on my shoulders, not on his platter." This is another example for the kind of tensions we had in this project, because we didn't quite know exactly what we were doing. We assumed a certain behavior. But "is it a horse, is it a camel, maybe something in between"—I didn't know.

Ringli After the pouring, the next big thing was to take all the support scaffolding down.

Tor When we took down the scaffolding and the formwork and released the whole roof, we had a sequence to follow in terms of where to start so that no unanticipated stresses would develop during the removal. We wanted to be very careful, do it very gradually and have it observed—also because the Port Authority was concerned after the cracks in the Pan Am Terminal. Pieces of steel were embedded in the roof concrete to serve as benchmarks for a survey of elevations to see how much the structure deflects. The initial plan was to start the decentering on the first day of a long holiday weekend. So I said, "We need a crew of surveyors checking the elevations of the points over a two-week period, just to see how it moves daily." The contractor said he could not do it. Due to the labor union rule, he was not allowed to put people on overtime during the holiday weekend. And they had already started taking down the scaffolding! "In that case, bring it back up," I said. They didn't love me for it. But they had to do it, because I wouldn't take the responsibility. I was concerned that at some point the deflections would be over and above what we expected. I didn't

We were not sure, because we had never done anything like this before.

even think about what I would have done, especially because the window mullions were already fabricated. We had to have enough sliding capability in the mullions. We were not sure, because we had never done anything like this before. If you do something new you never know. And the feeling here was a little "huiii" [makes a sound to express the uncertainty]. If we had had computer modeling, we could have tested the behavior of the structure. Here the design was based on certain assumptions.

Ringli What assumptions?

Tor We started from the first principles of structural equilibrium, i. e., each element has to be in equilibrium with the adjacent ones. We "sliced" the vaults transversely into approximately three-foot-wide [91 cm] slices—like you slice a salami. In all of those pieces the sum of the horizontal forces, of the vertical forces, and of the moments has to be zero. These are the basic three equations of equilibrium. So you have many equations of equilibrium at the joints, at the imaginary slicing planes. I had a couple of young Indian engineers who filled three thick ring binders with the calculations. We assumed that the structure works as a cantilevered curved beam along the lines of the ridges. In the transverse direction we assumed that those slices work as arches kicking out on the edge beams. We assumed that these kicks can be evaluated based on the equilibrium of this two-foot-deep [61 cm] piece of arch, and those kicks act as forces on these edge beams, which in turn act as inclined arches. How are they kept in place? Because along the spine—if you take the three-foot slice— you have forces acting along the ridges both in the longitudinal and transverse directions. These forces are keeping the arch from falling down. On the one hand, you have forces that push out from the slice as a reaction on this inclined arch. On the other hand, they are being held back. So that's how we worked it out. It's explained in detail in the proceedings of the 1962 World Conference on Shell Structures in San Francisco where I presented the structural design. The element I spent a lot of time and thought on was the design of that hub at the center where the four vaults meet. That was a critical point where we had to make sure that all the forces are in equilibrium and can be transferred smoothly. In case of any local failure each vault would be unstable on its own; the two side vaults would collapse inward, the other two out. We spent a lot of effort and time to make sure that the reinforcement not only fit its need but also that the concrete could be poured and properly vibrated. If you don't have enough space between the bars, it won't work.

Ringli Idlewild was once a marshy tract of land. Did this influence the foundations?

Tor All foundations are on piles. Some of the piles were vertical, but a large percentage of the piles were inclined to take the horizontal kicks into the foundations. And in addition to that the footings, the pile

The concrete is extremely well-controlled until this very day. If you go down you won't see a crack.

caps, were tied together so that the forces would be equalized. In the end it all worked out. Once we had the readings of the deflections [ninety days vertical displacement between 0.0 and 2.0 inch / 0.0 and 5.1 cm], they were within a quarter inch [6 mm] of the assumed values.

Ringli I would like to pick your brain about the PR part of my work.

Tor All I can tell you is that right after this terminal was opened to the public, TWA immediately started renting it out for advertising. They used it quite often as a background for advertising products. Also I remember someone at TWA named Don Keogh [probably a manager of facilities construction] telling me that the ridership of TWA went up significantly in the first two years after the terminal was built. However, some years later they realized that the building did not keep up with the growth in traffic. Originally they just built one bridge and one satellite—the building was limping on one leg. By the time they built the other satellite, they didn't build it according to the original plan—they made it much bigger.

Ringli Why wasn't the second satellite built in the initial project?

Tor See, TWA put up a big sign, "A 12.5-million-dollar terminal is going to be built here." Then the bills started coming in. When they reached the 12.5 million, maybe they decided to do it in stages because of costs. There were additional costs because of the fact that the architect wanted those ridges that I explained to you. The other cost item was the non-reusability of the formwork for the roof. The cost of that roof was about 15 dollars per square foot [0.1 m^2]. Half of it went into the forms. So, the fact that they insisted on certain things like not having joints forced us to do night pours. We did a thirty-hour continuous pour on the side shell. Working under night conditions cost extra money, because people had to work overtime. It was very impressive working at night with all those lights. They poured the concrete in the middle of the night. The concrete is extremely well-controlled until this very day. If you go down you won't see a crack.

Sometimes I would get a little frustrated, because most of the designers were young architects. They didn't have experience.

Ringli Eero Saarinen had mock-ups built for some other buildings. Did you consider building one for TWA?

Tor They just made a mock-up for the formwork to make sure that it works. Just partially, to get the sense of the concrete not sliding down during the pour on sharply curved surfaces.

Ringli How was the project team organized?

Tor Saarinen had a very specific way of handling projects. Kevin Roche was involved in the design; John Dinkeloo was involved in everything that had to do with the construction. Sometimes I would get a little frustrated, because most of the designers were young architects. They didn't have experience. So I talked to Eero Saarinen. Why don't you hire more experienced people so that they won't go off in a direction where you only have to pull them back? His answer was, "I don't want to clip their imagination." However, some of the people on the design team had previously been on the team that did the working drawings so that they could talk to the others. Other firms didn't have that kind of defined separation.

Ringli How was the project team at Ammann and Whitney organized? How many people were involved?

Tor I would say six or seven people. Maybe three or four engineers and two or three draftsmen. Boyd Anderson, an inspired and inspiring engineer and mentor, was the partner in charge of the Special Structures Division. Within this unit I had my "boutique" and reported directly to Boyd Anderson. At that time Mr. [Othmar] Ammann was still active. The second deck of the George Washington Bridge, anticipated in his original plans of the 1920s, and the Verrazano [Narrows] Bridge were on his desk. He was in charge of his Bridges Division and not concerned with the TWA Terminal.

You know, did Bilbao know that they wanted all this stuff? The Guggenheim constitutes this great image and really put Bilbao on the map for a lot of tourists. This is actually the same story. ... Today, people would hire Frank O. Gehry because of the excitement of that, because of the publicity, because... it's the thing to do. You're collecting architects. Sure, it really has a lot to do with publicity.

Interview with Kevin Roche
Former Associate at ES&A

May 5, 2008
Kevin Roche John Dinkeloo and Associates
20 Davis Street, Hamden, CT

Ringli Yesterday I had the opportunity to talk to Abba Tor, the project manager at Ammann and Whitney.

Roche Boyd Anderson was the chief engineer and Tor worked under him. Boyd Anderson was the key figure. Tor was the one who did the calculations. Boyd Anderson was a brilliant engineer. He was very encouraging, the perfect kind of engineer to work with, because he never said no.

Ringli Which was important . . .

Roche On the subject of identity and TWA and all of that: you know, I think the corporate identity was not an intention in the beginning. TWA had a strong identity with the letters, and of course they had a crazy owner at the time, Howard Hughes. He was never involved in this project, as I think I told you before.

Ringli Yes, you mentioned that you mainly dealt with one person . . .

Roche . . . I cannot remember this person.

Ringli Yesterday Abba Tor mentioned the name Don Keogh. Does that ring a bell?

Roche No. But you know, TWA was a very large corporation at the time. They were sort of the cutting-edge airline at that time. They initiated many things in terms of service, attitude, and all of that. But I think the TWA Terminal was really low on the corporate vision. They didn't go and say: here we'll make a big statement. All of that came from Eero. All of the buildings at Idlewild under the master plan of Harrison and Abramovitz were supposed to be low-key buildings, and the central building, which was the International Arrivals Building, was supposed to be the main feature. So the idea that each airline would make a big statement didn't exist. According to Harrison's master plan the central building was important. The other buildings were two-story-high buildings. Pan Am broke the mould with their oval-shaped building.

Ringli That was the first one after the International Arrivals Building.

Roche That's right, and that sort of broke the mould of the master plan. As I think I explained to you before, Eero saw the opportunity to exploit the potential of the site with a symmetrical building. The site for TWA was one of the worst sites from an airline operations point of view. I don't quite know why they ended up with that site. I think they might have been late getting there or something.

Ringli One reason was because TWA had an international and a domestic service. So they needed to be next to the International Arrivals Building where customs was located.

Roche So, it was not considered a very good site because of the curve. The idea back then was that you had a building with fingers. This was before the loading bridge was developed. It was being developed, but it hadn't been used. That was one development that was not quite there yet. The other was the idea of the satellite, where you have a building here [sketches] and you have a satellite, and then you have the loading bridges around it, which would facilitate the maneuvering of the jets. The first step was a building like that, and then the plane was pulled in like that [draws one long rectangular building and planes standing next to each other along the building]. And that was 200 feet [61 m] for each one. Then they led the bridge out. So you could get more 200-foot sections. That was the second phase. The third phase was to create a satellite around which you could group six planes. And so, with that in mind, when you look at TWA's site it doesn't lend itself to the usual planning at that time.

Ringli Because it was in a curve of the Idlewild loop . . .

Roche . . . it was not regarded as an ideal site. Eero looked at the site and then realized that there was an opportunity. He had come back from Sydney, had been impressed by [Jørn] Utzon's forms. And he started off with the . . . You know the old grapefruit story—which is actually true.

Ringli Yes, you told me last time we met.

Roche But I think how the story really goes is that he was explaining it to his wife at breakfast. He had the idea, and he was explaining it to his wife. It wasn't that he turned the grapefruit over and then he had the idea. It was a way of explaining to Aline [Saarinen] what he was proposing to do. At the office he went back to a very old working method—certainly in this country and of course also in the Beaux-Arts system. He got some clay and built this flared-up form at his desk.

Ringli Was this typical?

Roche No, very unusual. He had never done this before. He had done it at school but not in the office up to that point. Because in fact, the buildings up to then were all rectangles. There was no reason to use clay. There was no form.

Ringli Not even for the hockey rink?

Roche Not for the hockey rink [David S. Ingalls Hockey Rink, 1958] either. That was influenced by the cattle sheds in North Carolina. And the arch was really influenced by . . . I wouldn't say the arch was influenced by [Jørn] Utzon, but maybe . . . To get back to your initial question: the fact that what he did became a major symbol for TWA and gave them a tremendous amount of publicity was an accident. They didn't ask for it. They got it, and, of course, naturally they embraced it fully.

Ringli Was that true for other projects as well—Eero Saarinen coming up with a design the client didn't expect but gladly exploited for their PR?

Roche It was true for the rink, and it was true for Concordia. Nobody seems to think about it, because it seems so retro. It's actually true for all of his projects, and it's true for any architect . . .

Ringli True for any architect . . . ?

Roche Like [Daniel] Libeskind or [Frank O.] Gehry or . . .

Ringli . . . Nowadays.

Roche Nowadays, yes, yes. But then not so much.

Ringli Can you explain the difference between now and then, between architects like Libeskind or Gehry and Mies van der Rohe or Harrison and Abramovitz?

Roche Well, Mies, of course, was the architect of the moment in the late 1940s and 1950s. He was trying to create a universal architecture—much like classical architecture, so that the forms, the detailed forms, the planning criteria, and all of the aspects of architecture would be predetermined as they were in classical architecture. In classical architecture there were certain kinds of axial arrangements, there was a choice of columns, there were certain proportions that you followed, corners, domes, central areas, arches . . . There was a vocabulary. And Mies was, I think, establishing a vocabulary of modern architecture, modern industrial architecture as opposed to [Alvar] Aalto and Le Corbusier. They were not trying to establish a universal architecture. They were expressing themselves more as artists. But Mies was establishing a universal language so that everybody could follow it. You had these dicta that you shouldn't do this, you shouldn't do that. Just as in classical architecture. So, it was entirely different from today. And that meant if you hired an architect who had been trained in the Mies system, you could pretty much predict what kind of a building you were going to get. It was certainly going to be a flat roof; it was certainly going to be exposed steel with details on the corners and all those kinds of things. So, what Eero was doing was really quite unique—not establishing a universal language, but saying that each problem had a possible artistic, sculptural, technical, or humanistic answer.

TWA had a strong identity with the letters, and of course they had a crazy owner at the time, Howard Hughes.

Ringli Do you think this was something the clients were looking for? Do you think this was a reason why they commissioned Eero Saarinen?

Roche In general, clients don't know what they are looking for. They don't. I mean they are not in the profession. What they do know is that an architect has done some buildings, has a certain reputation. Can he stay inside the budget? Can he deal with the program? Does it fall down? Does it leak? There are those criteria, very pragmatic criteria, very important, but very pragmatic criteria, which are usually taken into consideration. Is it somebody I know? Is it somebody someone mentioned in the club? It's a referential kind of world. IBM came to Eero because of Eliot Noyes. Eliot Noyes was the design guidance counselor, and he recommended Eero, but they didn't really know what they were going to get. They had some specifics, a certain area, certain distances from the windows—those kinds of things. TWA had its own specifics. You had to accommodate a jet. But they didn't really know. They didn't say, "We want a bird in flight, we want you to give us . . ." That was all contributed by Eero. You know, did Bilbao know that they wanted all this stuff? The Guggenheim constitutes this great image and put Bilbao on the map for a lot of tourists. This is actually the same story.

Ringli Do you think it is the same today as in those days?

Roche I think it . . . Eero unfortunately didn't live long enough. Today people would hire Frank O. Gehry because of the excitement, because of the publicity, because . . . it's the thing to do. You're collecting architects. Sure, it really has a lot to do with publicity. But more so today. Yet, TWA was fairly unique in those days. See, [Wallace] Harrison was not a great designer. I say that with some reservations, because I think Wally Harrison tried very hard. Max Abramovitz was a very good designer, he won the Rome Prize. But the typical architects like Emery Roth in New York or Albert Kahn in Detroit, or the people who preceded Mies in Chicago were kind of workaday architects who did a credible job, I would say. John Russell Pope and all those classical architects, of course, were very skilled at a particular vocabulary. Once that began to fall out of favor for a lot of reasons, all of which you know, the architects who picked up the modern style didn't quite know what they were doing. They had no guides. Frank Lloyd Wright certainly knew what he was doing and certainly had a principal philosophy for the whole thing. Mies was trying to establish the guide for that universal architecture. But artists like Aalto and Le Corbusier and [Sven] Markelius and all these people were working on their own in an environment where there wasn't much else going on. You know, they were singular. Nowadays, there are so many architects worldwide who are doing unusual, exciting, and very good work. But there is still a large body of architects who are just doing the everyday kind of work. But now we've gotten off the track of TWA. So just to restate: it was a unique moment in time, it was a unique solution to a difficult site, and it provided a whole series of benefits for the ownership, which they really had not anticipated.

Ringli I would like to talk about the form of TWA. It was designed to express a movement.

Roche You know, if you think of a sculptor, he has ideas, but these ideas are in terms of form. They are not in terms of words. The words always come afterwards. And the words belong to the literary world. The forms belong to the sculptural world and the architectural world as well. A sculptor couldn't make an argument saying "now we have to do this, then we have to do that." A sculptor is thinking in terms of form, which maybe contains some image or some idea of flight, or happens to be a bird or similar. You know, these are all ephemeral things. A creative mind doesn't say, "Oh, I'm going to design it like a bird!" It doesn't start like that. That is the literary explanation afterwards. You always have to separate the writer from the sculptor. Eero had the concept of a form which happened to fit with this arrangement. The form comes out of your artistic aim, and then the arguments are made afterwards. And sometimes the form is suggested subsequently to accommodate the arguments. The initial form idea is one that comes from the self.

A creative mind doesn't say, "Oh, I'm going to design it like a bird!" It doesn't start like that. That is the literary explanation afterwards.

Ringli How did TWA react when they first saw Eero Saarinen's design?

Roche I wish I could remember this vice president, because he was very positive. Very positive. The actual form developed in detail over quite some time with the big models and all of that. He was a very good client. He was very good. And, as I said, my feeling is that this never went back to Howard Hughes until it was all pretty much done. He was preoccupied. This was very small, you know. Very small. It wasn't a big deal from Howard Hughes' point of view.

Ringli Most people primarily see the shape of the building, but the functional aspects were equally important. It was not just a form statement.

Roche That was Eero's particular characteristic. Not only did he have the sculptural sense but also a very scientific and pragmatic approach to technical problems, to operating problems and all of those things. Well, you know the story about the stopwatch. How long will it take to get there? How do you get to the bathroom? Where do you get information? Where do you get a cup of coffee? How long does it take to get out to the satellites? Should there be a restroom if that takes too long? Should there be a coffee shop? Where are the bathroom windows? Where's the place to sit, and how many seats should you have? You know, all of those things. Because in that moment of time there was no precedent. There was really no precedent. Because the jet hadn't arrived yet. The jet came up just about the time the building was finished. The jets were just beginning to come into being. And they constituted an entirely different passenger-handling problem. Both in terms of size and in terms of the . . . With the earlier planes you got off and you walked across the runway. With the jets you were up in the air. So the second level was becoming a reality in terms of passenger operations. When we started the project for Dulles, we knew that one would arrive on the airport level to depart, and upon arrival one would leave for the city on a lower level. Departure was on the upper level, and arrival was on the lower level. So that was another aspect of general terminal design which was beginning to evolve. Because up to that point, the original buildings were just on one level. You went in, you showed your ticket, you walked out, and got on the plane.

Ringli But the TWA terminal already accommodates this two-level concept with the elevated tubes leading to the satellites.

Roche Well, TWA precedes it, and of course it was part of the problem, because the master plan didn't say anything about the two-level requirement, because jets hadn't arrived yet. So the international terminal was on one level, the other departure on one level. But then, when the jets came, one had to get up to the second level. One had to get up stairs to that second level to get onto the plane. It was a transitional thing. When the design started, the jets weren't there and these fingers—the departure lounges—weren't really established. The first one—I think I told you—was in San Francisco. That was United Airlines. We went down and looked at that. But if another architect had designed TWA, he would have done a one-story building. And then reality would have struck at some point when the building was finished, and they would have realized that they had to go up to the second level. But up to that point there would have just been a one-story building—as was tradition.

Ringli The two levels came from the San Francisco terminal?

Roche From the idea of the jet, the increased volume of traffic, the separation of ticketing and baggage, the problem of the loading finger or the departure satellite. This was all happening at the same time. In a period of about three or four or five years all of these things just kicked in. O'Hare Airport was the first one to install the loading bridge. I went out to O'Hare to look at it, and there was just one loading bridge. There were three gate positions at O'Hare at the time. And they had decided to go up on the second floor. So they were one of the very first ones to use the second level. All of these things were just evolving simultaneously. And they were impacted by, first of all, the jet, second, the size of the jet, as well as the number of passengers, which was a substantial increase in size and passenger count from the early propeller-driven planes. In 1948 I flew from Dublin to New York. We had to fly to Gander and then to Boston and then to New York. And it was all one level. That was fourteen flight hours. Only ten years later there was this tremendous change. There wasn't a precedent. Everything was evolving. There wasn't any technical precedent that we could have followed.

Ringli Some Saarinen researchers see TWA in a line starting with the MIT auditorium, continuing with the Yale Hockey Rink, and ending with the terminal. What connection is there between these designs?

Roche What was happening concurrently was the evolution of the shell. Several engineers had been experimenting with that before the war. And mostly they were single vaults. Actually, there was a Spanish engineer called [Rafael] Guastavino who had developed an interlocking tile, which you could install and pour the concrete on top of it. He used it in the approaches to the 59th Street Bridge [Queensboro Bridge] in New York. So that was one of the very early efforts . . . I can't give you an exact name of a precedent for MIT. That was a thin-shell concrete dome. But of course Eero violated the whole dome principle by cutting it into a triangle. That's why there had to be beams to restrain the pressure of the dome. The engineering of a dome is aimed at getting all of the resulting forces down into a ring. In churches they were tied together by a chain to hold the ring. So MIT violated every engineering principle. The next thing he was interested in was the cable, which came to be used for the rink. The third step, which is

There wasn't any technical precedent that we could have followed.

TWA, was also a violation of every structural principle, because you have these ridges—like on a Nordic helmet. The next problem was getting all of those forces to the ground. When I said it violates the structural principle, I referred to the four shells that are cut apart. So they didn't have the opportunity to counterbalance. An engineer wouldn't have done it that way.

Ringli Abba Tor told me yesterday that he was bewildered when he saw the initial design. So it seems that the aspect of violation is present in many of Eero Saarinen's designs.

Roche I'm using the word violation. Perhaps he [Eero Saarinen] never thought of it that way. He would be very upset. But in fact, that's what it was. He would think of it more as a challenge for the engineer. Because, of course, there were other precedents, like Erich Mendelsohn's Einstein Tower, which of course was never built in concrete but in plaster. The vision of that was very, very strong in the prewar years—that plasticity of Mendelsohn and the idea that you could build almost anything in concrete. As I said, in reality it was done in bricks and plaster. They weren't able to do it in concrete. So I think that kind of form-world opportunity was very much in the architects' minds. Corbu's Ronchamp chapel came later, but he also had these form ideas. So it was very much in the air then.

Ringli One of the main reasons Eero Saarinen faced harsh criticism from his colleagues was because his designs didn't represent one specific style. Sculptural and rectangular design coexisted. I feel that Eero Saarinen's work cannot be seen as a shift from rectangular designs to sculptural designs.

Roche When I was studying with Mies, he designed the IIT [Illinois Institute of Technology] campus—two-story flat-roofed buildings. He designed a chapel, and he designed a drive-in. And they could be interchangeable. They were universal spaces to be occupied by some function. So that is the absolute antithesis of Eero's attitude. To draw an analogy: costumes— in the Arabic world you wrap yourself in a sheet. You know, the inside of the robe can be anything. In the Western world you tailor everything. Everything is sewn and stitched. Everything is sort of . . . In the Arabic world, in the Islamic world you wouldn't do that, you have a simple robe. There is a difference between the two, parallel to that in architecture, where Mies is the sheet. He wraps everything, no matter what is inside. And the other one is custom-tailoring. That's a fairly barbarian analogy, but there you are.

Ringli I feel that the sculptural aspect in Saarinen's work was already there right in the beginning with his furniture . . .

Roche . . . Yes, sure.

Ringli At the end of his career there was the TWA Terminal. Would you say that his "appetite" for sculptural forms grew towards the end of his career?

Roche It's hard to say, because I think he would use it in response to a specific problem. Let me just go back for a second. We talked about MIT and TWA and the rink. But now in Dulles—which we didn't get to—he combines both the cable and the structural forms. So in Dulles we really see the combination of the two things in a much more specific way than in the rink.

Ringli You mean the combination of the shell and the cable?

Roche The extravagant poured form and the cable. So that's something. If you are tracing influences or connections between the two, they pretty much end up together in Dulles.

Ringli Cesar Pelli said that the design process for TWA was rather unsteady compared to other projects and that there were many changes.

Roche I would say there were changes, but there were always changes. I would not say there were any more of them than elsewhere. I would not say that it was unusual. It was in the nature of that kind of project.

Ringli I would like to talk about how the project was organized. Who were the designers involved?

Roche It went through a couple of phases. I worked on it initially. Then we decided we needed to work at a larger scale and we put together a team led by Cesar [Pelli]. Eero and I would come by every day. And then John Dinkeloo and some people started doing the basic drawings. John was actually the one who got into it and watched it every day. He hasn't been credited for that, but he was the one who managed to convince the contractors, who worked with the engineers. It was a very, very tough building to build. John and some other people really did a great job. That it was so successful is to a large extent his achievement.

Ringli That was his role in many projects.

Roche That was his role. He took a special interest in this. It was a lot of back and forth, and there were many people involved. But Eero guided every decision all the way through. It was still under construction on the day he died. As it happened, I was out there. I was on the site. But it was all designed. Eero really had his hands on everything, all the decisions. There's a tendency of some people to say I designed this, I designed that. That's not the way it was. Despite the growing size of his office he was not an administrator. We sat virtually every day; he was drawing, sketching . . . He was working long hours. He would come in at about ten o'clock in the morning and work till about eight o'clock at night. If he started at eight o'clock in the morning, he'd still work till eight in the evening. And he worked Saturday, Sunday, New Year's Day. I remember, one day he was very upset, because somebody hadn't come in that morning. We told him that it was New Year's Day. To which he said, "But he's not here!"

Eero had never really used models before that. Models were for presentation, they weren't for study. I think that is the thing that one remembers the most.

Ringli He had a very close eye on details in general.

Roche He had a very strong sculptural sense. You know, when you look at his career, as a young student he was very interested in sculpture. He might very well have gone into that direction as well.

Ringli His mother was a sculptor.

Roche His wife was a sculptor, too.

Ringli Ezra Stoller took photographs of most Saarinen buildings. On what basis did you choose a photographer?

Roche We hired Ezra Stoller to photograph all the buildings. So we would have a complete, consistent record by one photographer.

Ringli He was considered one of the best photographers of his time.

Roche He was the best. All the top-notch architects used him. There was also [Balthazar] Korab, who worked in the office. He was very interested in photography and started photographing things around the office. He wasn't really hired as a photographer until after he left.

Ringli As a last question, when you think of the TWA Terminal, what are your first thoughts?

Roche That's a very tough question. I suppose it would be the memories of the whole process of the design, from the small models as it graduated, evolved, you know, it was like an elephant being born—this gigantic thing suddenly growing. The whole process was very unusual. In other buildings you didn't need to do that. Eero had never really used models before that. Models were for presentation, they weren't for study. I think that is the thing that one remembers the most. A good deal of excitement about it, you know, because who knew if it was ever going to happen? We were all very young, hoping that something exciting was going to happen. But then again, at one point, things had moved on to other projects. Dulles was even more exciting, because it was a bigger project. So, it moved on from one project to the other. But it was a good time. Imagine! I can imagine the same thing happening in Gehry's office. Young people going there, gradually developed from doing a shopping center, and then suddenly there is Bilbao. I imagine that's pretty exciting. It's kind of similar.

I think the shapes of the TWA Terminal coincide with a futuristic theme and certain images that came to us through comic books. Those soft curves have been used in early comic books like *Flash Gordon* and in movies like *Things to Come*, where people were trying to express the future.

Interview with Cesar Pelli
Former employee at ES&A
and member of the design team
for the TWA Terminal

June 24, 2009
Pelli Clarke Pelli Architects
1056 Chapel Street, New Haven, CT

Ringli I'm trying to find out about the marketing aspects of the TWA Terminal Eero Saarinen and Associates designed for the airline. Do you know how the TWA project started for Eero Saarinen?

Pelli I do not know what TWA had in mind, but what you have to remember is that this was a brand-new airport—at that time it was called Idlewild—where each airline had to build its own terminal. There was very strong competition between the airlines. Each airline had to present its own image. So there was a sense of competition to start with. Also the situation was new, because jet planes didn't quite exist when the planning started. Jet planes were only introduced when we were already designing. Eero Saarinen was on one of the first jet flights and was given a diploma for having been on a 707 jet. The scheme of the TWA Terminal seemed pretty odd to some people, because it had these huge overhangs so that passengers could get out of their cars without getting wet. When TWA was designed, modern air travel was just in its beginnings, and many people were taking guesses about how the terminal should work. Unfortunately for Pan Am, shortly after their terminal was built, jets came into operation and were usually handled on "finger" piers, which rendered the roof of their building obsolete and a bit silly. But that happens to architects: when Saarinen designed the Dulles International Airport at Washington, D.C., he came up with the idea of a mobile lounge based on a certain idea how airports were supposed to function. Today airports don't function this way anymore. Unquestionably, Saarinen took the most sculptural and artistic solution to the problem. Most of the other terminals at Idlewild were very straightforward. American [Airlines], for instance, had a very simple, straightforward building, just with a kind of mural in front. So American wasn't very adventurous. National [Airlines] had a very handsome building, but Saarinen was by far trying the most to turn the building into art. Unquestionably, it was an artistic quest supported by structural design.

Ringli Do you think it was the idea of TWA to come up with a big statement? Or was it Saarinen's interpretation?

Pelli It was Saarinen's statement. I think TWA wanted a handsome building, and they went to Saarinen, but the way it developed was because of Saarinen. You may know the story: Saarinen finished the schematic design and took it to TWA. It had the same vaults, but it was a much simpler building. TWA approved it, but back in the office on the same day Saarinen was having second thoughts. He called TWA and said, "I cannot go ahead with this scheme." It took another year to finish the design for the terminal, which made the TWA people furious. The office didn't get paid for the additional design work and lost a lot of money. At that point I entered the project.

Ringli I have seen the presentation brochure you just mentioned. The structure Saarinen presented to TWA was a flatter version of what was actually built later.

Pelli The difference was that the structure had not yet been completed. The vaults were there all the time, but they rested on thin columns. When the engineers came into action, they concluded that the wind and snow loads asked for tilted columns. Unfortunately, they didn't match with conventional walls—the whole clarity of the scheme was lost. That's when I entered the project. Since the office was growing at that time and was running out of space, I was left alone in a small room at a service station near the office. That's where I designed the columns the way they were eventually built.

Ringli The Y-shaped columns?

Pelli Exactly. They combine the forces into a more sculptural form, which Eero liked. But the problem was: how would those columns look against straight walls? We examined that by making models. First small ones, then bigger ones, and finally the model had the size of this room. It took a great deal of time. But this was not what TWA had in mind, they had been happy with the first scheme.

Ringli Do you remember the year all of this happened?

Pelli I started working on the project in 1957. Before that Leon Yulkowski was responsible for all the more mechanical, functional aspects of the project, but Eero was not entirely happy with how he handled the aesthetic part. So when I came in, I was responsible for that, and Leon remained in charge of the technical issues.

Ringli What kind of technical problems had to be resolved?

Pelli We needed to solve the problem of baggage handling. How does it move? How do the arriving passenger get hold of their baggage? What security measures need to be taken? How do the people get from the taxi stand into the building and get their tickets? How do they proceed to the airplane? Many complex functional problems like these.

Ringli How did you know about these requirements?

Pelli Leon was in touch with somebody at TWA. All the requirements came from them. We initially got a set of requirements, but many questions arose during the design process. And sometimes there are conflicting situations in which you have to know the client's priorities.

The scheme of the TWA Terminal seemed pretty odd to some people, because it had these huge overhangs.

Ringli Who came up with the idea to install conveyor belts for the baggage and passengers, which was a rather unusual thing to do at the time?

Pelli The idea must have come from TWA.

Ringli Why do you think TWA asked Saarinen to do this building?

Pelli At that time there were relatively few firms that had a proven record for large, complex buildings for major companies. Saarinen's firm had just completed the General Motors Technical Center. He was also already designing other large projects. Many of his big projects, like the ones for IBM or Bell Telephone, started around 1955. This was a reassurance for TWA. But Saarinen had done nothing like an airport terminal before. Then again, all the major firms were relatively new and hadn't yet specialized in anything. Even Skidmore, Owings and Merrill had only started before the Second World War, and all of this was happening shortly after the war.

Ringli Apart from the project for General Motors, do you think TWA chose Saarinen for a particular reason?

Pelli I don't know. But the design for TWA was quite unlike anything Saarinen had done. They may have expected something like what he had done for General Motors, something much simpler or in the line of Mies van der Rohe, but Eero rarely repeated himself.

Ringli So I get the feeling it was really Eero Saarinen's interpretation and not TWA's idea to make a big statement.

Pelli No, it wasn't. But I'm sure they must have had some specific request. Have you talked with Kevin Roche about this?

Ringli Yes, I have.

Pelli He followed the project through all its stages. I was not there in the beginning and don't know about the exact requirements TWA had. I was brought in because the design process was stuck.

Ringli What can you tell me about the relation between the formal and the technical aspects of the terminal?

Pelli They were very much one thing, but I would say it was by and large an aesthetic goal that led Saarinen through the process. Not an aesthetic solution, but an aesthetic goal. He had this wonderful partner, John Dinkeloo, who was very good at finding technical answers to problems. You know, we never started with a technical aspect. The technical aspect was the solution to a problem that was usually of an aesthetic nature. But Dinkeloo was very good at finding new solutions or at suggesting things like the neoprene gaskets [that General Motors used for its cars and] that had never been used in a building before. Until then the only thing available was putty. General Motors invented the gaskets, but when Dinkeloo brought up the idea we saw in them a great opportunity for architecture.

Often clients want an image, something that makes for a story about a building—and the "bird" makes for a very good story.

Ringli So Saarinen's approach was primarily aesthetic, and the building technology was defined as a solution for an aesthetic problem?

Pelli Right. Unquestionably, the technical solution affected the aesthetics. In the project for the Morse and Stiles Colleges at Yale University Eero wanted the buildings to blend with the existing structures and their stone walls, but he had very little money at hand. So he put Dinkeloo on the task of finding a technology that would allow building a stone wall for very little money. Once that technology was found, it had aesthetic qualities which Saarinen had to adapt to his buildings. Technology and aesthetics reinforced each other, but in my experience with Saarinen it always started with an aesthetic goal—not necessarily with an aesthetic vision that implies some sense of form before he started the design. Saarinen's aesthetic goal would lead him through the process of how to solve a problem aesthetically.

Ringli What was that goal in the project for TWA?

Pelli Eero wanted an extraordinary building that would express the sense of flight to everybody who saw it. That was the goal. Ammann and Whitney, one of the largest structural engineering firms in the USA at the time, handled the structural part of the building. I think Dinkeloo was involved with how to provide sun shades for the sloping [curtain] wall. But this was a secondary problem that occurred very late in the design process. Apart from that, as far as I remember, there were no particular technical problems.

Ringli Looking at the building, many people see a bird. Saarinen, however, said the fact that the building resembles a bird was entirely coincidental.

Pelli He actually knew that the building looked like a bird. We prepared a small book to show the design to TWA . . .

Ringli . . . yes, I know it.

Pelli [Balthazar] Korab designed a cover full of birds in flight—and Saarinen was happy with it, which means that for him the image was there, at least as an image that he could sell to TWA. Often clients want an image, something that makes for a story about a building—and the "bird" makes for a very good story, although it may not have been there when the project started. According to Eero, he had the initial idea when he was having a grapefruit for breakfast . . . you know the story. I don't know if it's true, but that's the story.

Ringli In a book by Richard Knight [*Saarinen's Quest: A Memoir*, San Francisco, CA: William Stout Publishers, 2008] the story is supported by one of your former colleagues at Saarinen's office, Jimmy Smith . . .

Pelli . . . because it's a good story. That's why Eero told it, but I have no idea if it's true. Today nobody will ever be able to find out if it's true or not. But another thing that comes to my mind is that while we were designing the terminal, Eero went to Australia, to judge the Sydney Opera House competition. Later he told me that he had arrived late and found that the other jurors had already discarded a project he liked very much—it was [Jørn] Utzon's project. Eero was impressed by the shapes Utzon had designed and managed to convince the jury. After he returned from Australia, he added a "crease" to the domes [of the TWA Terminal] so that they would be easier to read. If this was because of Utzon one can only assume. Eero never spoke much, he would rather draw.

Ringli Mr. Roche also said that the design changes you just mentioned came after Sydney. He also said Saarinen compared the vaults to a Norse helmet.

Pelli [Laughs] Yes, the Norse helmet had an influence. Indeed, it helped to clarify the form. It was a good device. Structurally the domes were not the most efficient. They are very thick and not the kind of domes somebody like [Pier Luigi] Nervi would have designed at that time. Eero was not particularly interested in that kind of engineering work. Structurally, Saarinen's domes weren't the most elegant solution,

In general, Eero was guided by an aesthetic goal. There's no doubt about that, and it's probably true for all of his projects.

but they served the aesthetic effect he wanted. Each of the four domes is supported by only two legs; the structure as a whole is stabilized because the domes hook into each other—engineering-wise quite tricky and complex, particularly at a time before computers.

Ringli Mr. Tor, who was the project manager at Ammann and Whitney, confirmed to me that the vaults were very difficult and complex to calculate.

Pelli I can imagine. Because of the shapes of the domes the forces have many different directions—and the concrete and the steel had to support these.

Ringli So the fact that engineering had to support Saarinen's aesthetic requirements is also in a way proof that technology came after the form was established.

Pelli The structure followed the aesthetic form, but if the structural engineer requested something, Eero took it very seriously, unless he could come up with a counter-solution. But in general, Eero was guided by an aesthetic goal. There's no doubt about that, and it's probably true for all of his projects. He had an aesthetic objective in his mind. But after that he was very American, very pragmatic about how to solve the problems and how to get there.

Ringli In the sense that . . . ?

Pelli In the sense that he was not concerned with the purity or simplicity of the structure. He wanted to achieve a certain look, and he would go whichever way to get it.

Ringli Was he PR-minded?

Pelli No, PR was secondary in his firm. You know, other firms spent a great deal on PR. Eero was concerned about his image, his fame, his glory, his position in architecture books.

Ringli He was concerned about that?

Pelli I assume he was. He never said that, but I'm quite sure he was. Actually, most well-known architects have that concern very much. Philip Johnson couldn't think of anything else. But Philip said everything that came to his mind, whereas Eero—as I said before—spoke very little. Very Finnish . . . [chuckles]

Ringli What was Aline Saarinen's role?

Pelli At the beginning Aline Saarinen used to come and make comments on the design. But something happened, there was a clash, and Aline never showed up again during design. By the time we were designing TWA, she almost never showed up, and when she did she was quiet. She must have gone home and told Eero what she was thinking. She indeed organized some of his PR at a very high level. But even all her efforts didn't compare to those of SOM or I. M. Pei. In terms of PR, those firms were much more organized than Eero Saarinen's ever was, even including Aline.

Ringli Was the PR-mindedness of some of the architecture firms a new phenomenon then in your opinion?

Pelli I don't know. That's a very good question. It would be interesting to know how much PR by architecture firms there was before the Second World War . . . I do not know. Very good question. I never thought about it. By the time I became involved in architecture in America in the late 1950s, all firms were doing PR. They may always have needed some person to respond to the requests of the press. Today the role of our PR person [at Pelli Clarke Pelli Architects] includes not just responding to the press but to requests from outside in general, like yours for this interview, but we do very little promotion, like Eero Saarinen. But some firms like SOM were very promotion-minded, and one of their partners, Nat Owings, dedicated himself almost entirely to PR.

Ringli So what did Nat Owings do for PR?

Pelli He dined and played golf with the press and with politicians. Eero Saarinen never did anything like that. Do you know Gene Kohn?

Ringli No, I don't.

Pelli Eugene Kohn of Kohn Pedersen Fox Associates. He's a master of PR. Once we [Pelli Clarke Pelli Architects] were competing with SOM and some other firm for a project for General Reinsurance in Stanford, and Gene Kohn [whose firm had not been invited] introduced himself to the company's president and sold his firm to him. Kohn Pedersen Fox were not among the three in consideration first, but [ultimately] they were selected. There are many stories like that. We have never done that, Saarinen never ever did that. Yet many firms such as SOM had partners that they selected because of their social connections. But this was more PR towards getting new work; being published was secondary for them, because many clients never read what the press writes.

Ringli In the 1950s Saarinen became some kind of a celebrity. He was on the cover of *Time* magazine.

Pelli Yes, he was on the cover of *Time* magazine. But that was because he had done this incredible project for General Motors just after the Second World War, when most architects didn't have work. In terms of technology and look, the General Motors Technical Center was one of the first large-scale modern projects. So for Saarinen this was a major project, but also for General Motors, which was one of the largest corporations at that time. So all of this had a huge effect. That was primarily where his fame came from.

Aline Saarinen used to come and make comments on the design. But something happened, there was a clash, and Aline never showed up again during design.

Ringli Going back to the TWA Terminal, it seems to me that it matched the needs of the client very well.

Pelli Saarinen worked very hard, and he felt responsible for what was needed. Saarinen's buildings normally work extremely well in a functional sense at all levels. The clients got all they needed in terms of image, function, reception, everything.

Ringli The image was always important for Saarinen?

Pelli Yes, the projection of an image was important for Saarinen in all his projects, but the meaning of image varied a great deal among his clients. General Motors wanted to give an impression of cutting-edge technology and to represent an up-to-date company. So what Saarinen gave General Motors suited them perfectly at that time. But this was very different from what he gave TWA or the Lutheran Concordia College, which conveys a very romantic image.

Ringli Why do you think did the TWA Terminal serve the airline's image well?

Pelli Well, two separate reasons. One, Eero had this idea in mind of what an airport should be, and he wanted to express this sense of flight with a building that is barely touching the ground. Two, the plans were developed so that all of the functions TWA required were covered adequately. Unfortunately, air travel was changing so quickly that the terminal could not function anymore the way Eero had foreseen. The rest area didn't have enough space, because there were many more people flying than anyone had projected. And the board with flight information quickly became obsolete, because it was replaced by TV screens.

Ringli The information boards were not in use for long? When were they replaced?

Pelli They were used for about a year or two and then replaced by television screens.

Ringli The oval-shaped boards . . . ?

Pelli Yes, the huge oval-shaped board near the entrance. Like in all airports they were replaced by TV screens, which didn't exist at the time of building. So the whole technology of flying has kept on changing. Eero thought he had learnt his lesson when he did Dulles International, which is quite different from the work he did for TWA. Dulles responds better to certain things. Eero for instance provided for its expansion, and today the terminal has doubled in size, after SOM expanded it [in 1997]. In many respects the changes in technology were impossible to foresee—by anybody. And I guess this will keep on happening.

Ringli When you look at how TWA tried to promote the terminal, for example its technology and mechanization, or the complexity of the building process, would you say that was in contrast to what Saarinen actually intended to express with the building? In other words, was the look of the terminal more important to him than its functionality?

Pelli No, for Saarinen all those functional aspects were extremely important. He would make all necessary changes to ensure the functionality of the terminal. Function was never sacrificed in any of Saarinen's buildings. But there is this peculiar combination of a functionality that is very well resolved and [at the same time] aesthetically driven.

Ringli The building has a futuristic appeal. Where do you think it stems from?

Pelli Well, most architects at that time were looking towards the future. So designing a building with a feeling of what things would be in future was not uncommon during that period. Of course, the interpretations of what this future would be varied greatly. But the TWA Terminal was not supposed to look more futuristic than any other of his buildings. Eero just wanted a very beautiful terminal.

Ringli What do you think it is that makes it look futuristic? The General Motors Technical Center was also depicted as a futuristic building, and yet it looks completely different than the TWA Terminal.

Pelli [Laughs] I think the shapes of the TWA Terminal coincide with a futuristic theme and certain images that came to us through comic books. Those soft curves have been used in early comic books like *Flash Gordon* and in movies like *Things to Come* [1936], where people were trying to express the future.

Ringli I also have a feeling that these images, as an important phenomenon of the Zeitgeist, could have had some influence on Saarinen, but so far nobody has analyzed this in detail.

Pelli Probably, but I have never thought about it. This connection of the shapes of the terminal and futuristic images is a new thought that just came to my mind. But you have a point, these things were very much in the air at that time.

Ringli Did Saarinen ever verbally express such an allusion?

Pelli No, not at all. If somebody had asked Eero, I think he would have dismissed it. If there is indeed such a connection, it was operating subconsciously in Eero's mind. It's absolutely possible; it's a very good point, because the terminal does have some of that futuristic feeling of comics and movies.

The terminal does have some of that futuristic feeling of comics and movies.

Ringli In 1960 TWA got a new corporate design by Raymond Loewy. Did that affect the design of the terminal in any way?

Pelli I don't know; it's a good question. I have no idea, though in 1960 the building was already designed. So Raymond Loewy's firm ... Raymond Loewy wasn't alive anymore then, was he?

Ringli Yes, he was ...

Pelli ... but his fame came from the 1930s. Raymond Loewy's firm was aware of what Saarinen had designed, but I have no idea if he got any instructions from TWA.

Ringli Loewy's firm designed the two restaurants and the bar of the terminal.

Pelli I think so, but I'm not sure. The restaurants were designed when I was no longer in the project.

Ringli So you worked on TWA from 1957 to ... ?

Pelli I was in the project about a year and a half, from early 1957 to late 1958. Then I was put in charge of the Morse and Stiles Colleges. Leon Yulkowski kept on following it. Interestingly, as soon as the contractor got the commission for the TWA Terminal, they hired a young Yugoslavian architect ...

Ringli ... his name was Vladimir Petrovitch.

Pelli I don't remember his name. He was very, very engrossed. He built his own model of the building, because he needed to design the scaffolding, which, at that time, was all wood. He had to figure out how to position the wood panels to achieve that form. So he did a large, very handsome model of the scaffolding.

Drawings

Plan of departure hall, entrance level, no scale, 34 ¾" × 26 ¼" (88.3 × 66.8 cm), ES&A, July 12, 1963

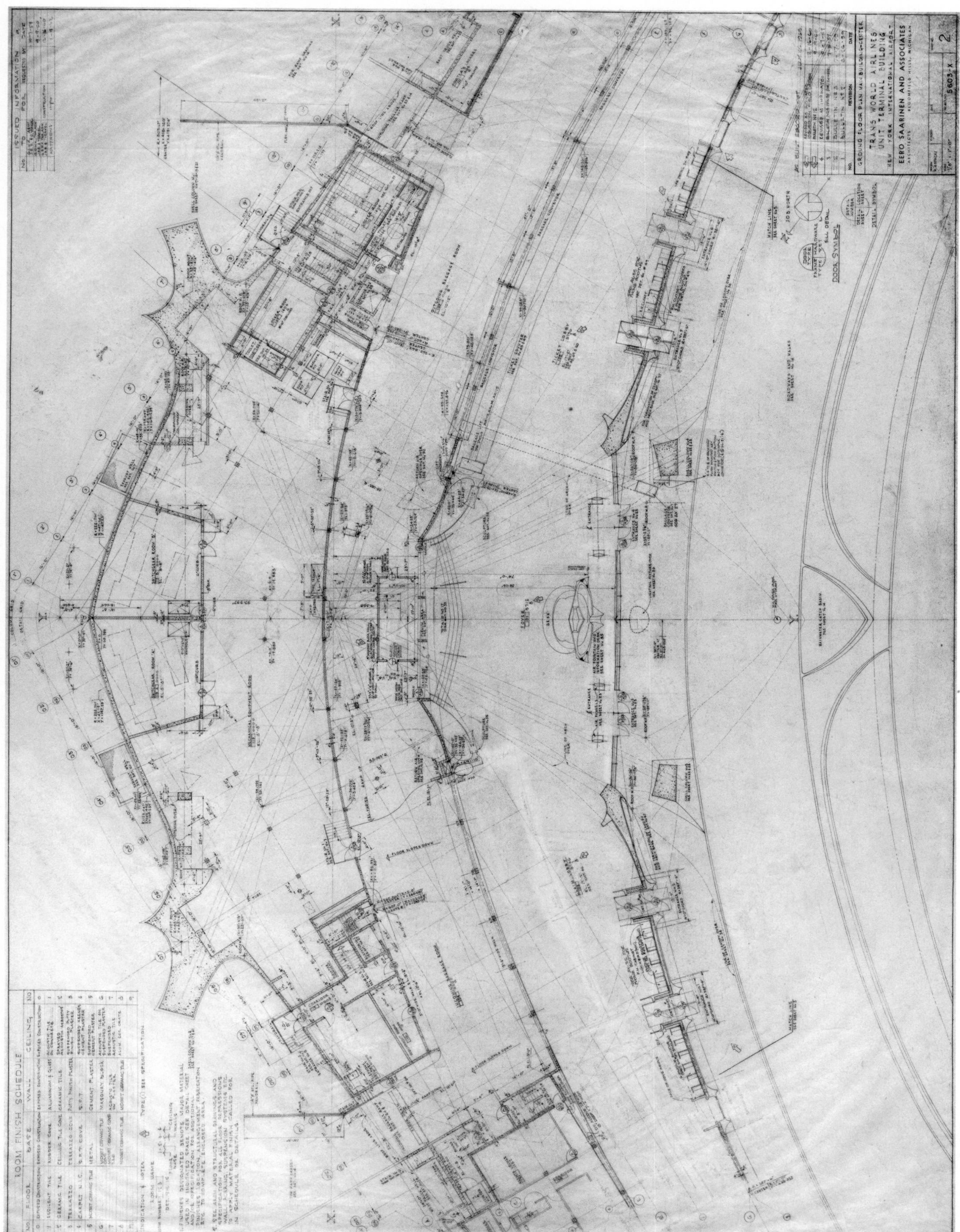

Plan of departure hall, main floor, no scale, 35⅝" × 26¼" (90.5 × 66.8 cm), ES&A, July 12, 1963

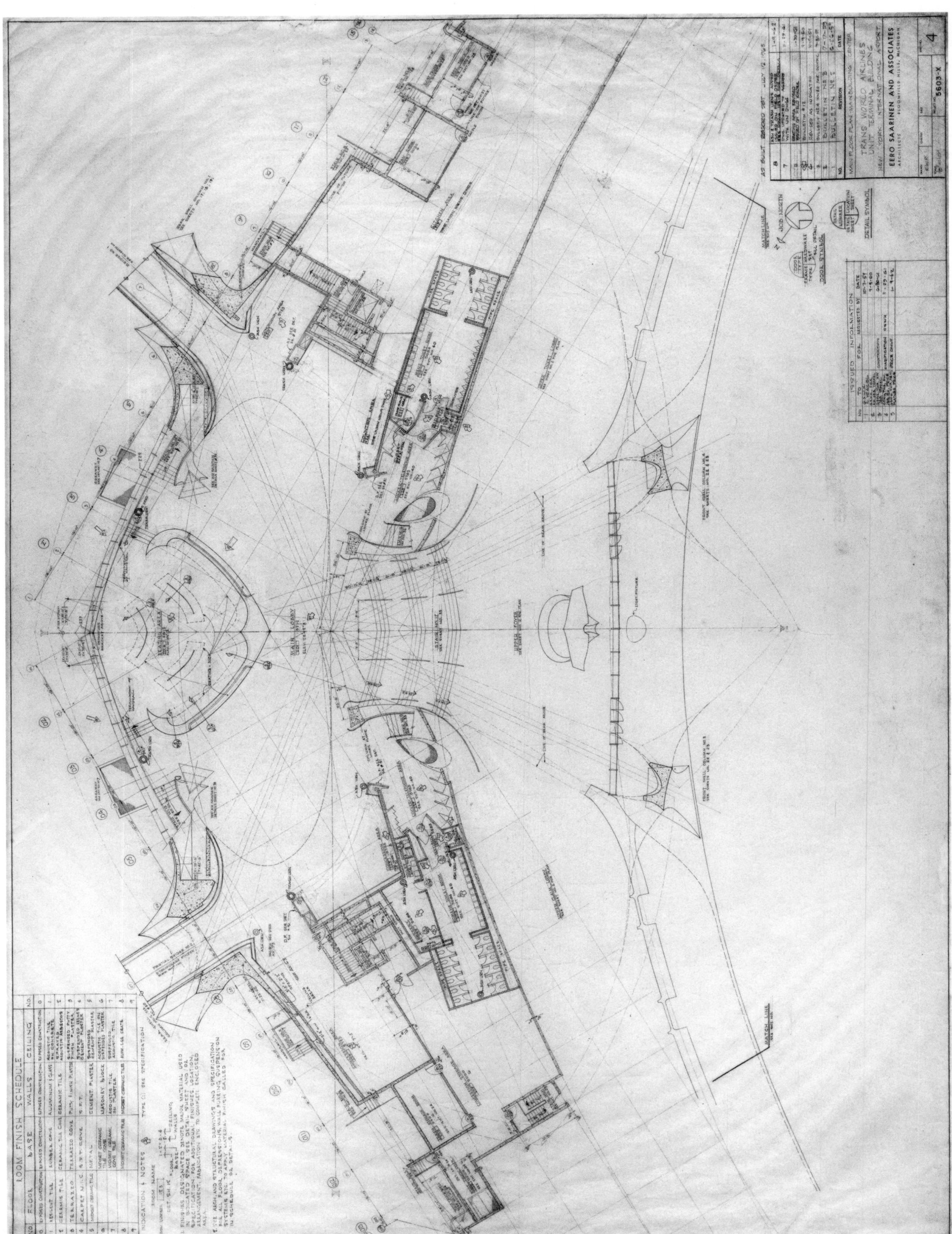

**Plan of departure hall, upper floor,
no scale, 35 5/8" × 26 1/4" (90.5 × 66.8 cm), ES&A, July 12, 1963**

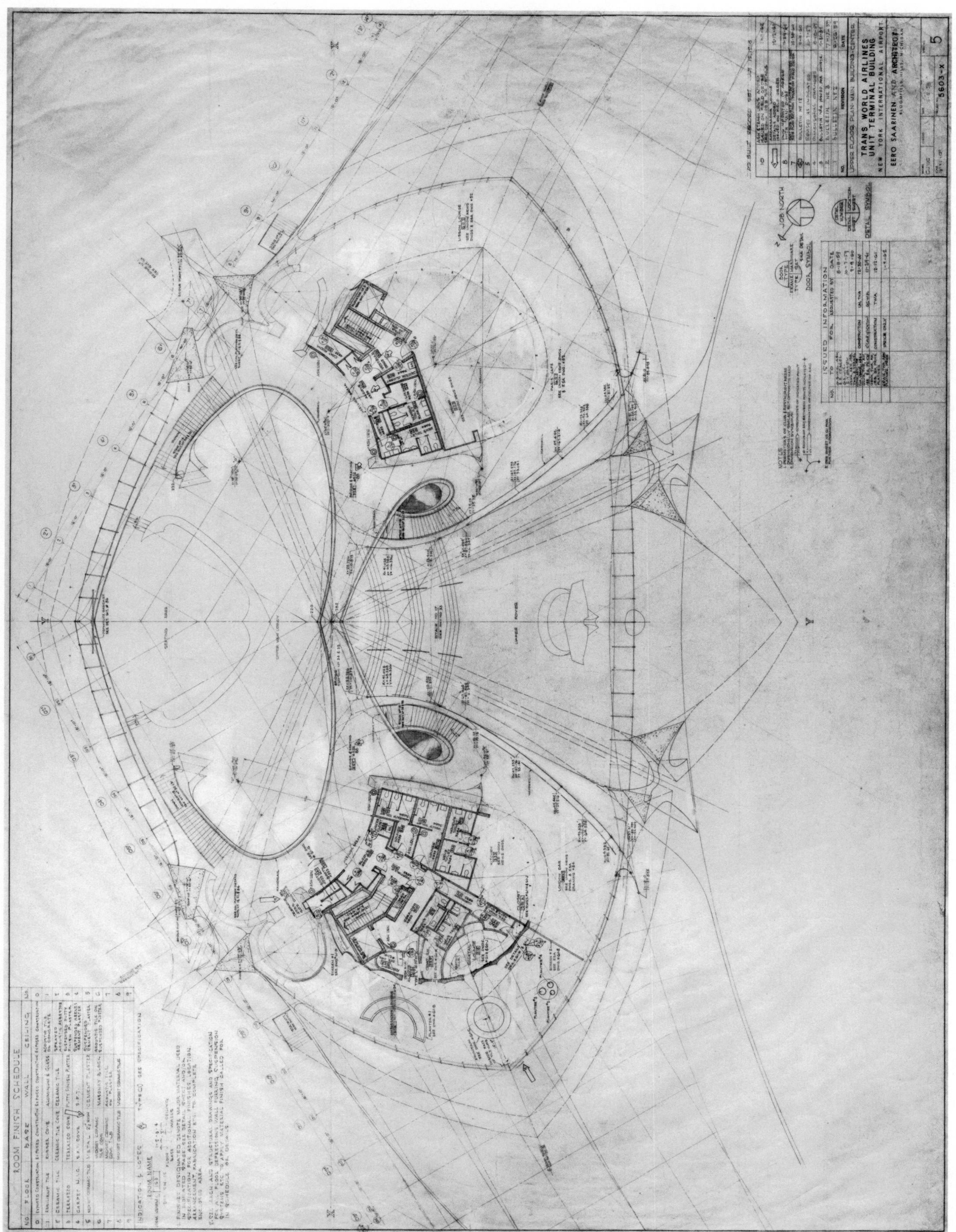

Longitudinal section of departure hall, no scale, 19 5/8" × 14 5/8" (50 × 37.1 cm), ES&A, July 12, 1963

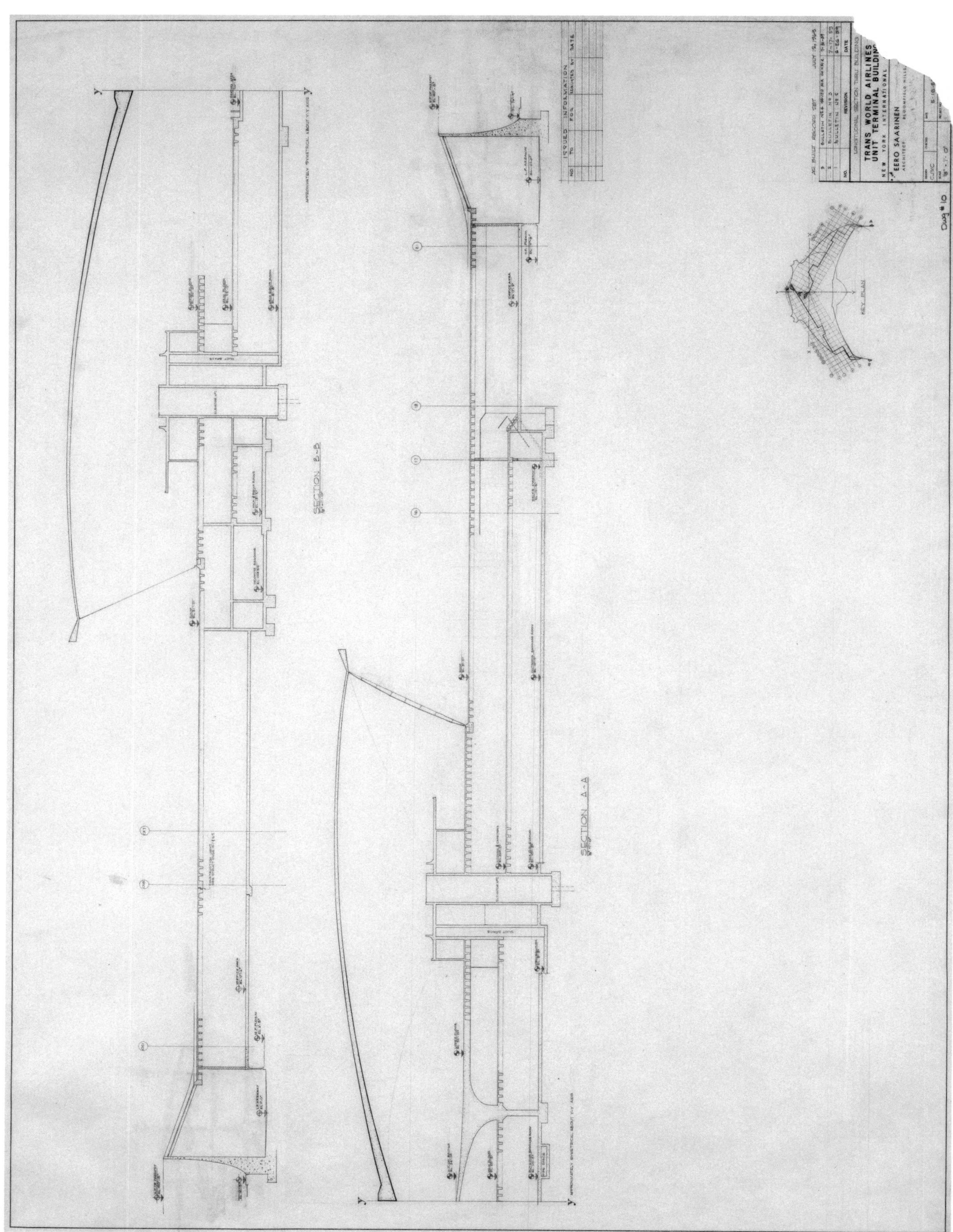

Section and elevation of stair in departure hall, no scale, 11⅛" × 14⅝" (37.9 × 28.3 cm), ES&A, July 12, 1963

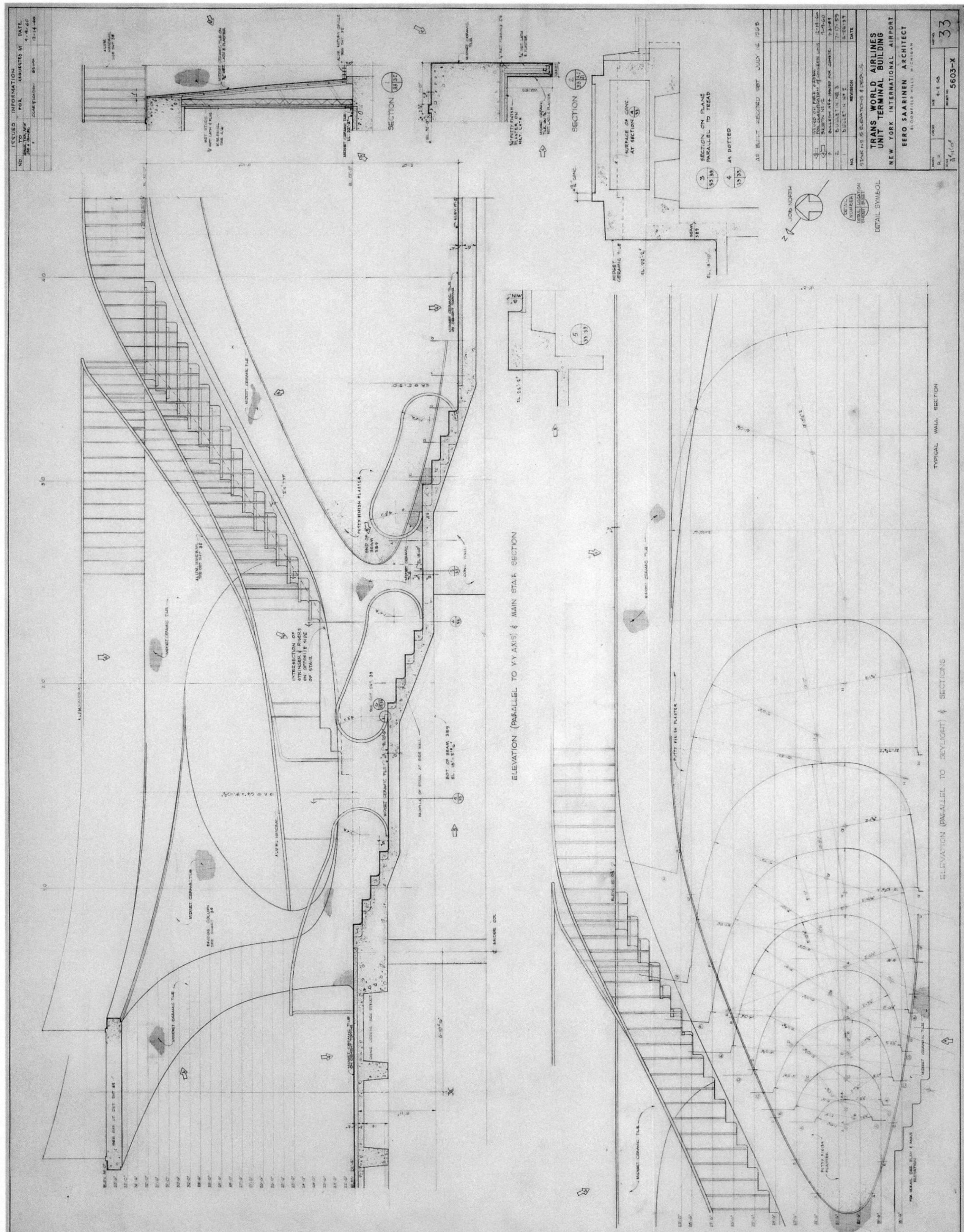

Plan, section, and elevation of information desk with arrivals and departures board, no scale, 35⅝" × 26¼" (90.5 × 66.8 cm), ES&A, July 12, 1963

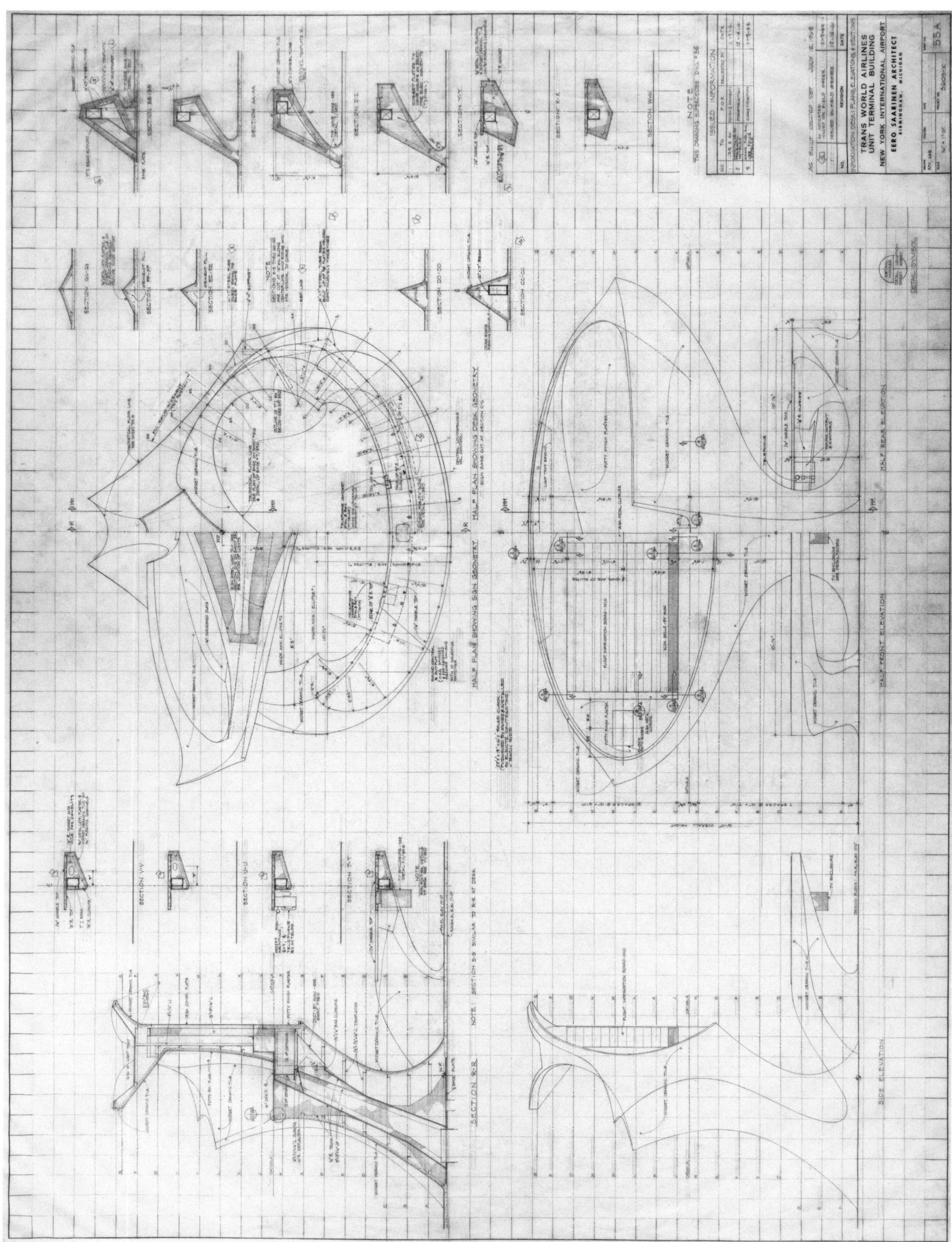

Details of suspended loudspeaker, no scale, 46 3/4" × 34 7/8" (118.7 × 88.6 cm), ES&A, July 12, 1963

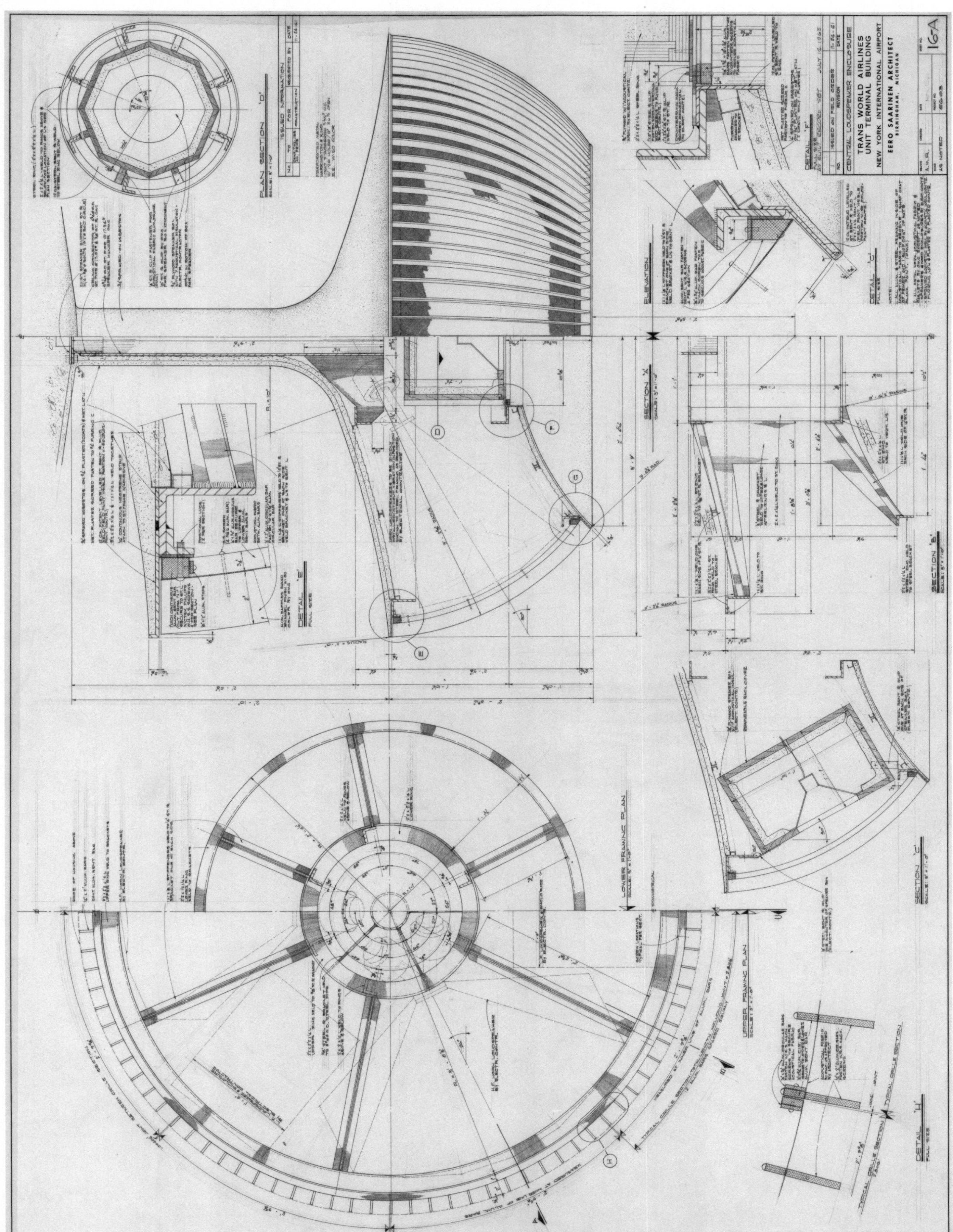

**Building signage,
no scale, dimensions unknown, ES&A, July 12, 1963**

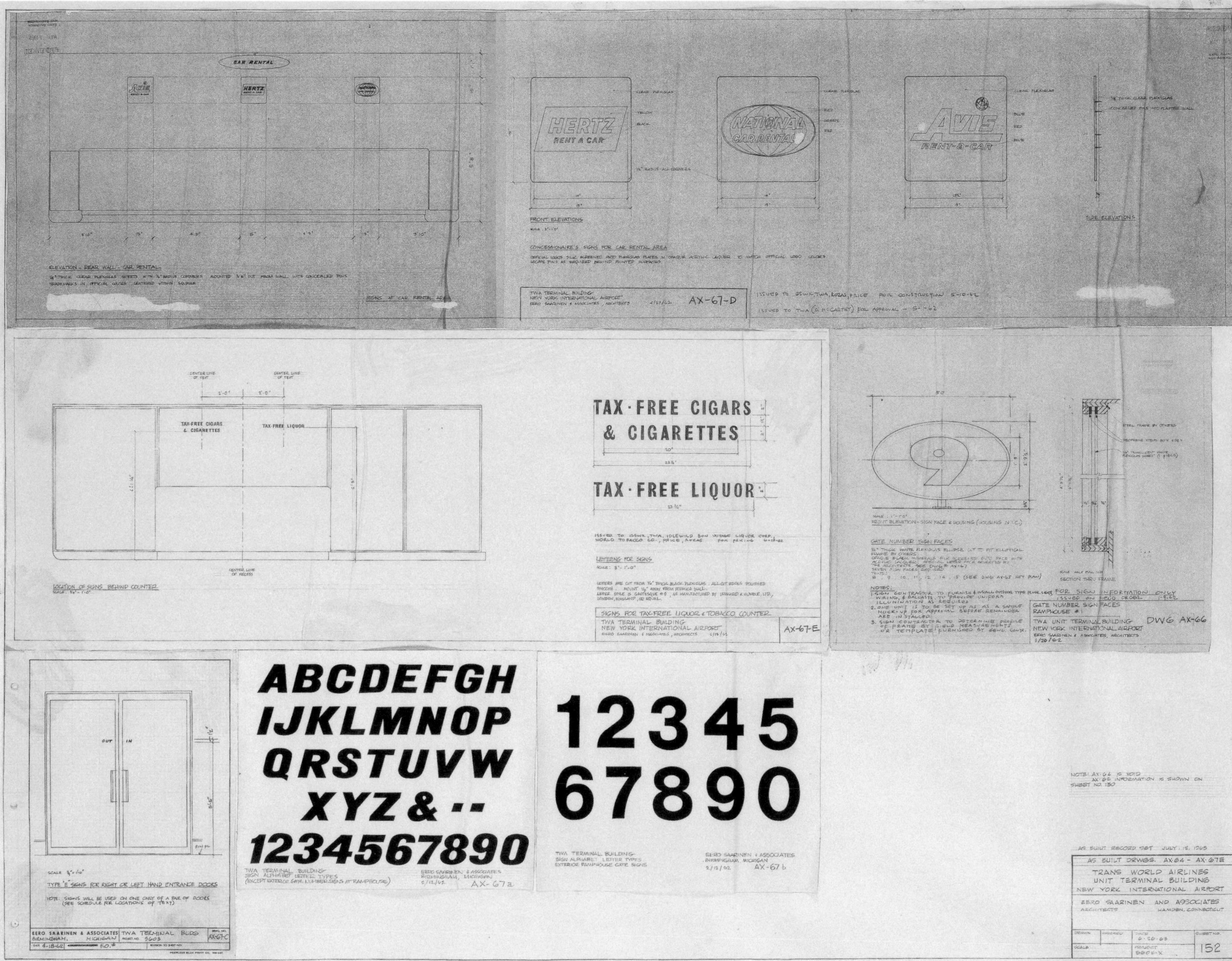

Vicinity map of John F. Kennedy International Airport, no scale, BBB, 2004–2005

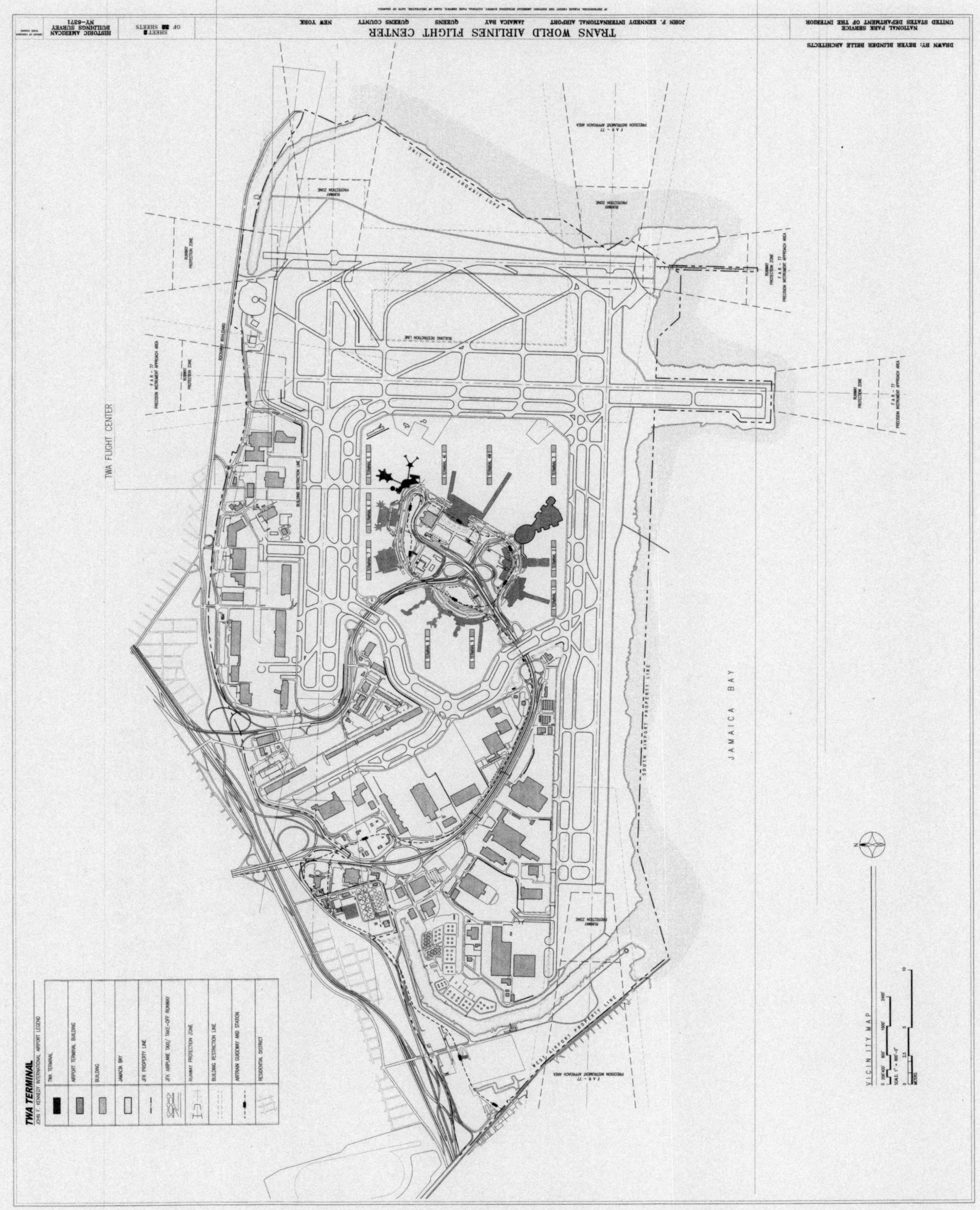

Plan of main floor, no scale, BBB, 2004–2005

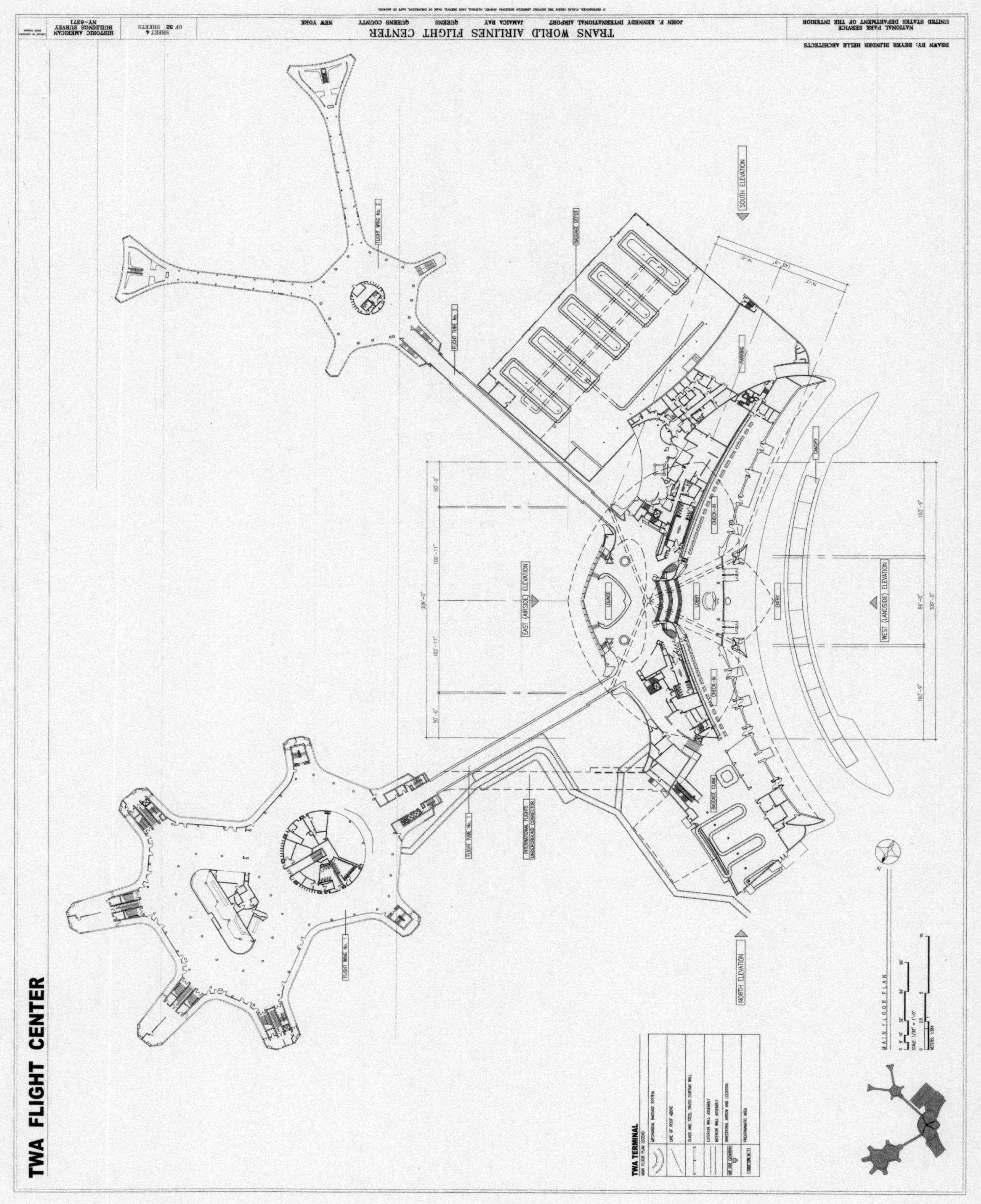

Plan of departure hall, basement level, no scale, BBB, 2004–2005

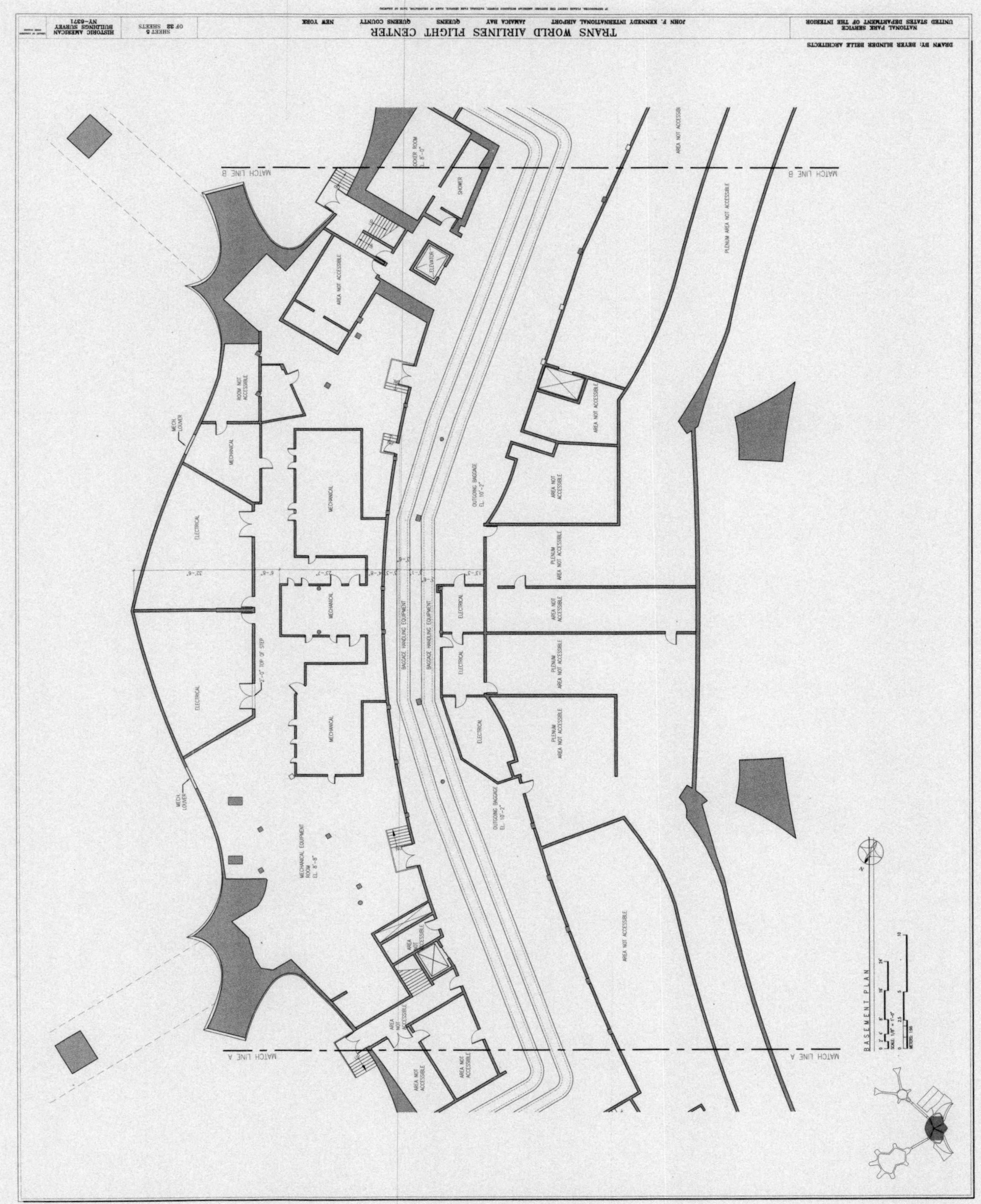

Plan of departure hall, main floor, no scale, BBB, 2004–2005

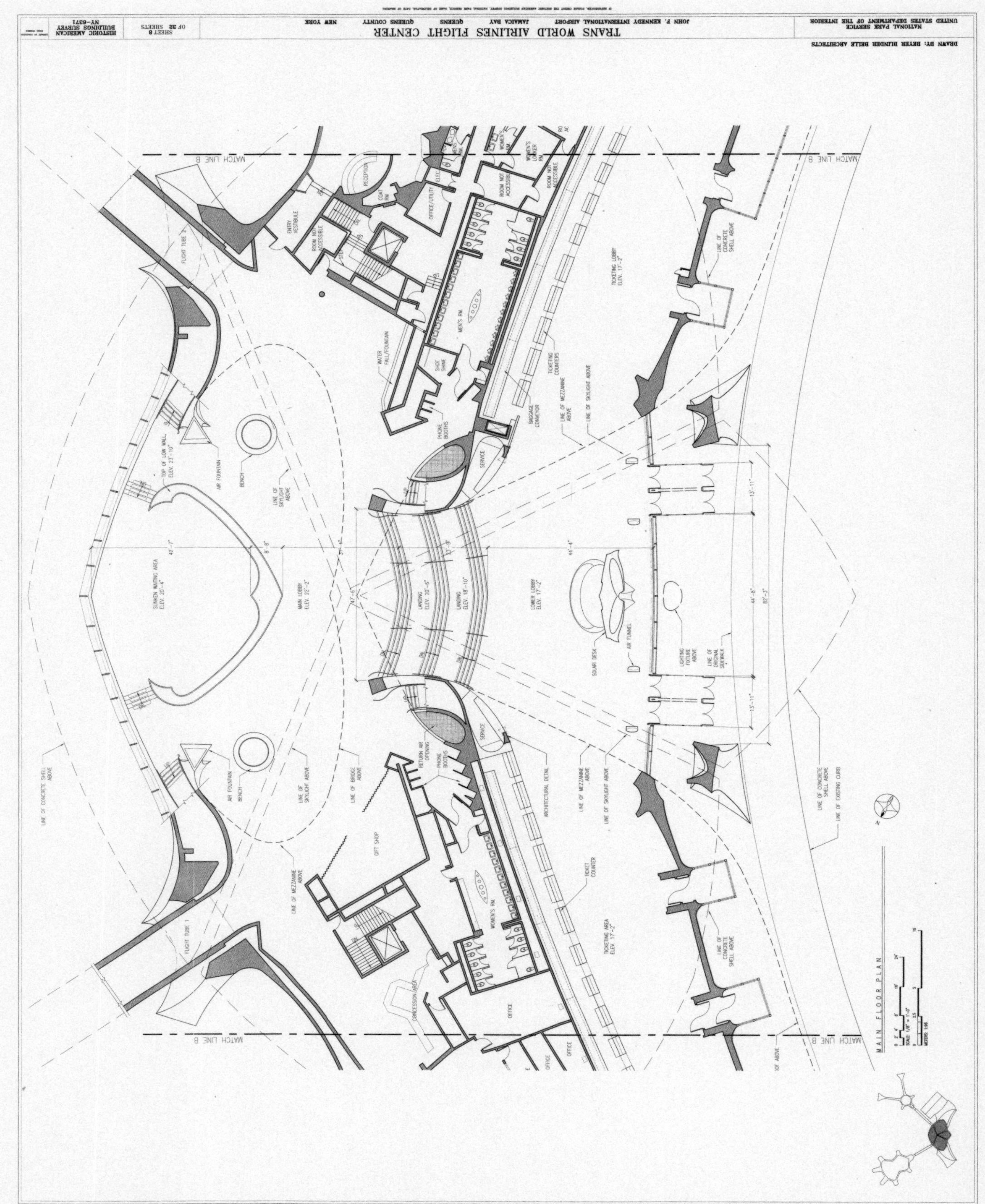

Plan of departure hall, upper floor ("Mezzanine"), no scale, BBB, 2004–2005

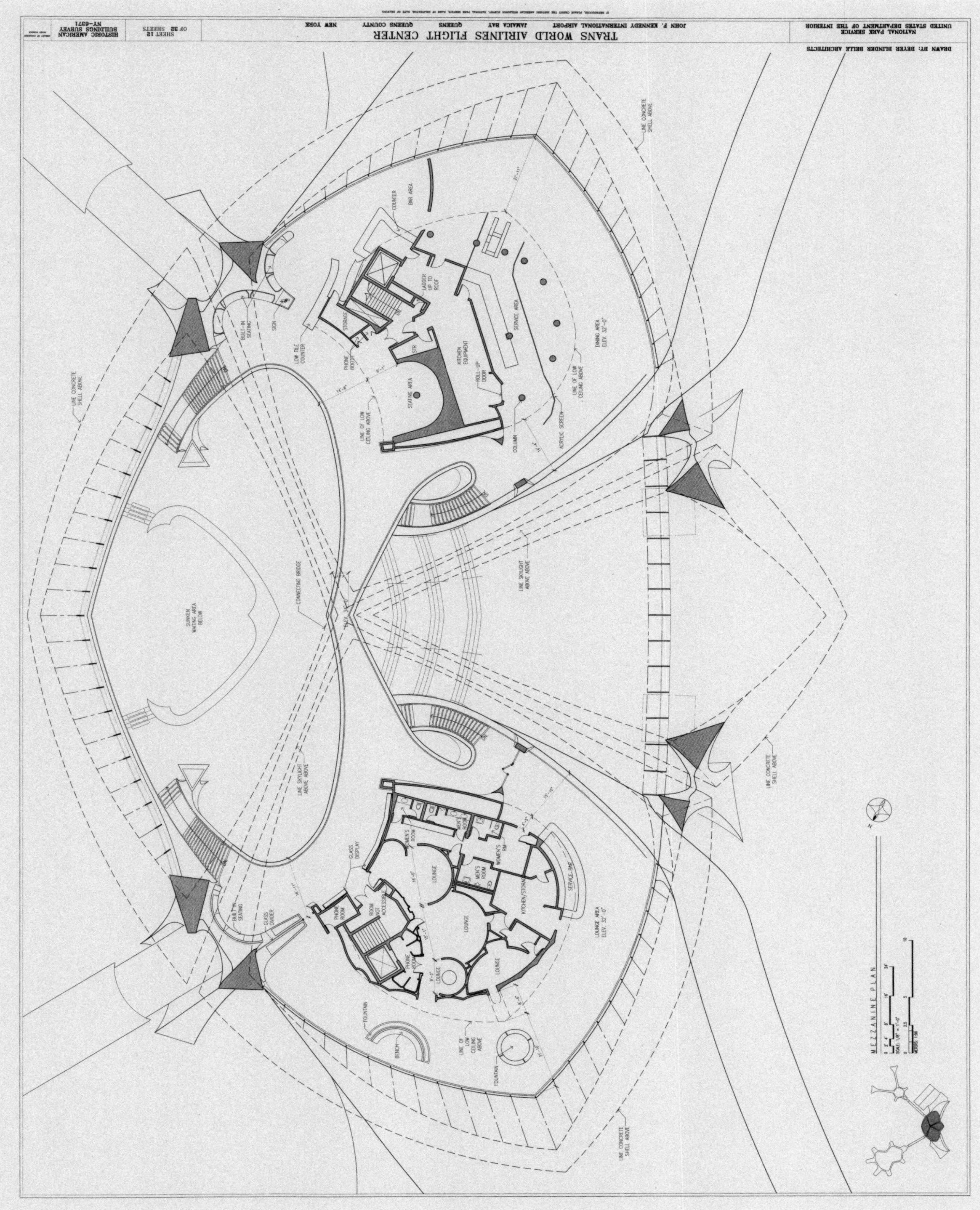

Transverse section and interior details of departure hall, no scale, BBB, 2004–2005

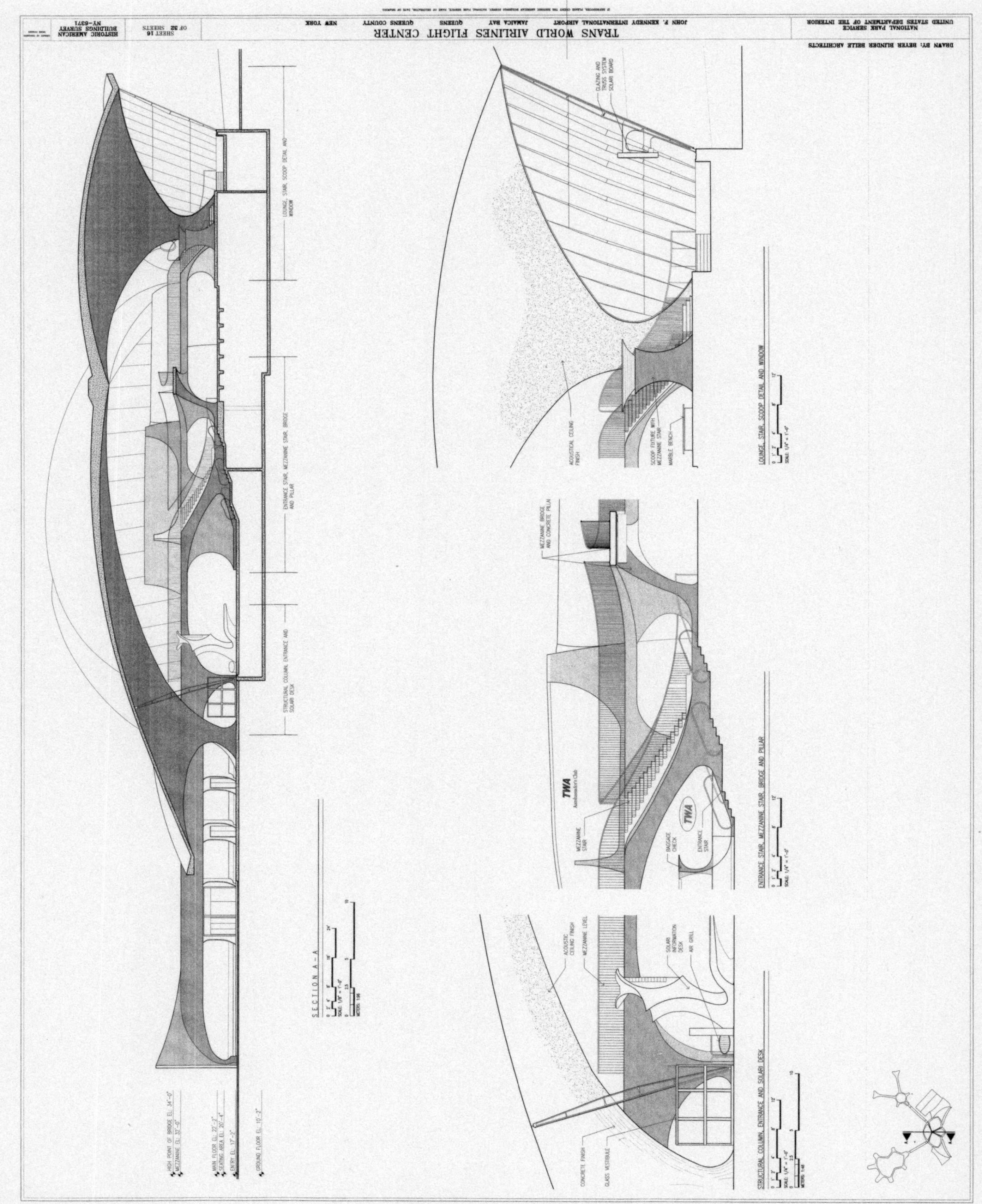

Plan, section, and elevation of connecting corridor (“Flight Tube No. 1”), no scale, BBB, 2004–2005

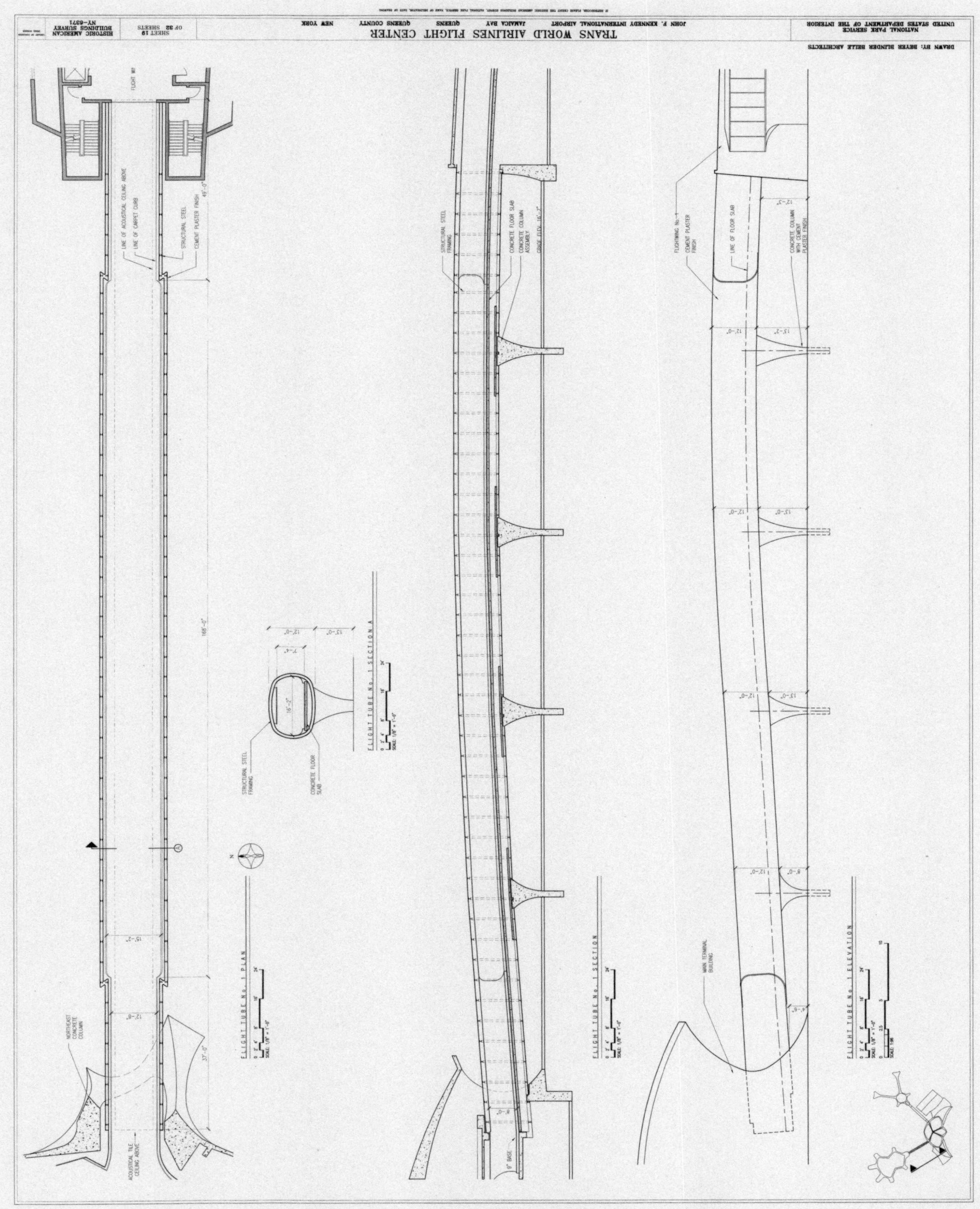

Plan of Flight Wing Two, no scale, BBB, 2004–2005

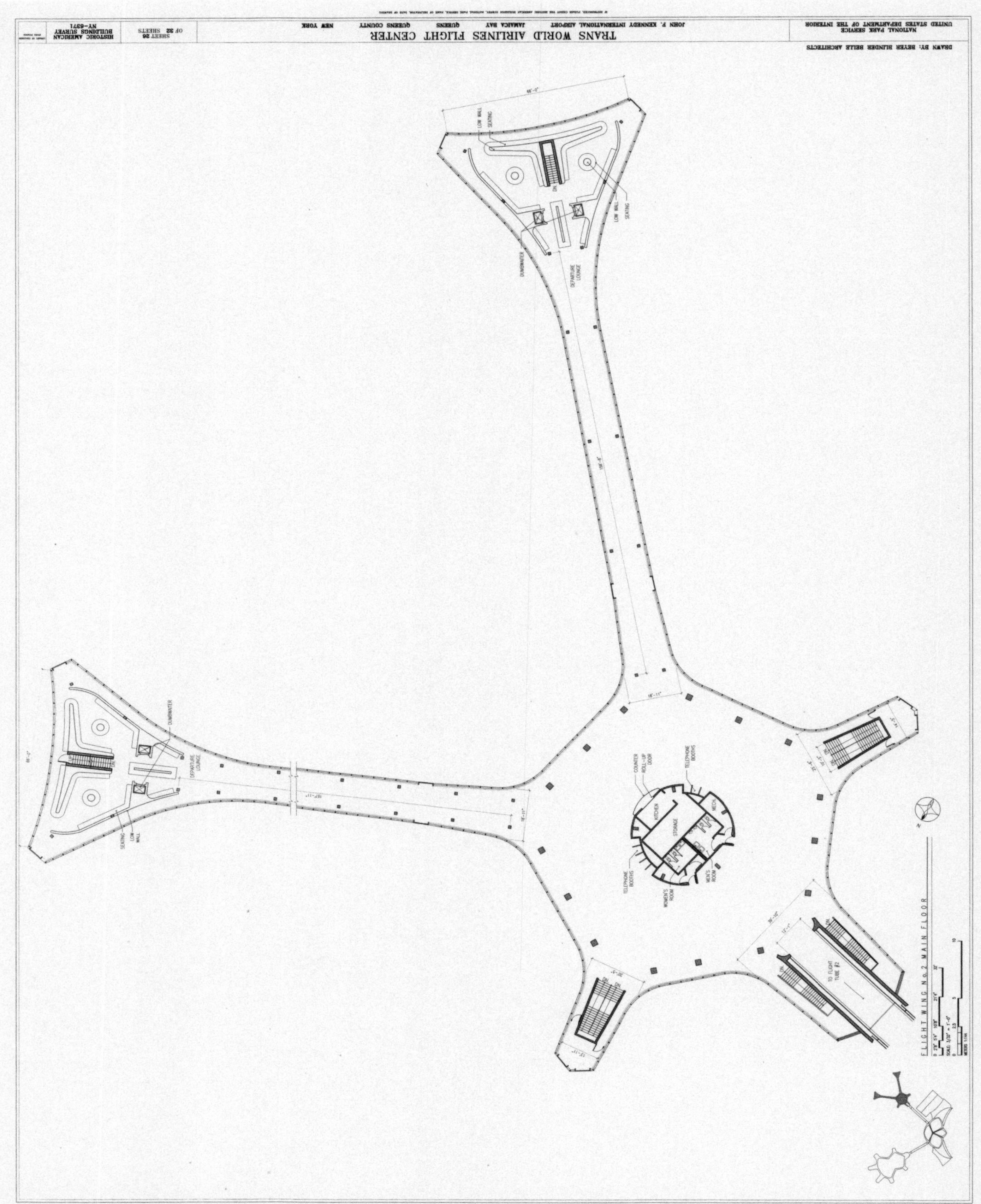

Building Chronology

February 1955 The Port of New York Authority (PONYA) presents its concept for Idlewild. Like the other major airlines in the US, Trans World Airlines (TWA) gets the opportunity to build its own terminal.

Late 1955 The real estate board of TWA, led by President Ralph S. Damon, concretizes its construction plans and decides to commission Eero Saarinen.

January 4, 1956 Damon dies unexpectedly of pneumonia. As Chief Executive Officer, John A. Collings takes over the duties of the president (but does not officially have the same status).

February 1956 The first approaches to finding a solution are developed. In addition, Eero Saarinen and Associates (ES&A) study numerous planning guidelines and different airports.

March 1956 First entry for TWA project number 5603 in ES&A's time–cost ledgers.

June 1956 Eero Saarinen explains the design idea to his wife Aline with the help of a grapefruit and makes a small clay model at the office.

October 15, 1956 Structural engineers from Ammann and Whitney have joined the project team. The partner in charge is Boyd Anderson. The roof consists of a single, continuously undulating concrete slab. The architects call the design at this stage "the flying brassiere." The chief structural engineer, Abba Tor, instructs the architect that the terminal cannot be built that way, because cracks would develop. ES&A subsequently split the roof into four parts and inserts elongated skylights in between.

January 2, 1957 Eero and Aline Saarinen embark on a month-long trip to Southeast Asia. After stops in Indonesia, Thailand, and Cambodia, the couple reach Sydney, where Saarinen serves as a juror in the competition for the new opera house. According to legend, Saarinen arrives late and brings Jørn Utzon's design, which has already been eliminated, back into consideration. Impressed by Utzon's design, upon arriving home Saarinen gives the roof of the terminal stronger contours. Proceeding from there, the interior is also designed to be rich in curves.

January 1957 Carter L. Burgess becomes the new president of TWA, only to resign at the end of the same year.

November 12, 1957 TWA unveils its plans for the new terminal at a press conference in New York's Barbizon Plaza Hotel (now Trump Parc). A fruitful collaboration between Aline Saarinen and the communications department of TWA begins. As for the design, the roof's shape corresponds to the later built form. At this time, the terminal is expected to open mid-1959. TWA wants to install moving sidewalks, but omits them over the course of the project.

April 1958 With a slight delay, ES&A complete their work on the construction drawings. The opening is planned for 1960.

July 1958 TWA decides to use passenger boarding bridges (jetways). The decision to move the boarding level to the upper floor leads to a redesign of the satellites. The departure hall remains unaffected by these changes. Charles S. Thomas becomes the new president of TWA. Around the same time, given its precarious financial situation, TWA fundamentally reconsiders the decision to build.

April 1959 TWA announces awarding the construction work to Grove Shepherd Wilson and Kruge. Jaros, Baum and Bolles are the mechanical engineers, Bolt, Beranek and Newman are the acoustic consultants, and Stanley McCandless is responsible for the lighting design.

June 9, 1959 Groundbreaking takes place and construction starts. TWA proceeds on the premise that both satellites will be built. The airline subsequently forgoes one of them, but must consequently concede capacity constraints.

September 1959 The concrete foundations are in place. Construction workers are in the process of assembling the concrete formwork for the four supports.

November 1959 The supports are cast and stripped of the formwork. Now the laborious job of making the formwork for the vaults and then adding the reinforcing begins. The opening is expected for 1961.

June 1960 All the concrete formwork is ready with the exception of the northern side vault.

July 28, 1960 After only two years in office, President Thomas announces his resignation and the former interim management committee takes over again.

September 1960 At the beginning of the month, the formwork and the reinforcement are ready. The construction workers now place the water and power lines into the formwork. One difficulty is to account for shrinkage of the concrete during the curing process and to position outlet openings for the utility lines within the nearest centimeter. Thus the construction site is ready in mid-September for casting of the vaults. Because they are to appear as if made of one piece, the casting process must be carried out without interruption. First, the middle junction slab is concreted, then the workers cast the vault on the air side. Work continues around the clock. After twenty-two hours, the first form is fully poured. Next, the vault above the entrance ramp is cast and finally the side roof sections. After about 120 hours of continuous work, the last of the four vaults is poured. Now the curing period ensues.

December 8, 1960 The steel shoring under the vaults is removed. As Saarinen sees the concrete shell, he says to Abba Tor: "If this were to fall on my head now, I would die a happy man." Now the finishing work begins. The opening is expected at the end of 1961.

March 1961 Charles C. Tillinghast, Jr. assumes the office of president and keeps the post until 1969, when he becomes chairman (until 1976). Because of the many changes in leadership, the building is called "the five chairmen terminal."

September 1, 1961 Eero Saarinen must undergo brain surgery and dies from complications. A few days before, he had been diagnosed with a tumor. In addition to the TWA Flight Center, eight other major projects are still unfinished.

March 19, 1962 Trial operations begin for the first satellite ("Flight Wing Two"). Passengers enter it via TWA's previous terminal.

May 17, 1962 The array of events preceding the official start of operations begins with a press tour, for which TWA flies in 150 to 200 media representatives from around the country. On May 22, a "Grand Opening Charity Ball" is held "for the glitterati of New York society, business community and news media." The next day, there is a viewing for invited guests on the agenda, and an open house for the general public is held on May 26.

May 28, 1962 The big opening day has arrived. The Trans World Flight Center is put into operation with a ceremonious gala. In addition to the TWA board of directors, two senators and numerous representatives from business, media, and culture are on the guest list. President Tillinghast leads 400 invited guests through the opening ceremonies. Aline Saarinen unveils a commemorative plaque for the deceased architect of the terminal.

June–July 1962 The terminal's restaurant facilities, the Paris Cafe, the Lisbon Lounge, and the London Club, go into operation.

December 24, 1963 A few weeks after the assassination of President Kennedy, the Mayor of the City of New York and PONYA rename Idlewild Airport as John F. Kennedy International Airport.

June 1967 TWA announces construction of the second satellite ("Flight Wing One"). After the opening, Aline Saarinen had still assumed that construction of the second satellite would go ahead without interruption.

July 1967 Construction of the second satellite begins. It was designed by Kevin Roche John Dinkeloo and Associates. At the same time, the south wing of the existing terminal is expanded in order to provide additional space for offices, retail stores, and baggage handling. In so doing, the floor area of the Flight Center is almost doubled, from 170,000 to 339,000 sq. ft. (15,800–31,500 m²). Completion is expected in the fall of 1969.

March 19, 1970 "Flight Wing One" goes into operation. An underground luggage tunnel joins it to the main building. In the same year, both wings are expanded.

1969–1970 TWA has the Le Monde Restaurant incorporated within the ground floor, and the existing cafe on the upper floor is expanded. The architect is Warren Platner, who formerly worked for Saarinen, in collaboration with Kevin Roche John Dinkeloo and Associates. Artist Sheila Hicks designs the textile wall surfaces in Le Monde.

1981 TWA takes over the National Airlines Terminal and opens it as a the TWA Domestic Flight Center (Terminal B). Saarinen's terminal is renamed TWA International Terminal (Terminal A). The two adjacent terminals are connected via an above-ground corridor. TWA gets the brunt of the deregulated aviation market and struggles with severe economic problems. By mid-decade the airline is taken over by the investor Carl Icahn. He adopts a rigorous divestiture strategy.

1990 A roadway canopy is constructed on the land side for passengers, and a baggage canopy is built on the air side.

1992 TWA has to file for bankruptcy. Even though the demise of TWA can eventually be averted in 1995 and despite various attempts to restructure, the airline never entirely frees itself of its corporate difficulties.

1994 The terminal is placed under landmark protection, much to the disfavor of TWA, which sees the action as restricting their operational freedom.

1997 TWA renovates the Royal Ambassador Lounge in the terminal.

2000 Additional baggage carousels are installed in "Flight Wing One," and an extension to the southern wing is built for baggage handling.

April 2001 TWA is taken over by American Airlines. Because the new owner already has its own departure building at the airport, the days of service are numbered for Saarinen's terminal.

October 6, 2001 With the departure of TWA flight 481, Saarinen's terminal ceases operations. After the plans to demolish the airport terminal become known, professional circles successfully oppose them.

2002 The terminal serves as a backdrop for *Catch Me If You Can* by Steven Spielberg, the most popular movie filmed there to date.

October 1, 2004 An exhibition entitled *Terminal 5,* curated by Rachel K. Ward and initially scheduled to remain on view in the airport terminal until the end of January 2005, is closed immediately after a rowdy opening reception. The exhibition was named after the Port Authority's official designation for the terminal.

December 2005 The Port Authority implements its expansion plans. A new terminal that leaves Saarinen's main building untouched is constructed for low-cost carrier Jet Blue, according to plans of the firm Gensler. The satellites, however, are demolished.

November 16, 2006 The *New York Times* reports that the Port Authority expects proposals from developers by month's end for how the airport terminal could be used in the future.

October 22, 2008 Jet Blue puts their new terminal into operation. Meanwhile, the fate of Saarinen's building remains unknown.

February 2011 The Port Authority publicly announces plans to build a boutique hotel on the narrow strip of land between the Saarinen building and the Jet Blue terminal. The TWA Flight Center is to serve as its lobby.

September 2013 It is made known that hotelier André Balazs is designated to carry out the transformation. But the partnership with the Port Authority fails, as announced by the latter in January 2014.

August 8, 2014 The Port Authority issues a request for proposals in its search for a developer who is capable of converting the landmarked building into a luxury ("high-quality") hotel.

April 14, 2015 Jet Blue and its partner, hotel developer MCR Development LLC, have emerged as the preferred bidder and are in advanced negotiations with the Port Authority for the rights to turn the terminal into a hotel. Up to the time of printing, no announcement has been made about awarding a contract.

165 **Plans for a Guggenheim Museum in Helsinki are critically opposed in 2015 by the group The Next Helsinki with their own competition. With their submission entitled "Terminal Velocity," the architects Thibaut de Ruyter, Esther Mysius and Camille Rouaud propose transporting the disused TWA Terminal from New York to Helsinki by sea.**

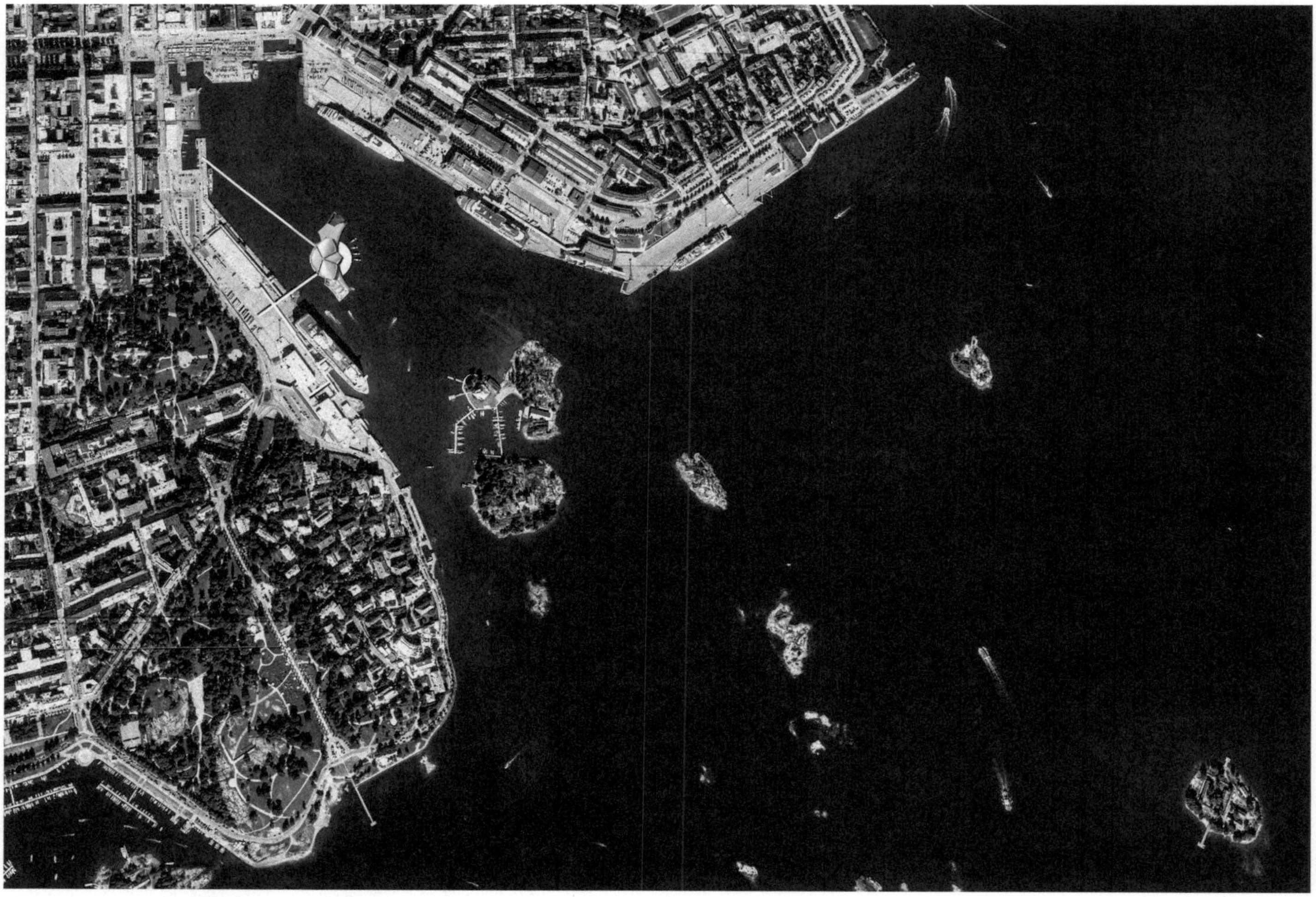

166 **Once relocated in Helsinki's harbor basin, the terminal takes on a new use: Joined to the shore via connecting passages, it becomes a restaurant and lobby for an art museum and conference center. The adaptive reuse of disused landmark buildings catches on as the "Helsinki effect."**

Index

List of Illustrations

Every effort has been made to identify and contact the copyright owners. The author apologizes for any unintentional omissions or errors and will be pleased to insert the appropriate acknowledgements to companies or individuals in any subsequent editions of this book.

Division, Balthazar Korab Archive at the Library of Congress, LC-DIG-krb-00617
Fig. 60 Library of Congress, Prints & Photographs Division, Balthazar Korab Archive at the Library of Congress, LC-DIG-krb-00613
58 **Fig. 61** Illustrator unknown/*Skyliner,* vol. 20, no. 30 (November 21, 1957), p. 3
64 **Fig. 62** ©The Nick DeWolf Foundation
65 **Fig. 63** Illustrator unknown/*Holiday,* vol. 11, no. 4 (April 1952)
Fig. 64 ©Mike Machat. Reproduced with kind permission
Fig. 65 ©Terry Waddington/Jon Proctor Collection
66 **Fig. 66** Illustrator unknown/*Skyliner,* vol. 23, no. 21 (November 20, 1960), p. 8
67 **Fig. 67** Illustrator unknown/Kornel Ringli Collection
Fig. 68 Photographer unknown/*Skyliner,* vol. 23, no. 17 (August 18, 1960), p. 1
Fig. 69 Photographer unknown/Trans World Airlines (TWA) Records (KC0453), WHMC-KC, University of Missouri, Box 234
68 **Fig. 70** Eero Saarinen Collection (MS 593). Manuscripts and Archives, Yale University Library
69 **Fig. 71** Robert Day/*Saturday Review,* April 25, 1970, p. 54
70 **Fig. 72** Balthazar Korab/Eero Saarinen Collection (MS 593). Manuscripts and Archives, Yale University Library
71 **Fig. 73** ©Richard G. Knight/Richard Gamble Knight Papers (MS 1999). Manuscripts and Archives, Yale University Library
Fig. 74 Library of Congress, Prints & Photographs Division, Balthazar Korab Archive at the Library of Congress, LC-DIG-krb-00572
72 From top left to bottom right:
Figs 75.1–75.5 ©Abba Tor
Figs 75.6–75.10 Richard G. Knight/Eero Saarinen Collection (MS 593). Manuscripts and Archives, Yale University Library
73 **Fig. 76** ©Richard G. Knight/Richard Gamble Knight Papers (MS 1999). Manuscripts and Archives, Yale University Library
74 **Fig. 77.1** Library of Congress, Prints & Photographs Division, Balthazar Korab Archive at the Library of Congress, LC-DIG-krb-00584
Fig. 77.2 Library of Congress, Prints & Photographs Division, Balthazar Korab Archive at the Library of Congress, LC-DIG-krb-00585
75 **Fig. 78** Illustrator unknown/Eero Saarinen Collection (MS 593). Manuscripts and Archives, Yale University Library
Figs 79–80 Eero Saarinen Collection (MS 593). Manuscripts and Archives, Yale University Library
76 **Fig. 81** Claude de Forest/Cranbrook Archives, AD.22.165. Reproduced with kind permission
Fig. 82.1 Photographer unknown/Eero Saarinen Collection (MS 593). Manuscripts and Archives, Yale University Library
Fig. 82.2 ©Ezra Stoller/Esto
77 **Fig. 83** Eero Saarinen Collection (MS 593). Manuscripts and Archives, Yale University Library
Fig. 84 Herbert Matter; photographer unknown/Eero Saarinen Collection (MS 593). Manuscripts and Archives, Yale University Library
Fig. 85 Photographer unknown/Eero Saarinen Collection (MS 593). Manuscripts and Archives, Yale University Library
78 **Fig. 86** Alan Dunn/**Dunn**, Alan: *Architecture Observed,* New York: Architectural Record Books, 1971, p. 129
79 **Fig. 87** Photographer unknown/*Skyliner,* vol. 27, no. 5 (March 2, 1964), p. 8
Fig. 88 Photographer unknown/*Aviation Week & Space Technology,* vol. 77, no. 4 (July 23, 1962), p. 35
80 **Fig. 89.1** Photographer unknown/**Davies**, R. E. G.: *TWA: An Airline and Its Aircrafts,* McLean, VA: Paladwr Press, 2000, p. 67
Fig. 89.2 Photographer unknown/San Francisco International Airport (SFO), Aviation Museum & Library Collection, Accession no. 2011.032.1967
Fig. 90 Photographer unknown/Kornel Ringli Collection
81 **Fig. 91** Photographer unknown/*Life* Photo Archive hosted by Google
Fig. 92 ©Roy Stevens/Getty Images
Fig. 93 Library of Congress, Prints & Photographs Division, Balthazar Korab Archive at the Library of Congress, LC-DIG-krb-00114
82 **Fig. 94** Photographer unknown/Eero Saarinen Collection (MS 593). Manuscripts and Archives, Yale University Library
83 **Fig. 95** ©Ezra Stoller/Esto
Fig. 96 Photographer unknown/General Negative Collection, North Carolina State Archives
Fig. 97 Manfred Beier/Deutsches Bundesarchiv (German Federal Archives), Sammlung Beier, N 1648 Bild-KD02449
Fig. 98 Charles Trefts/The State Historical Society of Missouri
84 **Fig. 99** Photographer unknown/Archivo Torroja, Cehopu-Cedex
Fig. 100 Photographer unknown/Avaloncm; flickr.com (June 13, 2015)
85 **Fig. 101** Illustrator unknown/**General Motors Corporation**: «1959 Cadillac Data Book», Detroit, MI: Cadillac Motor Car Division, 1959, p. 6A/GM Heritage Center
86 **Fig. 102** ©Richard Shirk/Cranbrook Archives, RS-95
87 **Fig. 103** Photographer unknown/University of Nevada, Las Vegas, University Libraries. Martin Stern Photo Collection
Fig. 104 ©Bob Proctor/Jon Proctor Collection
Fig. 105 Library of Congress, Prints & Photographs Division, New York World-Telegram and the Sun Newspaper Photograph Collection, LC-DIG-ds-00100
88 **Fig. 106** Designer unknown/Kornel Ringli Collection
Fig. 107 Designer unknown/San Francisco International Airport (SFO), Aviation Museum & Library Collection, Accession no. 2009.161.010 a c
94 **Fig. 108** Bernice Clark, Joe Clark (HBSS Studio)/Eero Saarinen Collection (MS 593). Manuscripts and Archives, Yale University Library
95 **Fig. 109** Aline and Eero Saarinen Papers, 1906–1977. Archives of American Art, Smithsonian Institution, Dig. ID 17594
Fig. 110 Walter Daran/Eero Saarinen Collection (MS 593). Manuscripts and Archives, Yale University Library
Fig. 111 Photographer unknown/Eero Saarinen Collection (MS 593). Manuscripts and Archives, Yale University Library
96 **Fig. 112** Library of Congress, Prints & Photographs Division, Balthazar Korab Archive at the Library of Congress, LC-DIG-krb-00576
97 **Fig. 113.1** Library of Congress, Prints & Photographs Division, Balthazar Korab Archive at the Library of Congress, LC-DIG-krb-00562
Fig. 113.2 Library of Congress, Prints & Photographs Division, Balthazar Korab Archive at the Library of Congress, LC-DIG-krb-00561
98 **Fig. 114** Photographer unknown/Eero Saarinen Collection (MS 593). Manuscripts and Archives, Yale University Library
98 **Fig. 115** Library of Congress, Prints & Photographs Division, Balthazar Korab Archive at the Library of Congress, LC-DIG-krb-00566
99 **Fig. 116** Library of Congress, Prints & Photographs Division, Balthazar Korab Archive at the Library of Congress, LC-DIG-krb-00569
100 **Fig. 117** ©John Pickett/**Walker**, Andrew Lee; **Ward**, Rachel K. (eds): *Terminal 5,* New York: Lukas & Sternberg, 2004, pp. 26–27
Fig. 118 Photographer unknown/*Architectural Record,* vol. 130, no. 3 (Sept. 1961), p. 163
101 **Fig. 119** Library of Congress, Prints & Photographs Division, Balthazar Korab Archive at the Library of Congress, LC-DIG-krb-00596
102 **Fig. 120** Photographer unknown/Eero Saarinen Collection (MS 593). Manuscripts and Archives, Yale University Library
103 **Fig. 121.1** Top left: Photographer unknown/*Skyliner,* vol. 20, no. 30 (November 21, 1957), p. 3
Fig. 121.2 Middle left: Photographer unknown/*Skyliner,* vol. 20, no. 30 (November 21, 1957), p. 3
Fig. 121.3 Bottom left: Photographer unknown/*Skyliner,* vol. 25, no. 12 (June 4, 1962), p. 1

Works Cited

A

Adams, Don: "Filling Those Seats: US Airlines Try New Publicity Baits to Lure the Passenger," in: *Flight International*, vol. 80, no. 2735 (August 10, 1961), p. 190.

Albrecht, Donald: "The Clients and Their Architect," in: **Pelkonen**, Eeva-Liisa; **Albrecht**, Donald: (eds): *Eero Saarinen: Shaping the Future*, New Haven, CT: Yale University Press, 2006, pp. 44–55.

Anderson, Boyd G.; **Tor**, Abba; **Yeakel**, Ralph W., Jr.: "Design and Construction of Shell Roof for the New York International Airport TWA Flight Center," in: *Proceedings World Conference on Shell Structures, October 1–4, 1962, San Francisco, CA*; Washington, D.C.: National Academy of Sciences—National Research Council, pp. 319–328.

Angélil, Marc: "Terminal Space: Gedanken zur zeitgenössischen Flughafenarchitektur," in: *archithese*, vol. 32, no. 5 (2002), pp. 8–13.

Anonymous: "21 Country Salute to Modern Design," in: *House Beautiful*, vol. 83, no. 10 (October 1941), pp. 50–51.

Anonymous: "Air Terminal for Jet Travel: Choosing a Terminal Plan," in: *Progressive Architecture*, vol. 42, no. 11 (November 1961), pp. 128–129.

Anonymous: "Airports Turn to the Engineers," in: *Business Week*, no. 1287 (May 1, 1954), pp. 92–98.

Anonymous: "Anti-Hijacking System Being Used by TWA," in: *Aviation Week & Space Technology*, vol. 91, no. 25 (December 22, 1969), p. 32.

Anonymous: "Boeing Shows Luxurious 707 Interior," in: *Aviation Week*, vol. 64, no. 23 (June 4, 1956), pp. 80–83.

Anonymous: "Design for the Jet Age," in: *Time*, vol. 80, no. 22 (November 30, 1962), pp. 50–51, 53.

Anonymous: "Details of Automatic Plane Parking Device," in: *Aviation Week*, vol. 56, no. 4 (January 28, 1952), pp. 59–60.

Anonymous: "Dream of Jet Age Airports Still Far from Reality," in: *Business Week*, no. 1474 (November 30, 1957), pp. 90–92, 94, 96.

Anonymous: "Europe, Here They Come," in: *Life*, vol. 38, no. 26 (June 27, 1955), pp. 34–39.

Anonymous: "Fourteen Corporation Staff Designers," in: *Contract Interiors*, vol. 124, no. 12 (July 1965), pp. 85–105.

Anonymous: "Giant Lockheed Air Transport Makes Test Flight in California," in: *Washington Post*, January 10, 1943, pp. 1–2.

Anonymous: "Good Architecture is Good Promotion," in: *Architectural Forum*, vol. 113, no. 1 (July 1960), pp. 88–89, 186–187.

Anonymous: "Grand Central of the Air," in: *Architectural Forum*, vol. 104, no. 5 (May 1956), pp. 106–115.

Anonymous: "Neues Flight Center in New York-Idlewild," in: *Neue Zürcher Zeitung*, June 22, 1962 (evening edition), no. 2491, p. 6.

Anonymous: "New for Idlewild Airport," in: *Chicago Tribune*, December 8, 1957, p. D16.

Anonymous: "New Furniture: Top American Designers Make It Simple, Slim and Comfortable," in: *Life*, vol. 25, no. 20 (November 15, 1948), pp. 115–118.

Anonymous: "New World of Shells," in: *Time*, vol. 73, no. 10 (March 9, 1959), p. 50.

Anonymous: "New York's Modern Wonder: T.W.A.'s Flight Center dramatizes Jet Age," in: *Boston Globe*, May 13, 1962, p. 59.

Anonymous: "Pan Am Ticket Office: An Airy Sweep of Sculptured Space," in: *Architectural Forum*, vol. 119, no. 2 (August 1963), pp. 98–101.

Anonymous: "Queens Chamber Cites Air Center," in: *New York Times*, December 2, 1962, pp. 1, 4.

Anonymous: "Saarinen Challenges the Rectangle: Designs a Domed Auditorium and a Cylindrical Chapel for MIT's Laboratory Campus," in: *Architectural Forum*, vol. 98, no. 1 (January 1953), pp. 126–133.

Anonymous: "Saarinen's TWA Flight Center," in: *Architectural Record*, vol. 132, no. 7 (July 1962), pp. 129–134.

Anonymous: "Saarinen Designs Terminal for TWA," in: *Progressive Architecture*, vol. 38, no. 12 (December 1957), pp. 66–67.

Anonymous: "Sculpture in Concrete," in: *Concrete Construction*, vol. 6, no. 10 (October 1961), pp. 282–284.

Anonymous: "Shaping a Two-Acre Sculpture," in: *Architectural Forum*, vol. 113, no. 2 (August 1960), pp. 118–123.

Anonymous: "Terminal City Rises at Idlewild," in: *Business Week*, no. 1610 (July 9, 1960), pp. 86–89, 90, 92.

Anonymous: "The Airport Scramble," in: *Architectural Forum*, vol. 104, no. 6 (June 1956), pp. 116–131.

Anonymous: "The Word Is Soar," in: *Time*, vol. 81, no. 13 (March 29, 1963), p. 48.

Anonymous: "TWA Unveils Terminal Plans," in: *Washington Post*, December 22, 1957, p. E19.

Anonymous: "TWA's Concrete, Wing-Roofed Terminal Now Ready for Flight," in: *Engineering News-Record*, vol. 168, no. 22 (May 31, 1962), pp. 48–50.

Anonymous: "A Jet Age Icon is Threatened," 2001, http://www.jetsetmodern.com/twa.htm (accessed February 3, 2015).

Arroyo, Nicholas R.; **Grisdale**, John; **Heino**, Albert F.; **Meisch**, Francis R.; **Prokosch**, Walther: "Airport Terminal Buildings," in: *Progressive Architecture*, vol. 34, no. 5 (May 1953), pp. 69–121.

Ashford, Norman; **Wright**, Paul H.: *Airport Engineering*, New York: Wiley, 1979.

B

Bacon, Roger: "Straight and Level," in: *Flight International*, vol. 95, no. 3138 (May 1, 1969), p. 736a.

Banham, Reyner: "The Fear of Eero's Mana," in: *Arts Magazine*, vol. 36, no. 5 (February 1962), pp. 70–73.

Banham, Reyner: "The Obsolescent Airport," in: *Architectural Review*, vol. 132, no. 788 (October 1962), pp. 252–253.

Banham, Reyner: "The Trouble with Eero," in: *New Statesman*, vol. 64, no. 1654 (November 23, 1962), pp. 745–746.

Bayley, Stephen: *Harley Earl and the Dream Machine* (series: "Design Heroes"), London: Trefoil Publications, 1990.

Bilstein, Roger E.: *Flight in America: From the Wrights to the Astronauts*, Baltimore, MD: Johns Hopkins University Press, 1994 (second ed.).

Blacklock, Mark: "Bridging the Gap," in: *Airways*, vol. 13, no. 10 (December 2006), pp. 44–49.

Blacklock, Mark: *Recapturing the Dream: A Design History of New York's JFK Airport*, London: M. Blacklock, 2005.

Blake, Peter: "Modern Architecture: Its Many Faces," in: *Architectural Forum*, vol. 108, no. 3 (March 1958), pp. 76–81.

Blanck, Katherine: "Hostess Couture, Classrooms Go Modern: New in Look and Book," in: *Skyliner*, vol. 23, no. 17 (August 18, 1960), p. 4.

Borcherdt, Helmut: "Planung des TWA-Flughafengebäudes in New York," in: *Baukunst und Werkform*, vol. 13, no. 5 (May 1960), pp. 256–263.

Borcherdt, Helmut: *Architekten: Begegnungen 1956–1986,* Munich: Langen Müller, 1988.
Borger, J. G.: "Jet Transport Economics: Influence on Airport and Airway," in: *ASCE Proceedings*, vol. 79, no. 241 (1953), pp. 1–12.
Boyd, Robin: "The Counter-Revolution in Architecture," in: *Harper's Magazine*, vol. 219, no. 10 (September 1959), pp. 40–48.

C
Canty, Donald: "Architecture for the Jet Age: New Buildings, New Problems, New Solutions," in: *Architectural Forum*, vol. 117, no. 1 (July 1962), pp. 66–83.
Carlson, Walter: "Advertising: How T.W.A. Got Off the Ground. Ailing Airline Found Key to Recovery in Research," in: *New York Times*, June 4, 1965, p. F12.
Chermayeff, Serge: "History of Thin Concrete Shells," in: **Massachusetts Institute of Technology** (ed.): *Proceedings of a Conference on Thin Concrete Shells*, Cambridge, MA: MIT, 1954, pp. 2–4.
Christian, George: "Comfort in Airline Cabin Design Makes Dollar Sense," in: *Aviation Week*, vol. 64, no. 20 (May 14, 1956), pp. 92–101.
Christian, George: "Loadair Dock Goes into Operation," in: *Aviation Week*, vol. 62, no. 3 (January 17, 1955), pp. 63–64.
Clark, Robert Judson (ed.): *Design in America: The Cranbrook Vision 1925–1950,* New York: Abrams, 1983.
Clausen, Meredith L.: *The Pan Am Building and the Shattering of the Modernist Dream*, Cambridge, MA: MIT Press, 2005.
Colomina, Beatriz: "Saarinen's Use of the Media" [lecture at the conference "Eero Saarinen: Beyond the Measly ABC"], October 11, 2008, Walker Art Center, Minneapolis, MN, http://channel.walkerart.org/play/eero-saarinen-symposium-beatriz-colomina/ (accessed February 3, 2015).
Colquhoun, Alan: "TWA Terminal Building, Idlewild, New York," in: *Architectural Design*, vol. 32, no. 10 (October 1962), pp. 465–469.
Conley, Gordon: "TWA Hopes to Double Tourist Volume," in: *Aviation Week*, vol. 63, no. 10 (September 5, 1955), pp. 97–98.
Cook, Robert H.: "Idlewild Sprawl Poses Transfer Problems," in: *Aviation Week & Space Technology*, vol. 79, no. 5 (July 29, 1963), pp. 33–34, 37.
Cooper, Michael H.; **Maynard**, Alan K.: *The Price of Air Travel* (series: "Hobard Paper," no. 53), London: The Institute of Economic Affairs (IEA), 1971.
Cosley, Jerry W.: "What Be Shakin', Nagwa?," TWA Seniors Club, January 3, 2004, http://twaseniorsclub.org/memories/contrails/shakin.htm (accessed February 3, 2015).
Creighton, Thomas H.: "The New Sensualism [I]," in: *Progressive Architecture*, vol. 40, no. 9 (September 1959), pp. 141–147.

D
Damon, Ralph S.: "Trans World Airlines," in: *Flight International*, vol. 61, no. 2260 (May 16, 1952), p. 591.
Davies, R. E. G.: *A History of the World's Airlines*, London: Oxford University Press, 1964.
Davies, R. E. G.: *Airlines of the United States since 1914*, London: Putnam, 1972.
Davies, R. E. G.: *TWA: An Airline and Its Aircrafts*, McLean, VA: Paladwr, 2000.
Dean, Andrea O.: "Eero Saarinen in Perspective: A Generation After His Loss. A Discussion of His Work and Influence," in: *AIA Journal*, vol. 70, no. 13 (November 1981), pp. 36–51.
Dietrich, Fred; **Cieszynski**, Horst: *Große Leistungen der Technik*, Gütersloh: Bertelsmann, 1961.
Dixon, John Morris: "Air Terminal for Jet Travel: New Problems and Trends," in: *Progressive Architecture*, vol. 42, no. 11 (November 1961), pp. 128–131.
Dixon, John Morris: "Star-chitects of the 1950s," in: *Docomomo New York/Tri-State Newsletter*, winter 2007, pp. 4–5.
Dixon, John Morris: "Can JFK's Terminal 3 Be Saved?" May 19, 2013, www.docomomo-nytri.org/2013/05/19/can-jfks-terminal-3-be-saved (accessed February 3, 2015).
Dommann, Monika: "'Be Wise—Palletize': die Transformationen eines Transportbretts zwischen den USA und Europa im Zeitalter der Logistik," in: *Traverse: Zeitschrift für Geschichte*, vol. 16, no. 3, "Gesteuerte Gesellschaft" (2009), pp. 21–35.
Dorr, Maude: "Portraits in Architecture: A Review of the Most Recent Buildings of the Late Eero Saarinen," in: *Industrial Design*, vol. 10, no. 5 (May 1963), pp. 62–71.
Drexler, Arthur; **Green**, Wilder: "Architecture and Imagery: Four New Buildings," in: *Museum of Modern Art Bulletin*, vol. 26, no. 2 (1959), p. 1.
Dreyfuss, Henry: *Designing for People*, New York: Simon and Schuster, 1955.
Drummond, Alanya: "Architects on the Cover of *Time* Magazine," in: *The International Journal of the Image*, vol. 2, no. 1 (2012), pp. 83–98.
Duncan, Ian: "TWA's 'Terminal of Tomorrow': An Architectural Showpiece," in: *Airliners*, no. 75 (May/June 2002), pp. 40–49.
Dunlap, David W.: "A Move to Make a Silent Air Terminal Hum Again," November 16, 2006, http://www.nytimes.com/2006/11/16/nyregion/16blocks.html (accessed February 3, 2015).
Dunlap, David W.: "Unusual Planning Duel over Kennedy Terminal," November 28, 2002, www.nytimes.com/2002/11/28/nyregion/blocks-unusual-planning-duel-over-kennedy-terminal.html (accessed February 3, 2015).

E
Eisenbrand, Jochen: "Fluggesellschaften und Corporate Design," in: **Vegesack**, Alexander von (ed.): *Airworld: Design and Architecture for Air Travel*, Weil am Rhein: Vitra Design Museum, 2004, pp. 144–174.
Entwistle, Joanna: "Fashion Takes Flight: The Air Stewardess and Her Uniform," in: **Vegesack**, Alexander von (ed.): *Airworld: Design and Architecture for Air Travel*, Weil am Rhein: Vitra Design Museum, 2004, pp. 176–210.

F
Fisher, Thomas: "Landmarks: TWA Terminal," in: *Progressive Architecture*, vol. 73, no. 5 (May 1992), pp. 96–101.
Fitton Hauss, Barbara: "A Trip through Time in the Aircraft Cabin," in: **Vegesack**, Alexander von (ed.): *Airworld: Design and Architecture for Air Travel*, Weil am Rhein: Vitra Design Museum, 2004, pp. 82–122.
Franck, Georg: *Ökonomie der Aufmerksamkeit: ein Entwurf,* Munich: Hanser, 1998.

G
Garrison, Glenn: "TWA Forecasts Jet Costs, Operations," in: *Aviation Week*, vol. 67, no. 15 (October 14, 1957), pp. 38–40.
Gordon, Alastair: *Naked Airport: A Cultural History of the World's Most Revolutionary Structure*, New York: Metropolitan Books, 2004.
Gössel, Peter; **Leuthäuser**, Gabriele: *Architecture in the 20th Century,* Cologne: Taschen, 2005.
Gusrae, G. B.: "Moving Sidewalks," in: *Architectural Record*, vol. 119, no. 7 (June 1956), pp. 220–222, 233.

H
Hake, Bruno H.: "Baggage Handling: Passenger and Baggage Processing at Air Terminals," in: *Journal of the Aero-Space Transport Division* (series: "Proceedings of the American Society of Civil Engineers"), vol. 39, no. 3677, AT (October 1963), pp. 29–44.
Haskell, Douglas: "Architecture and Popular Taste," in: *Architectural Forum*, vol. 109, no. 2 (August 1958), pp. 104–109.
Haskell, Douglas: "Googie Architecture: Los Angeles Does Its Bit," in: *House and Home*, vol. 1, no. 2 (February 1952), pp. 86–88.
Heino, Albert F.: "Designing the Large Terminal," in: *Architectural Record*, vol. 97, no. 4 (April 1945), pp. 80–83.
Hewitt, Ed: "The Shrinking Airline Seat," n. d., www.independenttraveler.com/travel-tips/travelers-ed/the-shrinking-airline-seat (accessed February 3, 2015).
Hitchcock, Henry-Russell: "American Architecture in the Early Sixties," in: *Zodiac*, no. 10 (1962), pp. 4–17.
Houghton, Norris: "The Designer Sets the Stage: Norman Bel Geddes and Vincente Minnelli," in: *Theatre Arts Monthly*, vol. 20, no. 10 (October 1936), reprint: *Theatre Arts*, New York: Arno Press, 1971, pp. 776–788.
Huber, Benedikt: "Projekt für den TWA Terminal in Idlewild, New York," in: *Werk*, vol. 47, no. 2 (February 1960), pp. 53–54.
Hudson, Edward: "Bold Design Is Set for Air Terminal: Trans World Airlines Plan a Terminal at Idlewild," in: *New York Times*, November 13, 1957, p. 37.
Hudson, Edward: "Unfinished T.W.A. Terminal Is an Elegant Causeway," in: *New York Times*, April 22, 1962, p. 14.
Hudson, Edward: "Unusual Terminal for Idlewild: Startling Effect," in: *New York Times*, November 17, 1957, p. 37.
Hughes, Lawrence W.: "It's Happiness Time," in: *Airline Management and Marketing*, vol. 3, no. 6 (June 1969), pp. 73–75.

Hunt, Dudley, Jr.: "Idlewild: New York International Airport," in: *Architectural Record*, vol. 130, no. 3 (September 1961), pp. 151–190.
Huxtable, Ada Louise: "Idlewild: Distressing Monument to Air Age," in: *New York Times*, November 25, 1962, p. 25.

I
Isler, Heinz: "Moderner Schalenbau," in: **Henn**, Ursula (ed.): *Zum Werk von Felix Candela: die Kunst der leichten Schalen* (vol. 18), Cologne: Müller, 1992 (series: "Arcus"), pp. 50–66.

J
Jacobus, John M.: "John Deere Office Building, Moline, IL, USA," in: *Architectural Review*, vol. 137, no. 5 (May 1965), pp. 364–371.
Jacobus, John M.: "Reviewed Work(s): Eero Saarinen on His Work by Aline B. Saarinen; Eero Saarinen . . . ," in: *Journal of the Society of Architectural Historians*, vol. 22, no. 4 (December 1963), pp. 237–239.
Jencks, Charles: *The Iconic Building: The Power of Enigma*, London: Frances Lincoln, 2005.
Johnson, George: *The Abominable Airlines*, New York: The Macmillan Company, 1964.
Jones, Cranston; **Connery**, Donald S.: "The Maturing Modern," in: *Time*, vol. 68, no. 1 (July 2, 1956), pp. 50–57.

K
Kaufmann, Edgar, Jr.: "Inside Eero Saarinen's TWA Building," in: *Interiors*, vol. 121, no. 7 (July 1962), pp. 86–93.
Kieran, Stephen: "The Architecture of Plenty: Theory and Design in a Marketing Age," in: *The Harvard Architecture Review*, vol. 6, "Patronage" (1987), pp. 102–113.
Knight, Richard: "Once upon a Time . . . ," in: **idem**: *Saarinen's Quest: A Memoir*, San Francisco, CA: William Stout Publishers, 2008, pp. 17–64.
Korab, Balthazar: "Remembering Eero Saarinen: The Bloomfield Hills Office, 1955– 58," in: **De Long**, David G.; **idem** (eds): *Eero Saarinen: Buildings from the Balthazar Korab Archive*, New York: W. W. Norton, 2008, pp. 410–411.
Kovári, Thomas: "Die Stadt als Marke: Planung und Architektur im Dienst des City Branding," in: *archithese*, vol. 35, no. 6 (2005), pp. 44–49.
Kruse-Etzbach, Dirk: *New York*, Dormagen: Iwanowski, 2010 (sixth ed.).

L
Larrabee, Eric; **Vignelli**, Massimo (eds): *Knoll Design*, New York: Abrams, 1981.
Lawrence, Mary Wells: *A Big Life in Advertising*, New York: Touchstone, 2003, pp. 34–37.
Leslie, Thomas: "The Pan Am Terminal at Idlewild/Kennedy Airport and the Transition from Jet Age to Space Age," in: *Design Issues*, vol. 21, no. 1 (winter 2005), pp. 63–80.
Lessing, Lawrence: "The Diversity of Eero Saarinen," in: *Architectural Forum*, vol. 113, no. 1 (July 1960), pp. 94–103.
Loewy, Raymond: "Design Thoughts and Theories . . ." in: *Skyliner*, vol. 23, no. 21 (October 20, 1960), pp. 1–2.
Louchheim, Aline B.: "Now Saarinen the Son," in: *New York Times*, April 26, 1953, pp. 26–27, 44–45.
Love, Tim; **Schindler**, Susanne: "Von Museum bis Condominium: das Phänomen *signature building* in den USA," in: *Bauwelt*, vol. 96, no. 46 (December 2, 2005), pp. 12–15.

M
Makovsky, Paul [interview with Jayne Merkel]: "Reconsidering Eero," in: *Metropolis*, vol. 25, no. 2 (October 2005), pp. 134–139, 173.
Makowsky, Paul; **Pedersen**, Martin C.; **Lanks**, Belinda; **LaBarre**, Suzanne: "Team Eero," in: *Metropolis*, vol. 28, no. 4 (November 2008), pp. 70–79.
Martin, George; **Hornsby**, Jeremy: *All You Need Is Ears*, New York: St. Martin's Press, 1994.
Martin, Reinhold: *The Organizational Complex: Architecture, Media, and Corporate Space*, Cambridge, MA: MIT Press, 2003.
Maxfield, William: "TWA Standardizes Paint: New Painting Chart Guides Base and Terminal Crew," in: *Aviation Week*, vol. 40, no. 11 (November 1941), pp. 62–63, 168.
McHale, John: "Der Plastik-Parthenon," in: **Dorfles**, Gillo (ed.): *Der Kitsch*, Tübingen: Wasmuth, 1969, pp. 97–110; originally published as "The Plastic Parthenon," in: *Dot Zero Magazine*, no. 3 (spring 1967), pp. 4–11.
McQuade, Walter: "Eero Saarinen: A Complete Architect," in: *Architectural Forum*, vol. 116, no. 4 (April 1962), pp. 102–127.
McQuade, Walter: "The Exploded Landscape," in: *Perspecta*, no. 7 (1961), pp. 83–90.
Mecklin, John: "U.S. Airlines: Into the Wild Blue What?," in: *Fortune*, vol. 73, no. 5 (May 1966), pp. 146–151, 187–188, 192, 194.
Meikle, Jeffrey L.: *Twentieth Century Limited: Industrial Design in America, 1925–1939*, Philadelphia, PA: Temple University Press, 1979.
Meisch, Francis R.: "Architecture and Air Transportation," in: *Pencil Points*, vol. 24, no. 11 (November 1943), pp. 36–69.

N
New York Landmarks Preservation Commission: "Trans World Airlines Flight Center at New York International Airport," in: **ibid.**: *New York Landmarks Preservation Commission: Designation List; 259, LP-1916*, New York: The Commission, 1994.

P
Packard, Vance: *The Hidden Persuaders*, New York: Pocket Books, 1958 (fifth ed.).
Pearman, Hugh: *Airports: A Century of Architecture*, London: Laurence King, 2004.
Peter, John [interview with Eero Saarinen]: *The Oral History of Modern Architecture: Interviews with the Greatest Architects of the Twentieth Century*, New York: Abrams, 1994.
Peter, John: "Eero Saarinen: Second-Generation Genius," in: *Look*, vol. 22, no. 20 (September 30, 1958), pp. 66–68.
Pneu Michelin: *Les Guides verts: New York*, Paris: Michelin, 1968.
Podrecca, Boris: *Almanac of Architecture: Spatial Analysis*, Salzburg: Anton Pustet, 2009.
Pompl, Wilhelm: *Luftverkehr: eine ökonomische und politische Einführung*, Berlin: Springer, 2002.
Price, Cathy (ed.): *Saarinen Swanson Reunion Proceedings*, Bloomfield Hills, MI: Cranbrook, 2001.
Prokosch, Walther: "Airport Design: Its Architectural Aspects," in: *Architectural Record*, vol. 109, no. 1 (January 1951), pp. 112–117.

R
R. J. B.: "T.C.A. and the Viscount," in: *Flight International*, vol. 67, no. 2412 (April 15, 1955), pp. 502–503.
Raney, Don: "People and Planes! Can Airports Bridge the Gap?," in: *Progressive Architecture*, vol. 50, no. 9 (September 1969), pp. 92–115.
Rhoades, Dawna L.: *Evolution of International Aviation: Phoenix Rising*, Aldershot: Ashgate, 2003.
Riesman, David; **Larrabee**, Eric: "Autos in Amerika," in: **Riesman**, David (ed.): *Wohlstand wofür? Essays*, Frankfurt a. M.: Suhrkamp, 1966, pp. 202–238; Engl. original title: *Abundance for What? And Other Essays*, New York: Doubleday, 1964.
Ringli, Kornel [interview with Abba Tor, engineer in charge at Ammann and Whitney]: "Der Ingenieur von Kahn und Saarinen: ein Gespräch mit Abba Tor," in: *archithese* , vol. 41, no. 5 (2011), pp. 54–59.
Ringli, Kornel: "Planned Myth: The Building Plans for Eero Saarinen's TWA Terminal as Marketing Tool," in: **Spiro**, Annette; **Ganzoni**, David (eds): *The Working Drawing: The Architect's Tool*, Zurich: Park Books, 2013, pp. 298– 300.
Román, Antonio: *Eero Saarinen: An Architecture of Multiplicity*, New York: Princeton Architectural Press, 2003.
Rummel, Robert: *Howard Hughes and TWA*, Washington, D.C.: Smithsonian Institution Press, 1991.

S
Saarinen, Aline B.: "Four Architects Helping to Change the Look of America," in: *Vogue* [US edition], vol. 126, no. 8 (August 1955), pp. 118–121, 149–150.
Saarinen, Aline B.: *Eero Saarinen on His Work: A Selection of Buildings Dating from 1947 to 1964 with Statements by the Architect*, New Haven, CT: Yale University Press, 1968 (second ed.).
Saarinen, Eero: "Architecture of the Future," in: *Cleveland Engineering*, vol. 46, no. 19 (May 7, 1953), pp. 6–8, 10–11.
Saarinen, Eero: "Function, Structure, and Beauty," in: *Architectural Association Journal*, vol. 73, no. 814 (July/August 1957), pp. 40–51.
Saarinen, Eero: "The Challenge to the Arts Today," in: *Yale Daily News*, 1953, pp. 112–113, 191.
Saarinen, Eero: "What Is Architecture?," in: *Perspecta*, no. 7 (1961), pp. 29–42.
Schönberger, Angela (ed.): *Raymond Loewy: Pioneer of American Industrial Design*, Munich: Prestel, 1990.
Scullin, George: *International Airport: The Story of Kennedy Airport and U.S. Commercial Aviation*, Boston, MA: Little Brown and Co., 1968.
Scully, Vincent J.: *American Architecture and Urbanism*,

London: Thames and Hudson, 1969.
Serling, Robert J.: *Howard Hughes' Airline: An Informal History of TWA*, New York: St. Martin's Press, 1983.
Serraino, Pierluigi: "Modernism beyond Reasonable Doubt: Model Making and Photography in Eero Saarinen and Associates," in: **Knight**, Richard: *Saarinen's Quest: A Memoir*, San Francisco, CA: William Stout Publishers, 2008, pp. 151–159.
Shapiro, Irving D.: "From the 20's to Automation," in: *Progressive Architecture*, vol. 38, no. 6 (June 1957), pp. 201–203.
Simmons, Jean: "A New Look for Playland," in: *Dallas Morning News*, October 28, 1962, p. 6.
Spade, Rupert: "Introduction," in: **Futagawa**, Yukio (ed.): *Eero Saarinen* (series: "Library of Contemporary Architects"), New York: Simon and Schuster, 1971, pp. 7–20; Japanese original edition in the series "Gendai Kenchikuka Shirizu," 1968.
Spode, Hasso: "'Let Us Fly You Where the Sun Is': Air Travel and Tourism in Historical Perspective," in: **Vegesack**, Alexander von (ed.): *Airworld: Design and Architecture for Air Travel*, Weil am Rhein: Vitra Design Museum, 2004, pp. 12–34.
Stalder, Laurent: "Monumente der unmittelbaren Zukunft," in: **Ruhl**, Carsten (ed.): *Mythos Monument: urbane Strategien in Architektur und Kunst seit 1945*, Bielefeld: Transcript, 2011 (series: "Urban Studies"), pp. 63–75.
Stalder, Laurent: "Turning Architecture inside Out: Revolving Doors and Other Threshold Devices," in: *Journal of Design History*, vol. 22, no. 1 (2009), pp. 69–77.
Stoller, Ezra: "Preface," in: **idem** (ed.): *The TWA Terminal* (series: "Building Blocks"), New York: Princeton Architectural Press, 1999, pp. VII–VIII.

T
Temko, Allan: Eero Saarinen (series: "Makers of Contemporary Architecture"), New York: Braziller, 1962.
Thomis, Wayne: "Idlewild: 'Showcase Airport' Born of an Afterthought," in: *Chicago Tribune*, September 24, 1960, p. 8.
Thompson, Arnold W.: "Evolution and Future of Airport Passenger Terminals," in: *Journal of the Aero-Space Transport Division* (series: "Proceedings of the American Society of Civil Engineers"), no. 4064, AT 2 (October 1964), pp. 127–134.
Tillinghast, Charles C., Jr.: "Grandeur: Trans World Flight Center," in: *Jetage Airlanes: The International In-Flight Magazine*, vol. 27, no. 6 (June 1962), pp. 9, 15.
Tough, John M.; **O'Flaherty**, Coleman A.: *Passenger Conveyors: An Innovatory Form of Communal Transport*, London: Allan, 1971.
Transworld Airlines Flight Operations Department: *Legacy of Leadership: A Pictorial History of Trans World Airlines*, Marceline, MO: TWA/ Walsworth Publishing Company, 1971.
TWA: [Untitled news item], in: *Skyliner*, vol. 26, no. 11 (May 27, 1963), p. 6.
TWA: "All-Time Atlantic Travel Mark Set," in: *Skyliner*, vol. 11, no. 41 (October 12, 1950), p. 1.
TWA: "By Design (Rex Werner's), TWA Projects Proud Image," in: *Skyliner*, vol. 27, no. 5 (March 2, 1964), p. 8.
TWA: "Editor's Notes," in: *Skyliner*, vol. 26, no. 13 (June 24, 1963), p. 2.
TWA: "Introducing Trans World Service and Trans World Vacations," in: *Skyliner*, vol. 38, no. 5 (March 1975), p. 1.
TWA: "Las Vegas Opens New Air Terminal," in: *Skyliner*, vol. 26, no. 7 (April 1, 1963), p. 8.
TWA: "Meet the Architect," in: *Skyliner*, vol. 20, no. 30 (November 21, 1957), p. 3.
TWA: "Miniature Flight Center is Minidomm's Aerodrome," in: *Skyliner*, vol. 30, no. 10 (May 8, 1967), p. 4.
TWA: "Modernistic New Terminal Planned to Capture Spirit of Flight During Jet Age," in: *Skyliner*, vol. 20, no. 30 (November 21, 1957), p. 3.
TWA: "Name Chosen for Terminal," in: *Skyliner*, vol. 25, no. 1 (January 1, 1962), pp. 1–2.
TWA: "New Idlewild Terminal Designed by Saarinen Previewed in New York," in: *Skyliner*, vol. 20, no. 30 (November 21, 1957), p. 1.
TWA: "New Record High Set in September for Miles Flown," in: *Skyliner*, vol. 15, no. 41 (October 9, 1952), p. 1.
TWA: "Passenger Traffic Jumps 10 % as Business Booms in 1954," in: *Skyliner*, vol. 18, no. 1 (January 6, 1955), p. 1.
TWA: "Raymond Loewy Touch Is Added to TWA Design," in: *Skyliner*, vol. 23, no. 7 (March 31, 1960), p. 1.
TWA: "Saarinen's Genius, TWA's Bold Vision Are Cited at Flight Center Dedication," in: *Skyliner*, vol. 25, no. 12 (June 4, 1962), pp. 1, 5.
TWA: "The Terminals at Our Flight Hubs," in: *TWA Ambassador*, July 2000, p. 68.
TWA: "Three-Pronged Air Advertising Effort Helps Keep Name of TWA before Public," in: *Skyliner*, vol. 17, no. 25 (June 24, 1954), p. 2.
TWA: "Tourist Mileage Hiked on Jan. 9 Schedule Pattern," in: *Skyliner*, vol. 17, no. 1 (January 7, 1954), p. 1.
TWA: "Trans World Flight Center Opens at Idlewild May 28," in: *Skyliner*, vol. 25, no. 7 (March 26, 1962), p. 1.
TWA: "Travel Center, Flight Center Pair Off as Three-Stars," in: *Skyliner*, vol. 31, no. 17 (August 12, 1970), p. 1.
TWA: "TWA Ads Featured in Top National Magazines," in: *Skyliner*, vol. 25, no. 2 (January 15, 1962), p. 1.
TWA: "TWA and New York Airways Fly World's Fair Helicopters," in: *Skyliner*, vol. 27, no. 13 (June 22, 1964), p. 1.
TWA: "TWA Plans Flight Hostess Academy: Suburb of Kansas City Chosen for 34-Acre Campus," in: *Skyliner*, vol. 30, no. 16 (July 31, 1967), pp. 1, 9.
TWA: "TWA's Flight Wing I," in: *TWA Ambassador*, January/ February 1970, pp. 32–33.
TWA: "TWA's Got a Whole New Way to Fly," in: *TWA Today*, vol. 33, no. 20 (October 19, 1970), pp. 1, 4.
TWA: "Werner Appointed Design Director," in: *Skyliner*, vol. 22, no. 26 (December 24, 1959), p. 5.
TWA: "Werner is Named Sr. Dir. of Design," in: *Skyliner*, vol. 27, no. 3 (March 17, 1964), p. 6.
TWA: "World's News Media Cover Flight Center," in: *Skyliner*, vol. 25, no. 12 (June 4, 1962), p. 3.

V
Vidler, Anthony: *Art, Architecture, and Anxiety in Modern Culture*, Cambridge, MA: MIT Press, 2000.

W
Whyte, William H.: *The Organization Man*, New York: Simon and Schuster, 1956.
Wigley, Mark: "The Architectural Cult of Synchronisation," in: *The Journal of Architecture*, vol. 4, no. 4 (1999), pp. 409–435.
Williams, J. E. D.: *The Operation of Airliners*, London: Hutchinson and Co., 1964.

Y
Yamashita, Tsukasa [interview with Cesar Pelli]: "Eero Saarinen and His Works," in: **Hozumi**, Nobuo (ed.): *Eero Saarinen* (series: "A&U Extra Edition"), Tokyo: A&U Publishing Co., 1984, pp. 226–230.
Yamashita, Tsukasa [interview with Kevin Roche]: "Eero Saarinen and His Works," in: **Hozumi**, Nobuo (ed.): *Eero Saarinen* (series: "A&U Extra Edition"), Tokyo: A&U Publishing Co., 1984, pp. 20–24.

Z
Zevi, Bruno; **Richards**, J. M.; **Giedion**, Sigfried: "Three Critics Discuss M.I.T.'s New Buildings," in: *Architectural Forum*, vol. 104, no. 3 (March 1956), pp. 156–157, 174, 178, 182.

Acknowledgments

Some time after completing my dissertation in 2012, I had scrapped the idea of publishing two or three essays with the most important results of my research. I wanted to make this book. "Now I'm doing it, too," I thought. (I still scoff at colleagues who, after just a few years of work, already publish a monograph with their first completed buildings and unjustifiably lost competitions.) But I could not be dissuaded from my plan of issuing a beautifully designed book with a highly abridged version of my dissertation and the best pictures.

I am indebted first of all to my doctoral advisor, Laurent Stalder at ETH Zurich, for the fact that this book, the first monograph on the TWA Terminal, now lies before you. I have learned a tremendous amount from him, and when I think back to my first tentative steps at scholarly work, I believe I must have greatly strained his patience. I also owe many thanks to my co-advisor Monika Dommann; her clear thoughts and valuable comments were priceless. I am grateful to Ákos Moravánszky, because he awakened in me an interest in architectural theory during my studies at the ETH.

Fundamental to my research were the helpful archivists, especially the late Laura Tatum and Stephen Ross at Yale University. I am very grateful to my interview partners Kevin Roche, Cesar Pelli, and especially Abba Tor, who granted me images from his personal archive. My heartfelt thanks go to translator David Koralek, copy editor and proofreader Lisa Schons, everyone at the publishing house Park Books, and especially to book designers Marina Brugger and Marco Walser of Elektrosmog for their great curiosity and passionate engagement with the subject of this book.

Many more have contributed to this book, including Dagmar Hirsekorn, Mark Jarzombek, Jan-Eric Mack, Neha Maheshwari, Alessandra Ponte, and Mirella Rizzo, but especially Béatrice Müller. My publication wish must have seemed to her like a bad dream. "Not again!" may have been the words that went through her mind thinking back to the busy time of my dissertation. Her contribution to both works is immense, and this book is dedicated to her.

Lastly but importantly, huge thanks are due to all the companies, organizations, and private individuals who have made this publication possible through their financial support, as well as the 144 supporters of the crowdfunding campaign:

Kevin Roche John Dinkeloo and Associates LLC, Hamden, CT
Erich Degen-Stiftung, Zurich
Stiftung Edith Maryon, Basel
Susanna Züst, Zurich
Pelli Clarke Pelli Architects, New Haven, CT
Bearth und Deplazes Architekten AG, Chur
Markus Ringli, Wald
Ernst and Liselotte Müller, Männedorf
Spiro und Gantenbein Architekten ETH SIA AG, Zurich
Jürg Aerne, Zurich
Architonic AG, Zurich
Hansjürg Diener, Zurich
Gold Interactive, Zurich
Hämmerle und Partner, Zurich
Huggenbergerfries Architekten AG ETH SIA BSA, Zurich
Adrian Kloter, Basel
Albi and Martina Nussbaumer Gisler, Zug
Annette Ringli, Seon
Raphael Schenker, Zurich
Thomas Straubinger, Schlieren
Diego Wider, Zurich
Wild Bär Heule Architekten AG, Zurich
Mara Züst, Zurich
Adrian Streich Architekten AG, Zurich
Beat Jordi, Zurich
Markus Maeder, Rapperswil SG
Ursula and Giuliano Maestrini, Ebikon
Christoph Arm, Singapore
Ingrid Burgdorf, Zurich
Tobias Maestrini, Affoltern am Albis
Staufer und Hasler Architekten AG, Frauenfeld
Philip Albers, Zurich
Vrendli and Arnold Amsler, Winterthur
Can Asan, St. Gallen
Bakker und Blanc, Zurich
Jürg Bucher, Dällikon
Duplex Architekten AG, Zurich
Andi Hoppler, Zurich
Ralph Hut, Zurich
Michael Karli, Bern
LIIS Architektur GmbH, Marc Liechti und Antonella Sileno Liechti, Zurich
Lea Maestrini, Wildegg
Menzi Bürgler Architekten AG, Zurich
Gabriella and Lukas Meyer De Pasquale, Zurich
Michael Meier und Marius Hug Architekten, Zurich
Patrick Roost Planung Architektur, Zurich
Adrian Rehmann, Ennetbaden
Stefan Saner, Zurich
Bernd Steimann, Zurich
Jürg Steiner, Wettingen
Daniel Vuilleumier, Zurich
Hansjürg and Jolanda Walser-Dell'Era, Zurich
Stefanie Affolter, Fraubrunnen
Tristan Brenner, Ponte Capriasca
Ron Edelaar, Zurich
Marius Egger, Zurich
Mirjam Fischer, Zurich
Matthias Frei, Langenthal
Felix Gnehm, Zurich
Felix Gübeli, Zurich
Zohair Husain, Thalwil
Hanno Lietz, Zurich
Pia Mendez, Suhr
Elli Mosayebi and Christian Mueller Inderbitzin, Zurich
Jonas Ringli, Zurich

Alban Ringli, Zurich
Caspar Schärer, Zurich
Schenker Salvi Weber Architekten, Vienna
Anna Albisetti, Zurich
Lucas Bally, Zurich
Alexandra Banz, Zurich
Roger E. Baumann, Rüschlikon
Lorenz Baumann, Zurich
Marco Bazzani, Winterthur
Nott Caviezel, Bern
Maria Conen, Zurich
Berto Beat Dünki, Magden
Roman Egli, Lenzburg
Claudio Fetz and Ana Graciela Walser, Zollikon
Simon Frommenwiler, Basel
Mario Fuchs, Zurich
Marco Graber, Zurich
Felice Grella, Zurich
René Grüninger, Zurich
Esther and André Gstettenhofer, Zurich
Sandra Gubler, Wollerau
Guignard und Saner Architekten AG, Zurich
Janine Hächler, Zurich
Michael Hanak, Zurich
Martin Hauser, Zurich
Tilo Herlach, Basel
Andreas Hofer, Zurich
Manuela Hötzl, Vienna
Sabina Hubacher, Zurich
Werner Huber, Zurich
Isabelle Hunziker, Zurich
Philipp Irniger, Hausen AG
Martin Isler, Zurich
Margarethe Kämpf, Warth
Renato Käppeli, Bern
Maya Karácsony-Schüepp, Zurich
Manuela Kern, Zurich
Sean Khorsandi, Jackson Heights, NY
Christina Klausener, Basel
Stephanie Koch, Zurich
Jonathan Koellreuter, Basel
Daniel Kurz, Zurich
Agnès Laube, Zurich
Philipp Lischer, Zurich
Marc Loeliger, Zurich
Valentin Loewensberg, Zurich
Ashok, Asha and Neha Maheshwari, Bangalore
Balz Marti, Zurich
Martin Matter, Zurich
Andreas Meier, Winterthur
Béatrice Müller, Zurich
Pascal Müller, Zürich
Juho Nyberg, Zurich
Andrée Oberson, Wetzikon
Barbara Omlin, Schaffhausen
Franziska Pfyffer, Zurich
Mirella Rizzo, Wallisellen
Alain Roserens, Zurich
Barbara Schlauri, Zurich
Daniela Schmid, Zurich
Sandra Schmid, Zurich
André Schnider, Basel
Barbara Schwärzler, Biel
Daniel Silvestri, Kloten
Smarch, Mathys und Stücheli Architekten, Zurich
Priska Sonderegger, Volketswil
Laurent Stalder, Zurich
Lena Stocker, Zurich
Rebecca Taraborrelli, Zurich
Urs Buchmüller, Zurich
Johannes Vogel, Winterthur
Markus von Deschwanden, Zurich
Thomas Werder, Kilchberg
Vanessa J. Werder, Rapperswil SG
Roger Wernli, Buchs
Renate Wernli, Zurich
Tom Wiederkehr, Basel
Christoph Wieser, Zurich
Carlo Gaetano Zampieri, Luzern
Karin Zindel and David Zumstein, Zurich
Noëmi Züst, Zurich
Abba Tor, Hastings-on-Hudson, NY
Olivier Altenburger, Schaffhausen
Reto Andri, Habsburg
Alexander Baldele, Vienna
Montserrat Bellprat, Winterthur
Carmen Carfora, Zurich
Andrzej Egli, Zurich
Laure Fornasier, Zurich
Martin Ghisletti, Wiesendangen
Thomas Güntensperger, Zurich
Judith Herren, Zurich
Miyuki Inoue, Zurich
L3P Architekten ETH FH SIA, Regensberg
Reto Liechti, Zurich
Franziska Manetsch, Zurich
Michael Metzger, Zurich
Philippe Schär, Biel-Benken
Samuel Scherrer, Zollikofen
Christoph Schlachter, Zurich
Thomas Villiger, Niederurnen
Juan Carlos Zehnder, Zurich

Listed are those supporters who contributed at least 50 Swiss francs.

Author and Book Designers

Kornel Ringli (born 1972) earned his doctorate from ETH Zurich under Prof. Dr. Laurent Stalder with a dissertation on the TWA Terminal. He has been working in journalism since receiving his architectural degree from the same institution in 2001. He regularly publishes specialist articles in various magazines and newspapers. Ringli works full time for the City of Zurich's PWG Foundation, a nonprofit organization dedicated to preserving affordable residential and commercial space, where he is responsible for project development and communications. After completing his studies, he worked in project management and process design at a large company for several years. Kornel Ringli lives and works in Zurich.

Elektrosmog has established an excellent reputation for itself with numerous works for renowned book publishers and art houses. The graphic design studio has received awards and prizes for many of its book productions, including "The Most Beautiful Swiss Books" and the Jan Tschichold Award. Since 2012, Elektrosmog has been responsible for designing the tradition-rich architectural journal *werk, bauen+wohnen.* The firm was established in 1999 by Valentin Hindermann and Marco Walser, and since 2010 the latter has been serving as the sole creative director. Marco Walser (born 1973) studied at the Zurich University of the Arts and has taught at various universities. Designers Selina Bütler and Marina Brugger round off the small team that jointly develops Elektrosmog's work.

Translation
David Koralek, Berlin
Copy editing and proofreading
Lisa Schons, Zurich
Design and typesetting
Elektrosmog, Zurich
Marco Walser
and Marina Brugger
Lithography, printing, and binding
DZA Druckerei zu Altenburg
GmbH, Altenburg, Thuringia

English edition
ISBN 978-3-906027-75-3
German edition
ISBN 978-3-906027-83-8

Park Books
Niederdorfstrasse 54
8001 Zurich
Switzerland
www.park-books.com

DEPARTURES
FLIGHT DESTINATION TER TIME STATUS
FLIGHT DESTINATION TER TIME STATUS
Trans World Flight Center
Dedicated May the Twenty-eighth, 1962
Eero Saarinen, Architect

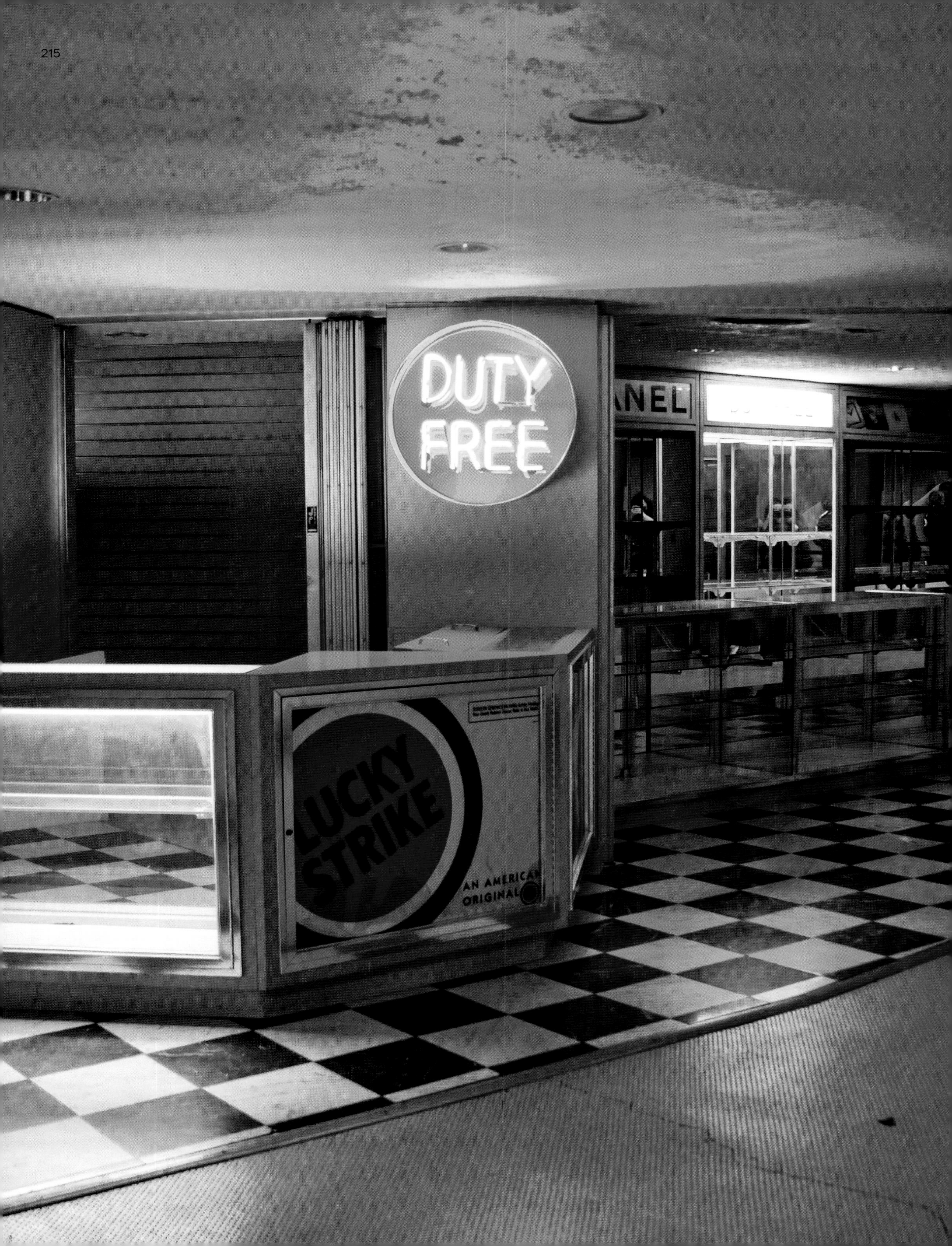
DUTY
FREE
LUCKY
STRIKE
AN AMERICAN
ORIGINAL

TWA
OFF
DUTY

Panasonic
TWA

UNAUTHORIZED PERSONS
PROHIBITED BEYOND THIS FENCE
VIOLATORS WILL BE PROSECUTED
THE PORT AUTHORITY
OF NJ&NY

jetBlu
CTI
38
104

15

WHAT'S NEXT

The best new looks are touching down ahead of time

Photographs by Terry Richardson